Traditional Chinese Leisure Culture and Economic Development

Huidi Ma • Er Liu

Traditional Chinese Leisure Culture and Economic Development

A Conflict of Forces

palgrave
macmillan

Huidi Ma
Institute of Chinese Culture
Beijing, China

Er Liu
Harbin Institute of Technology
Weihai, China

ISBN 978-1-137-59660-4 ISBN 978-1-137-59253-8 (eBook)
DOI 10.1057/978-1-137-59253-8

Library of Congress Control Number: 2017930495

Printed on acid-free paper

This Palgrave Macmillan imprint is published by Springer Nature
The registered company is Nature America Inc.
The registered company address is: 1 New York Plaza, New York, NY 10004, U.S.A.

Acknowledgments

We would like to express our gratitude to Karl Spracklen (Professor at Leeds Beckett University, UK), who has recommended and supported the project to write this book from the beginning and the colleagues of the Research Committee on Sociology of Leisure of the International Sociological Association. We also wish to give thanks to the anonymous peer reviewers for their suggestions, which brought us much fresh inspiration for writing. To Liu Mengxi (Director and Professor of the Institute of Chinese Culture), Feng Changgen (Chairman of Chinese Leisure Philosophy Professional Organization), Ren Xiaomei (Senior Editor of Foreign Language Teaching and Research Press), and Wang Xiaohui (Ma Huidi's daughter), who all gave us detailed comments, critiques, and suggestions. To Li Chunbo (a friend from Canada) who helped out with translating the second and third sections in the fifth chapter when we were on a tight schedule.

To Marjorie Miller (Former Dean and Professor, Department of Philosophy, Purchase College, State University of New York), and Stan Murai (Ma Huidi's English teacher), who critiqued some of the viewpoints in the draft, reviewed the full manuscript, and did part of the literature search for us. To all members of both our families for their support and assistance in the writing of the draft over the last two years. And to many other friends and colleagues, who have generously shared with us their information and views.

Contents

About the Authors

Huidi Ma is a Distinguished Researcher at the Institute of Chinese Culture of the Chinese Academy of Art and was an editorial director and senior editor for the journal *Studies in Dialectics of Nature* until 2006. Since 1995, she has been studying the leisure phenomenon from interdisciplinary perspectives, as well as acting as editor-in-chief and managing editor of the series *Chinese Leisure Studies*, at the same time publishing various books and translated works. She is a founder of the Center of China Leisure Studies and elected fellow of the American Leisure Academy (2006) and the World Leisure Academy (2010). She is also a board member of the Research Committee on Leisure of the International Sociological Association (2012).

Her representative works are: *Freedom and Aesthetics: The Two Wings of Leisure* (2014); *Yu Guangyuan and Ma Huidi's Dialogue Over a Decade: Basic Issues of Leisure Studies* (2008); *Toward a Leisure Economy with Humanistic Concerns* (2004); *Survey Studies of the State of Leisure Life among the Chinese Public* (2004); *Leisure: The Making of a Beautiful Home for the Human Spirit* (2004).

Er Liu has an MA in sociology from Princeton University and a PhD in classical Chinese literature from Harbin Teachers' University. He has been doing research in a variety of fields, including lifestyle and leisure studies. He is currently Professor in Chinese Language and Literature at Harbin Institute of Technology at Weihai.

CHAPTER 1

Introduction

Over time, leisure has imperceptibly nurtured the mind, the intellectual capacity, and the moral sense of human beings, like "an invisible drizzle that wets clothes, or flowers idly falling to the ground without a sound".[1] The history of the development of human civilization is also a history of leisure. Without leisure, it would be difficult to have real creativity, and human society would be no more than a machine that runs in cycles.

We can find grounds for leisure in both Eastern and Western cultures. For philosophers in ancient Greece, "leisure was not simply the freedom from the necessity of being occupied, nor was it time during which we could choose what to do. Leisure was an essential element in the realization of the ideals of the culture: knowledge leading to virtuous choices and conducts which, in turn, leads to true pleasure and happiness."[2] Likewise, for the ancient sages of China, "Having a day of carnival after a hundred days of hard work is a blessing. Working hard continuously without relaxation is something even the sages would not be capable of, whereas being always relaxed is something in which they would not indulge. Hard work interspersed

[1] From the poem "Bie Yan Shiyuan" (Farewell to Yan Shiyuan) by the Tang poet Liu Changqing.

[2] Thomas Goodale and Geoffrey Godbey, *The Evolution of Leisure: historical and philosophical perspectives.* State College, PA: Venture Publishing Inc., 1995, pp. 23–24.

Huidi Ma, Er Liu, *Traditional Chinese Leisure Culture and Economic Development*, DOI 10.1057/978-1-137-59253-8_1

with relaxation is the way of those great kings."[3] This is the common ground for culture, for human nature, and for human existence.

The intellectual breakthroughs in the "Axial Age" (according to Karl Jaspers) were related mainly to issues centered on human nature. In the period from about the eighth century BC to the fifth century AD, the Buddha Shakyamuni in India, Confucius and Laozi in China, and Socrates, Plato, and Aristotle in Greece, all expressed similar ideas on these issues.

In the Chinese word for leisure, *xiuxian* (休閒), the pictographic characters *xiu* (休) and *xian* (閒) have a kind of ingenuity, offering a clear interpretation of the profound meaning and great significance of leisure.

The pictograph *xiu* has a person leaning against a tree to rest, which expressively describes the harmonious relationship between humans and nature. And the pictograph *xian* portrays a scene as if from an essay by Lin Yutang: "On my estate there is a garden; in the garden there is a housing compound, in the center of which there is a courtyard; in the courtyard there is a tree; over the tree there is the sky; and in the sky there is the moon." With this we can almost see wise old Chinese men sitting in the courtyard, gazing at the moon through the gate and letting their imagination fly, out of which was born their philosophical ideas, their artistic achievements, and the technology of traditional China. But from *xian* are also derived many other meanings, including morality and law, as well as limit and constraint. Furthermore, *xian* is a phonetic loan for another character that means purity of thought and a peaceful mind that is the basis for a quality life.

The essence of *xiuxian* is the following: *xiu* means quietude, which facilitates one's self-cultivation and allows one to see far beyond the necessities of daily life; while *xian* means correctness of speech and action, and not breaking rules. The profound meanings of these characters had great influence on the basic philosophical ideas and attitudes in traditional Chinese culture for handling humans' relationship with nature, life, and society. These ideas and attitudes are well expressed in both Confucian and Taoist thinking.

The Confucians emphasized the role of rites in governing society and the importance of benevolent rule. They advocated a political philosophy of "starting from poetry, laying a sound foundation for society through rites,

[3] Sun Xidan. *Liji Jijie* (*Collected Annotations on the Book of Rites*). Beijing: Zhonghua Book Company, 1989, p. 1115.

and reaching the ideal society through music" ("Tai Bo" chapter of *Analects of Confucius*). This idea was embodied in the "six arts" of rites, music, archery, chariotry, writing, and arithmetic, which also constituted the highest level of aesthetic activity.

Laozi emphasizes "speculating in quietude to comprehend the dark mystery," that is, to attain to the Tao, thus highlighting the individual's ability to awaken to the Tao through introspection. This is aimed to achieve a harmony between the inner world of humans and the environment outside, which would allow us to gain insight and to cultivate the beauty of human nature.

Zhuangzi taught us to calm our inner tensions, to move in accord with time, and to identify with the world through *xinzhai* (spiritual fasting) and *zuowang* (sitting still to let all thoughts and desires diminish to the extent where one forgets the world and even oneself), so as to adapt to all kinds of circumstances. The *xiaoyao you* (free and easy wandering of the mind) advocated by Zhuangzi, where one "wanders beyond the four seas" and "appreciates the great beauty of heavens and earth" became the ultimate wisdom of the Chinese on leisure.

What is unique about the Chinese concept of leisure is that it suggests that leisure can exert an invisible and formative influence on people's lifestyles and their values. "The unity of humans and nature" lays the foundation for the concept of being and its values; "moral cultivation and propriety of conduct" provide the basis of the norms for the individual's social behavior; and "elegance and taste" enrich the world we live in and life itself.

Through the traditional leisure culture of China, we can still feel intimately the graceful leisureliness of the ancients in their natural philosophy, cultivation of character, aesthetic tastes, art and literature, and even good health and longevity. For them, leisure was Zen mingled with a tremendous creativity.

The ancient Chinese did not have material plenty in their lives, but they had a rich and colorful spiritual life. The large and ever-increasing body of Confucian classics, history, philosophy of different non-Confucian schools, and collections of work by individual authors were highly valued by generation after generation, and was gradually internalized by the Chinese. Thus it became an important factor influencing their individual temperaments, and also an important part of their cultural tradition.

In this rich tradition, two kinds of cultural elements stand out as the most splendid and long-lasting heritage of the nation. One is the "family instructions" (家訓), and the other is "womanly work" (女紅), both of which have provided much spiritual nourishment for people and profoundly influenced generation after generation of the Chinese people.

The family instructions were an important part of education in traditional China. They were easy to read, understand, memorize, recite, and put into practice. Closely related to the moral practice of ordinary people, they had a profound influence on popular ethical beliefs, norms for conduct, and rituals, and were model texts used to correct family moral standards and improve family reputations that have been passed on through generations.

China's cultural tradition stresses that the family, or the household, is closely associated with the state. The Confucians believed that self-cultivation of the individual serves as the basis for putting the household in order, which in turn is the basis for governing the state and pacifying the world, which implies that the self, the household, and the state are closely interrelated. The household is the foundation for the individual to attain harmony with society. Thus, family instructions have a special role in its education.

In the long history of China as an agrarian society, "womanly work," which usually meant needlework done by women, such as embroidery and sewing, contributed in a special way to the life and values of the Chinese. For thousands of years, "womanly work" had profound influence on "womanly virtues": first, "womanly work" could directly or indirectly foster "womanly virtues"; secondly, it helped to foster kindness and goodness in women; thirdly, it has played an important role in forming the role model of the mother for women, especially in their role of giving birth to the next generation, bringing up their children, and inheriting and passing on the feminine virtues through their own earnest practice; fourth, it was a good guide for the leisure life of the family. These are the reasons why "womanly work" has continued as a prominent part of Chinese culture for thousands of years.

Indeed, aesthetic taste and grace in leisure life was also nurtured by poetry, music, calligraphy, painting, and board games such as *go*, and such aesthetic taste and graceful leisure life were the foundations of China as "a land of courtesy and propriety" and promoted a tradition of "respecting teachers and valuing education."

The ancient Chinese had some standards for "affluence." In terms of material life, the standard was "two *mu* of land and an ox, together with a wife, several children, and a heatable brick bed to sleep on"; while the standard for a rich spiritual life is to have "learning and honesty to perpetuate the family." Knowing that "the tailorbird may build her nest deep in a huge forest, but the nest occupies but one branch; the mole may drink from the Yellow River, but he can take at most a bellyful," and that money was something external to the human self which one can neither bring at one's birth or take away with one when one dies, they tried to live a life that was moderate in terms of material wealth but spiritually rich.

In the Western world, the relationship between leisure and culture was also fully recognized. Starting with the Greeks, leisure was considered an important basis for a good life. Aristotle's statement that leisure is the pivot around which all things revolve had great impact on European culture and the Renaissance.

In his book *Leisure: the Basis of Culture*, the modern Swedish philosopher Josef Pieper points out that leisure is the basis for human culture; that, as an attitude in life, it means the state of peace and quietude in a human being; that it is the opportunity and ability for the human individual to immerse himself in "the whole process of creativity"; and that it is given to humans by God. While at leisure, human beings are not in possession of power to dominate the world, but are able to feel the joy of life because of the peace of mind attained in it.

The value of leisure is self-evident. Without leisure, even the natural growth of humans becomes problematic. The ancient Chinese believed that "with too much knowledge, one is likely to get entangled in a host of different opinions and be faced with many dilemmas; it would be better to be moderate even with acquiring knowledge" (*Laozi*), which means one needs to maintain peace and quietude of mind rather than trying to learn and do too many things, for then one would be highly stressed and likely to lose one's wits and go to extremes. The reason is that when one becomes very busy, one is likely to lose composure and become irritable and shallow, unable to keep calm and think carefully. When one becomes too busy, one is also likely to be short-sighted, unable to think far into the future while just enduring the hectic life.

Unfortunately, with the natural disasters, poverty, war, and rampant corruption on the part of the ruling elite that China has experienced in the last century, traditional leisure values have been mutilated and discarded. This is especially true of the decade of the Cultural Revolution.

Today, China is in a period of great social transformation. While people have focused solely on economic growth, the tradition of leisure culture has continued to become greatly diminished.

What does leisure mean today? Government policy has turned leisure into the "golden weeks" for tourism and a ready source of revenues; society has taken leisure to be a house of pleasure where one can live in luxury and dissipation; common people have taken it to be "TV + cellphone + chatting on the Internet." The mundane life of hustle and bustle, the earnest pursuits of material gains, greed, anxiety, and haste have become major themes in people's lives, and the whole scene has become one in which "humans are slaves to material goods" and "the mind is slave to the body."

Put into historical perspective, it is true that the Chinese now enjoy a great abundance of material goods. Nowadays not only people have a great range of goods to consume, but they have set for themselves the new goals of obtaining fancy food and clothes. But when the objects of aesthetic appreciation and philosophical reflection have become remote to people's lives, the nurturing role of leisure is bound to be looked down upon and become alienated.

Marx noticed long ago that the way humans make their living affects their body, their thinking, and their daily lives. Not only did he raise the issue of the "alienation of labor," but pointed out that we have sold our birthright for a mess of pottage. As Goodale and Godbey go on to say after quoting this sentence from Marx, "we seem to lack a sufficiently compelling idea, or a sufficiently refined taste, for anything else. In short, we lack a philosophy of leisure. Without one, we may never be satisfied."[4]

After Marx, Marcuse further discussed the problem of alienation. He believed Marx saw how "alienation" had enslaved the human body, but it bothered Marcuse that it now enslaved the mind and soul as well.

According to theories in the sociology of leisure, leisure has important influence on all stages of human life, especially on the individual's "becoming human" and his/her socialization, allowing him/her to obtain more freedom, aesthetic experiences, creativity, and opportunities to develop his/her interests, so that he/she can liberate him/herself, create his/her own life, incorporate his/her interests in life, and mold him/herself into a useful person in society.

One may ask: has China not experienced three splendid decades of economic growth without a need for the traditional leisure culture? This is a good question.

[4] Thomas Goodale and Geoffrey Godbey, *The Evolution of Leisure: historical and philosophical perspectives.* State College, PA: Venture Publishing Inc., 1995, pp. 87–88.

It is indeed true that China, as the second largest economy in the world now, is the country with the largest number of tourists visiting other countries, the greatest purchasing power in the area of luxury items, the largest number of entertainment projects, the greatest numbers of people going abroad for education, medical care, and recreation, and the largest number of middle-class people. It can even directly affect the direction taken by the world economy.

But China, a country with 1.3 billion people, still faces many challenges, for a population of 1.3 billion people is very large, and any tiny problem would become a huge one when multiplied by 1.3 billion, while any resource, when divided by 1.3 billion, would become very small. By the standards of the World Bank, there are still close to 200 million people living in poverty in China and it is the 83rd among 157 countries in the happiness rankings for 2013–2015.[5] Furthermore, the population of China is aging rapidly, with 212 million elderly people in 2015. There are more than 60 million children who stay in rural areas while their parent/parents are working in cities as migrant workers and 30 million adults who are bachelors; and one third of the population have health problems in need of treatment. Measures taken to tackle any one of these problems are likely to have repercussions for the whole society.

The most worrying problem is the weakness of the cultural capital of the whole nation. With people generally living in a great imbalance of work and leisure and in disorderly physical and mental states, the tradition of valuing education and culture has become very weak, and it is difficult to see grace and refinement in people's conduct. With a strong mentality for quick wealth, people are always hurrying, without stopping to make sound decisions, not knowing what the goals are for development. Both the "starry sky above" and the "moral law within" (Kant) are increasingly distant from people's lives.

Every day we talk about the "China dream" and the revival of Chinese culture, but both the natural and the humanistic ecology have greatly deteriorated in China. Both the development of society as a whole and the development of individual Chinese are in a distorted and unbalanced state, and the power for sustainable development is unfortunately insufficient. Is this not the price we have paid for losing our tradition of leisure

[5] John Helliwell, Richard Layard and Jeffrey Sachs, eds., *World Happiness Report 2016*, vol. 1, New York, Sustainable Development Solutions Network, 2016, p. 21.

culture? Leisure, it seems, does not increase GDP, but GDP growth without a leisurely temperament may well be transient or greatly distorted in nature.

Today, China is undergoing a great social transformation, with conflicts developing everywhere all the time. Proper handling of these conflicts would provide a new kind of power to propel the continuous progress of Chinese society. But in order to be able to handle them properly, national decision-makers would need to have not only superior wisdom, but also the courage of a warrior who cuts off his arm in order to preserve his human dignity.

CHAPTER 2

Leisure and Traditional Chinese Society

Leisure is a state of life and a form of existence for human beings. The meaning of leisure is part of the common cultural foundation for human existence. The basis for this point can be found in the sources of both Eastern and Western civilizations. The ancient Greeks believed that "leisure was not simply the freedom from the necessity of being occupied, nor was it time during which we could choose what to do. Leisure was an essential element in the realization of the ideals of the culture: knowledge leading to virtuous choices and conducts which, in turn, leads to true pleasure and happiness."[1] And "for leisure in Greek is *skole*, and in Latin's *scalo*, the English 'school'. The word used to designate the place where we educate and teach is derived from a word which means 'leisure'. School does not, properly speaking, mean school, but leisure".[2]

Likewise, Confucius once said, "Having a day of carnival after a hundred days of hard work is a blessing. Working hard continuously without relaxation is something even the sagacious Kings Wen and Wu would not be capable of, whereas being always relaxed is something they would not indulge in. Hard work interspersed with relaxation is the way of those

[1] Thomas Goodale and Geoffrey Godbey, *The Evolution of Leisure,* Venture Publishing Inc., State College, PA 1995, second printing, 1995, pp. 23–24.

[2] Ibid., p.19

Huidi Ma, Er Liu, *Traditional Chinese Leisure Culture and Economic Development*, DOI 10.1057/978-1-137-59253-8_2

great kings."[3] This is a common basis for culture and for human nature throughout history.

The two characters in the Chinese word for *xiuxian* (休閒), "leisure," have profound connotations in traditional Chinese culture. These characters express the basic philosophical ideas and attitudes in traditional Chinese culture for handling humans' relationship with nature, life, and society. Confucians and Taoists both affirm the positive values of leisure and their views in this respect often conflate and appear identical. The Confucian idea of the "golden mean," Laozi's "letting things take their own course," Zhuangzi's "carefree wandering," the Buddhist "state of self-oblivion," and folk sayings such as "the soul becomes clear after being purified just as things become clean after being washed" all succinctly reflect the essence of leisure activities.

What is unique about the Chinese concept of leisure is that it suggests that leisure can exert an invisible and formative influence on people's lifestyles and value systems. "The unity of Man and Nature" lays the foundation for the concept of being and its values; "moral cultivation and propriety of conduct" provide the basis for the norms of the individual's social behavior so that "elegance and taste" enrich both the world we live in and life itself.

Unity of Man and Nature

The idea that humans and nature are in a unity represents a basic approach of the Chinese in their philosophy of life. The ancients never placed themselves above nature. Zhuangzi, for example, claimed "Heaven and earth are parents to all things in the world."[4] The legend explains that the earth receives the seeds of the five grains and cares for the six domestic animals, enabling people to live in abundance, while the heavens bestow sunlight and rain, as well as the cyclic four seasons. The beauty of nature nourishes and edifies humanity. Harmony with nature is the foundation of humanity, and thus heaven, earth, and humans should be one in unity. The way of heaven is to "initiate all things"; that of earth, to "let all things grow"; and that of

[3] Sun Xidan. *Collected Annotations on the Book of Rites*. Beijing: Zhonghua Book Company, 1989, p. 1115.

[4] Cao Chuji. *A Simple Annotation of Zhuangzi* (revised ed.). Beijing: Zhonghua Book Company, 2000, p. 265.

humans, to "perfect all things." Each of the three has its own way, but, as Laozi points out, each way is an unspeakably mysterious way, for the way gives birth to all things, the way is indispensable for everything. The way of heaven and earth is particular about being generative and making offerings, while the way of humans is more inclined to being realistic and gainful. They are complementary to each other, and thus should treat each other with courtesy. In the cultural tradition of China, the doctrines of Taoism, Confucianism, and Buddhism all have the "unity of Man and Nature" as their foundation. Most of the popular festivals in China are joyous celebrations of nature while also working to build an ethical order of relationships among humans.

The Pictographs of Xiu *and* Xian

The two characters *xiu* 休and *xian* 閒, which together make up the Chinese word for "leisure," show the ingenuity of the ancients and have great significance for our understanding of the values of leisure. According to the *Kangxi Zidian*, an authoritative dictionary of classical Chinese compiled under the auspices of Emperor Kangxi in the early eighteenth century, the pictograph *xiu* portrays a person (人) leaning against a tree (木) to rest, which figuratively depicts the harmonious relationship between humans and nature and in a way embodies Zhuangzi's idea that "all things in the world are unified with me since heaven and earth were born together with me."[5] *Xiu* can also mean auspiciousness, joy, and blessing. Confucius felt this harmony of nature when he said, "Heaven never says anything, but all things grow naturally as the four seasons go in cycles in an orderly fashion."[6] Thus, when Zeng Xi, who was styled "Dian," said what he most wanted to do was "in late spring, when spring clothes are ready, together with a few friends and several disciples, I would like to take a bath in the Yi River (in Shandong), have my body dried at the dance altar, and then return home, singing songs along the way," Confucius could not help exclaiming: "I quite agree with Dian's idea!"[7] Harmony is brought about when humans

[5] Ibid., p. 29.

[6] Liu Baonan. *A Rectified Interpretation of Confucius' Analects*. Beijing: Zhonghua Book Company, 1990, p. 698.

[7] Zhu Xi. *Collected Annotations on Four Great Books of Confucianism*. Shanghai: Shanghai Bookstore, 1987, pp. 81–82.

follow heaven's natural course and blend with nature. This is the attitude of the ancients toward life, an attitude that shows their reverence for nature.

In the traditional script, the pictograph *xian* intuitively expresses this idea: one sits in the courtyard watching the moon (月) through the gate (門) and lets his imagination fly, being in a leisurely mood while enjoying life, just as Lin Yutang once wrote, "On my estate there is a garden; in the garden there is a mansion; in the center of the mansion there is a courtyard; in the courtyard there is a tree; over the tree there is the sky; and in the sky there is the moon—how happy I am for having such a place!"[8] But from *xian* are also derived other meanings, including having a broad view, morality, and law, as well as limits and constraint. Furthermore, *xian* is a phonetic loan for another character that means "gentle and refined, with purity in thought and a peaceful mind." Thus, our understanding of *xian* should not be limited to the temporal dimension of personal enjoyment of leisure time and recreation.

Thus, semantically speaking, the essence of *xiuxian* is the following: *xiu* means quietude, which facilitates one's self-cultivation and allows one to see far beyond the necessities for everyday life; while *xian* means correctness of speech and action, of living without breaking rules, and the cultivation of a life of high quality.

Three Relationships in Xiuxian (休閒) *in the Cultural Traditions of China*

First, we have the harmony between human beings and nature, with humans being considered part of nature. Thus, we should not wantonly offend nature, but should take for granted that humans should revere nature. In traditional China, people used the term *tiandi* 天地 ("heavens and the earth") to mean nature, and treated these things as divine. The earth receives the seeds of various grains and nourishes domestic animals, enabling people to live in abundance, while the heavens bestow sunlight and rain, as well as the cyclic four seasons. The beauty of nature nourishes and edifies humanity. Harmony with nature is therefore the very foundation of human life.

[8] Lin Yutang. *Selected Essays by Lin Yutang*. Tianjin: Baihua Literature and Art Publishing House, 1987, p. 265.

Secondly, we have harmony among people. In general, people all like to pursue auspiciousness, joyfulness, goodness, and blessings as their goals in life. Attainment to these goals is dependent on the sincerity, honesty, and purity of people's minds, and on rules and constraints in terms of morality and discipline. Therefore, *xiuxian* can help to maintain an order for human life and instill human virtues, thus creating harmonious relationships among people.

Thirdly, there is the harmony between the human individual and him/herself, which entails a balance between body and mind, between action and repose, and between being active and being at leisure. It also implies the pursuit of a happy life and a concern for spiritual life beyond material production. Only when one is in a state of leisure and inaction 無為 (*wuwei*) is one capable, as an individual, of feeling joy and harmonizing the myriad things of life. The inner harmony of the human individual is the basis for harmony among all things in the world.

The Conception of the "Unity of Man and Nature"

With the conception of the unity of humans and nature, the Chinese invented many festivals related to the natural cycle of things. For example, the 24 solar terms,[9] which originated in the Eastern Zhou Period, is a supplementary calendar the ancients invented to guide agricultural activities throughout the year. It is an interpretation of nature's mysteries, but also provides guidelines for life in an agrarian society in which people worked hard but also had joy and repose in accordance with nature's rhythms. Even the emperor had to worship the "Heavens" at each of the solar terms of every year. These rituals not only helped to make life more relaxed and joyous, but also instilled a reverence for nature in people's minds. The 24 solar terms represent not only a poeticized lifestyle of the literati who sang sentimental verses about flowers and the moon, but more importantly the understanding by common people of the value of leisure. When Confucius took his disciple Zigong to watch a festival of celebration after harvest, Zigong was worried that if people indulged in such joys they might forget their work. Confucius explained to him that since people

[9] The 24 solar terms are points in traditional Chinese calendar specified according to the position of the Earth on its orbit around the sun. Starting with the vernal equinox, the points are spaced 15° apart along the ecliptic. After a full cycle of 360°, the earth returns to the vernal equinox, ready to start another cycle.

had to labor in the fields year after year, it was good to let them relax once a while so that hard labor would be interspersed with periods of relaxation, which would actually help to promote production as well as allow them to live a better life. "Having a day of carnival after a hundred days of hard work is a blessing. Working hard continuously without relaxation is something even the sagacious Kings Wen and Wu would not be capable of, whereas being always relaxed is something they would not indulge in. Hard work interspersed with relaxation is the way of those great kings."[10] The system of solar terms embodies a symbiotic view of nature and humans in unity, with humans living in harmony with all things in nature, and for thousands of years this has been an integral part of the Chinese cultural tradition.

Benevolence 仁 (*ren*) is considered the core of Confucianism, which advocates a political philosophy of "starting from poetry, laying a sound foundation for society through rites, and reaching the ideal society through music," with poetry, rites, and music being used to educate people and to cultivate a healthy character. From the Zhou Dynasty on, the "six arts" of rites, music, archery, charioting, writing, and arithmetic were incorporated into the official educational system, making these "arts" required life skills. In the "Xueji" 學記 chapter of *The Book of Rites*, one of the five Confucian classics, it is stated, "The learning of the gentleman consists of taking rest from time to time and dabbling in various arts at ease (*you*) as well as actively absorbing knowledge and cultivating oneself."[11] In the "Shu'er" 述而 chapter of the *Analects*, Confucius says one can "playfully dabble in the (six) arts" in addition to the more serious task of "perfecting oneself through moral cultivation in order to attain to the Tao."[12] These comments reflect Confucius' idea that one should be cultivated in the Tao, morality, benevolence, and arts, which together constitute the foundation of human life.

Taoist philosophy, which was first developed by Laozi, has as its core idea the concept of *wu* (無), "nothingness." In his political thinking, he stressed "achieving order through *wuwei* (無為 inaction)," which actually means the ruler should let things take their natural course (which are in accord with the

[10] Sun Xidan. *Collected Annotations on the Book of Rites*. Beijing: Zhonghua Book Company, 1989, p. 1115.

[11] Chen Hao. *Collected Commentary on the Book of Rites*. Shanghai Classic Publishing House, 1987, p. 200.

[12] Zhu Xi. *Collected Annotations on Four Great Books of Confucianism*. Shanghai: Shanghai Bookstore, 1987, p. 46.

Tao), rather than take an activist approach 有為 (*youwei*) and forcibly interfere with them. Laozi's philosophy emphasizes "speculating in quietude to comprehend the dark mystery," in other words to attain to the Tao, thus highlighting the individual's ability to awaken to the Tao through introspection. "Things are generated from the Tao, maintained by virtues, shaped into physical objects, and perfected by right circumstances. This is why the Tao and virtues are most revered among myriad things. Such reverence is not commanded by anyone, but comes naturally,"[13] so that a harmony can be achieved between the inner world of humans and the environment outside. Laozi also teaches us, "Quietude can subdue rashness, and cold can overcome heat. Serenity is the right way for the world."[14] It is in serenity that one can obtain insight into human nature and attain to the beauty available to human beings.

The chapter "Xiaoyao you" 逍遙遊 ("Free and Easy Wandering") of *Zhuangzi* advocates the unity between humans and nature when humans are able to transcend all things and soar high in the realms of freedom. Many passages in that chapter have subtle meanings apart from their literal meanings, concluding with "the Perfect Man has no self; the Holy Man has no merit; the Sage has no fame,"[15] a remark full of a romanticism that combines reason, sensibility, and imagination.

Through *xinzhai* 心齋 (spiritual fasting) and *zuowang* 坐忘 (sitting still to let all thoughts and desires diminish to the extent where one forgets the world and even one's self), Zhuangzi also aims at the calming down of inner tensions, movement in accord with time, identification with the world, and thus adaptation to all kinds of circumstances. Thus, *xiaoyao you* as advocated by Zhuangzi, where one "wanders beyond the four seas" and "appreciates the great beauty of heavens and earth" became the ultimate wisdom of the Chinese with regard to leisure. The earliest concept of freedom in Chinese thinking can also be attributed to Zhuangzi.

The *Book of Poetry*, compiled two and half a millennia ago, is the oldest anthology of Chinese poems. It contains poems written in a period spanning about five centuries (from early Western Zhou to the middle of Spring and Autumn period, or *c.* eleventh–sixth century BC) that began a rich

[13] Huang Ruiyun. *The Original Meaning of Laozi*. Beijing: People's Literature Publishing House, 1995, p. 73.

[14] Huang Ruiyun. *The Original Meaning of Laozi*. Beijing: People's Literature Publishing House, 1995, p. 67.

[15] Watson, Burton, trans.. *Chuang Tzu: Basic Writings*. New York and London: Columbia University Press, 1964, p. 26.

tradition of poetry. Besides songs composed by musicians of the Zhou court and those presented as a tribute by the courtiers of various ranks, there are also many ballads that had been sung among common people.[16] Many of the poems in *The Book of Poetry* vividly depict scenarios of leisure activities of ancient China.

The Chinese conception of the unity between man and nature is also reflected in the traditional wedding ceremony, where the couple do obeisance first to heaven and earth, and then to their parents, before they do obeisance to each other, which shows the importance of nature in people's minds.

Confucianism and Taoism came to be the mainstream of Chinese culture from two millennia ago. A very important reason for this is that they passed on the ancients' conceptions of nature by making them into important philosophical ideas that have exerted great influence on the Chinese outlook on life for many generations.

In modern times, the famous writer Lin Yutang wrote, "Very much contented am I to lie low, to cling to the soil, to be of kin to the sod. My soul squirms comfortably in the soil and sand and is happy. Sometimes when one is drunk with this earth, one's spirit seems so light that he thinks he is in heaven."[17] And Xu Zhimo, an eminent Chinese poet in modern times, wrote, "Isn't it true that the roots of all great, profound, spirit-lifting, clear-sighted, and graceful thinking can be sought in the sound of wind, in clouds, in the mountains and the undulation of landscape, and in the colors and fragrance of flowers and grasses?"[18]

Lü *and* You*: Pursuits in Nature*

To the ancient Chinese, *lü* 旅 (to travel) and *you* 遊 (to wander) have great symbolic significance. The word *lü* not only denotes "to make an excursion," but also connotes "common" and "right conduct." In modern language, *lü* can be interpreted to mean when one makes an excursion, one should observe social norms and conduct oneself properly, for one's

[16] Yuan Xingpei et al., eds. *A History of Chinese Literature*. Beijing: Higher Education Press, vol. 1, 1999, p. 54.

[17] Lin Yutang. *The Importance of Living* (A John Day Book). New York: Reynal and Hitchcock, 1937, vii.

[18] Xu Zhimo. Notes at a mountain villa in Florence, *Modern Criticism*, 1925, 2 (30): 13–14.

conduct reflects not only one's self-cultivation, but also one's upbringing. *You*, on the other hand, means "to walk leisurely." Thus, the ancients believed the *you* means "dabbling in the six arts in one's leisure time"[19] and "unhurriedness."[20] Zhuangzi's "free and easy wandering" is the best form of going on a tour.

Confucius, Laozi, and Zhuangzi pioneered traveling and tourism for the Chinese. Confucius spent 14 years going to the different states of his time, traveling thousands of miles and passing through many difficulties in an attempt to find a ruler who would adopt the political measures he advocated. Though rejected almost everywhere, he still remained confident that his political ideal was the right Way, and was steadfast in teaching the Way and the arts to his disciples. He said, "Knowing something is not as good as being able to like it, and being able to like it is not as good as being able to enjoy it."[21] Although he traveled because of his political aspirations, he actually practiced the Way, and his traveling demonstrated his noble sentiments.

According to legends, when Laozi saw the Zhou Dynasty was in decline, he left his official position and traveled throughout the world on the back of his black ox, accompanied by a lad he took with him. When he reached the Hangu Pass and was about to go into the unsettled frontier region in the west from there, the chief of the guards at the pass asked Laozi to write something for him. Laozi obliged and wrote down a book of about 5,000 characters which then became the famous *Daodejing* 道德經, in which he used the concept "Tao" to explain the evolution of all things in the universe. In this book, he expounded the idea that "The Tao gives birth to the One, the One to Two (*yin* and *yang*, or the feminine and masculine principles), and the Two to the Three, from which the myriad things are derived." The Tao is not commanded by anyone, but comes about naturally. This is an ancient outlook on nature with its primitive simplicity.

Zhuangzi's idea about traveling is reflected in the concept "free and easy wandering," in which one is independent of mundane things, but becomes united with nature. One travels throughout the world free of all constraints,

[19] Zheng Xuan. *The Book of Rites, The Thirteen Confucian Classics with Annotations by Han and Wei Scholars*. Beijing: Zhonghua Book Company, 1998, p. 130.

[20] Liu Baonan. *A Rectified Interpretation of Confucius' Analects*. Beijing: Zhonghua Book Company, 1990, p. 257.

[21] Liu Baonan. *A Rectified Interpretation of Confucius' Analects*. Beijing: Zhonghua Book Company, 1990, p. 235.

transcending all secular ideas and reaching the highest level of spiritual freedom. Zhuangzi's "traveling outside the mundane world"[22] and watching "the great beauty of heaven and earth"[23] represent the highest wisdom of *lü* and *you*.

The spirit of these three sages with regard to *lü* (to travel) and *you* (to wander) have had a great impact on later generations. For example, Dong Qichang, an eminent painter and calligrapher of the Ming Dynasty, said, "Once you have read ten thousand scrolls of books and have traveled on foot ten thousand miles, and have washed off the mundane things in your heart, then mountains and valleys would naturally build up in your heart, and become as beautiful and majestic as those in Juancheng in Shandong and Ezhou in Hubei." He means, on the one hand, that one can gain much from traveling only if he has enough knowledge, and, on the other, that one has to read many books seriously in order to have fulfilling trips, for reading books can help one drive out the flippancy and impurity in one's heart, and increase one's knowledge of humanity and geography. With that, one can really attain to "free and easy wandering."

Xu Xiake, also of the Ming Dynasty, was a great traveler. Since he left home at the age of 22, he spent most of his life in traveling and in scientific investigation. He not only completed his *Travels*, the book that earned him the title "the ultimate traveler," but made many geographical, hydrological, geological, and botanical discoveries. He became "the ultimate traveler" also because, through his travels, he brought into being an aesthetic dimension and a standard for evaluating the grandeur of nature and the beauty of humanity.

From these examples, we can see how great an impact the idea of the unity of man and nature has had on the wisdom of life and the values of the Chinese people.

[22] Cao Chuji. *A Simple Annotation of Zhuangzi* (revised ed.). Beijing, Zhonghua Book Company, 2000, p. 9.

[23] Cao Chuji. *A Simple Annotation of Zhuangzi* (revised ed.). Beijing, Zhonghua Book Company, 2000, p. 320.

Spiritual Pursuits

The sages of ancient China believed that leisure is closely related to natural philosophy, cultivation of character, aesthetic taste, art and literature, and even good health and longevity. It was such spiritual pursuits that led to the production of the great works in Chinese culture, starting from *The Book of Change*, *The Book of Poems*, Laozi's work, *The Analects*, the chapter "free and easy wandering" in *Zhuangzi*, *The Songs of Chu*, through the different styles of poetry in various historical periods, to Yuan drama and the elegant essays of the Ming-Qing Period. These works helped to turn China into "a land of courtesy and propriety" and foster a tradition of "respecting teachers and valuing education."

The literati, or intellectuals of traditional China, had "self-cultivation, putting the household in order, governing the state, and pacifying the world" as the most important goals in life, but also considered abilities in music, *go*-playing, calligraphy, and painting as accomplishments required of a gentleman. They tried to set examples of strength and character for society by using their writings as carriers of the Tao, and by putting their knowledge into practice. They were the creators and transmitters of the cultural tradition of China. As a unique elite class, they had profound influence on public morals and social customs. It would be interesting to inquire into what forms of leisure activities they used to facilitate their self-cultivation and spiritual pursuits.

Subduing Dong 動 *(Motion) with* Jing 靜 *(Calmness)*

The concept of *jing* 靜 (calm, still, quiet, tranquil) occupies a very important position in China's cultural traditions. *The Great Learning*, one of the most important Confucian classics, starts with the following paragraph:

> What the Great Learning teaches, is—to illustrate illustrious virtue; to renovate the people; and to rest in the highest excellence. The point where to rest being known, the object of pursuit is then determined; and, that being determined, a calm unperturbedness may be attained to. To that calmness there will succeed a tranquil repose. In that repose there may be careful deliberation, and that deliberation will be followed by the attainment of the desired end.[24]

[24] Legge, James. *The Chinese Classics*, vol. 1 (*Confucian Analects*; *The Great Learning*; *The Doctrine of the Mean*). Taipei: SMC Publishing, 1991, pp. 356–357.

Laozi also places much emphasis on *jing*. Thus, "Who can by calmness, little by little, make troubled water turn clear?"[25] "Be completely empty, and be perfectly calm.... The return to the root is to be calm. To be calm is to accept what must be."[26] "Heaviness is the root of lightness; calm is the master of motion.... One loses his foundation by being light; and one loses one's master by moving in haste."[27] "The Way never actively does anything, but everything gets done.... Be calm without desiring anything, and all under heaven will settle down to peace."[28] "To be comfortable in the cold, keep moving; to be comfortable in the heat, remain calm. Calm and quietude are the master of the world."[29]

In the highly influential *Jiezishu* 誡子書 (*Admonitions to My Son*) by Zhuge Liang, the prime minister of the State of Shu in the Three Kingdoms Period, who has been considered the incarnation of wisdom in China, are the following words:

> The gentleman cultivates himself in quietude and nurtures his moral sense with a life of thrift. Without indifference to fame and wealth his ideal would not be made clear, and without tranquility of mind he would not be able to go far in realizing his ideal. A calm mind is necessary for studying, and ability has to be acquired through studying. Without studying one cannot enhance one's ability, and without a calm mind one cannot undertake fruitful study.[30]

This passage is representative of the great value accorded *jing* in traditional Chinese culture. The essence of this passage was later summarized into a proverb—"Cultivate yourself in quietude and nurture your moral sense with a life of thrift. Be indifferent to fame and wealth so as to clarify your ideal, and keep your mind tranquil in order to go far in realizing your ideal." This proverb became a very popular motto directing the Chinese in their self-cultivation.

[25] Chen Guying. *Laozi Annotated and Translated with Critical Notes.* Beijing: Zhonghua Book Company, 1984, p. 117.

[26] Ibid., p. 124.

[27] Ibid., p. 171.

[28] Ibid., p. 209.

[29] Ibid., p. 241.

[30] Zhang Lianke and Guan Shuzhen (annotated). *Collected Works of Zhuge Liang Collated and Annotated.* Tianjin: Tianjin Ancient Books Publishing House, 2008, p. 109.

Jing contains great power. When one stays calm, one can focus and concentrate; when one thinks in quiet, one can reach a more thorough understanding of things; when one lives quietly, one become gentle and refined; when one maintains quietude, one's mental capacity is greatly enhanced. That is why *yijing zhidong* 以靜致動 (attaining motion through tranquility) became a unique form of self-cultivation for the Chinese and also helped to promote social progress.

Yijing zhidong implies an emphasis on both the form and the spirit, both mind and body, both flesh and soul, and a mutual construction of the two elements in each pair. Through such techniques as sitting still, meditation, Taoist inner alchemy, Zen, and other forms of tranquil *gongfu* 功夫, one seeks to cultivate one's spirit, giving attention at the same time to breathing exercises and relaxation of the body and the mind. External forms of such self-cultivation include *qigong* 氣功, Taiji boxing, introspection, hobbies such as playing the Chinese zither or *go*, calligraphy, painting, writing poems, and the practice of Zen. The famous lines in a poem by Tao Qian of the Eastern Jin Period—"Picking chrysanthemum at the fence east to my abode, I chanced to see the mountains in the south" give expression to the ultimate state of *jing*, where one transcends the world of mundane things, forgetting both the world and oneself and reaches a state of quietude where everything one does comes naturally. This is a state of harmony between humans and nature, where one attains to both harmony with the external world and an inner harmony with oneself.

Jing is not total stillness with no motion at all, but is complementary with motion. Real *jing* actually facilitates motion, for it is the source of creativity, instilling power and passion in its practitioner. For example, Chinese *gongfu* include many forms of martial art, such as boxing and exercises with the cudgel, the spear, and the sword, and *gongfu* itself comes in many forms—external *gongfu* (which builds up muscles and bones), internal *gongfu* (which benefits the internal organs), hard *gongfu* (which makes the body extremely tough), light *gongfu* (which makes the body light and agile), and *qigong* (breathing exercises); but the essence of all these is "to calm the mind to attain quietude so as to gain enlightenment" and "to instill Zen into martial arts, and to learn martial arts as an effective approach to Zen." Taiji boxing, which has been popular in China for more than three centuries, is an outward expression of the ancient *yinyang* 陰陽 philosophy of China, for it embodies well the principles of the unity of man and nature.

Hermit Culture

Hermits (隱士) were a distinctive group in the cultural history of China. They "cultivated purity of mind and simplicity, and delved into literature as an art,"[31] and thus were also called *xianrenyin* 賢人隱 (virtuous recluses). "Lofty in character, they wanted to remain chaste and pure, and considered wealth and power as worthless."[32] They were talented and learned, and were qualified to be officials, but refused to seek a position in the officialdom against their own will. They can be considered intellectual elites who were learned and had moral integrity.

Though there had been well-known legendary and historical individual hermits from the earliest times in Chinese history, it was during the Wei and Jin Dynasties (AD 220–419) that hermit culture developed fully, with Tao Yuanming as an eminent representative. This culture was well in accord with the Taoist philosophy, which actively pursues an unconventional life with unrestrained sensual pleasures and much time devoted to conversations on metaphysical questions. Tao's recluse poems and essays were full of an immortal beauty that far transcends mundane concerns. They not only brought a new spirit to poetry and prose writing, but fostered a new outlook on life. These works are a monument in the history of Chinese culture and art, and have exerted great influence not only on literature and art, but also on people's leisure values. The first of a set of five poems entitled "Gui yuantian ju" 歸園田居 ("Returning to a Pastoral Life") reads as follows:

> Dimly I see a village in the distance encircled in a ring of embankment,
> With smoke from chimneys gently swaying in the wind.
> Dogs are barking in the long alleys,
> While chickens crow on top of mulberry trees.
> The courtyard in front of my house is dustless,
> And I spend much time in leisure in an empty room.
> Ah, long have I been imprisoned in a cage,
> But now I have returned to the natural world![33]

This pastoral poem sings of a return to life in quietude and represents the mind's pursuit of freedom and the poet's attempt to enrich life with leisure

[31] Xiao Zixian. *Nanqi Shu*. Beijing: Zhonghua Book Company, 1972, p. 925.

[32] Zhong Xianghong. "The hermit culture of traditional China." *Chinese Culture*, 1998(3).

[33] Tao Qian. *Collected Poems of Tao Jingjie*. Shanghai: Commercial Press, 1939, p. 6.

pursuits. Such individualistic spirit and self-cultivation became a model for people of intelligence today as well as those in traditional China, and symbolizes their integrity.

The eight great essayists of the Tang-Song Period (AD 618–1279), namely, Han Yu and Liu Zongyuan from the Tang Dynasty, and Ouyang Xiu, Wang Anshi, Su Xun, Su Shi, Su Zhe, and Zeng Gong from the Song Dynasty, represent another era of great achievements in the literary and artistic history of China. These figures were not strictly hermits, but most of them had experienced frustration and disappointment in their careers in the officialdom, and there were periods in their lives when they lived in a way similar to that of hermits. At such times, they were able to live a joyful life, touring many scenic areas with a carefree spirit. With their unique literary and artistic styles, they showed the romanticism and contentment of defiant eccentrics, lived a simple life following their own nature, with their minds well adapted to the circumstances. They were able to follow Confucius' precept to "be officials when the state is following the Tao, and be hermits when it is not."[34] With clear minds and high spirits, they were able to transcend the worldly and outshine their contemporaries. The peak of their literary creativity often came in periods of forced retirement to a pastoral life. There was the saying "Minor hermits hide themselves in remote areas, hermits of a medium level hide themselves in the marketplace, while the ultimate hermits are able to live a hermits' life while serving at the court." But wherever they were, the great essayists mentioned above were able to maintain purity of heart and look far ahead for quietude in their lives. When they sat quietly alone, a sobriety and calm filled their hearts, enabling them to see themselves and the myriad things of the world clearly. In such a state, they were able more thoroughly to understand the world, reaching ever higher wisdom as the quietude increased.

To some, the hermits seem to have just pretended to let their minds wander freely in harsh times that placed many constraints on them, but actually they had very independent thinking, lived simple lives, kept a low profile, and adhered to simplicity of mind. They would rather renounce officialdom than be restricted by the many requirements placed on officials. In the quietude of their lives, they cultivated their own talents and put them

[34] Liu Baonan. *A Rectified Interpretation of Confucius' Analects*. Beijing: China Bookstore, 1990, p. 617.

to work at appropriate times, which allowed them to create one period of high cultural achievements after another.

Family Instructions

Family instructions, denoting behavior passed down from generation to generation in many of the important families in traditional China, were a form of education aimed at self-cultivation, household management, and the governing of the state. "Cultivation of character" is the core of family instructions. An important feature of traditional Chinese culture is the concept that the individual, the household, and the state are closely integrated, and thus self-cultivation is carried out to serve the purpose of household management, which in turn provides a basis for the development of one's ability for governing the state. The household is both the basic unit of society to which the individual belongs and the basis for the state. Thus,

> The ancients, who wished to illustrate illustrious virtue throughout the kingdom, first ordered well their own States. Wishing to order well their States, they first regulated their households. Wishing to regulate their households, they first cultivated their persons. Wishing to cultivate their persons, they first rectified their hearts. Wishing to rectify their hearts, they first sought to be sincere in their thoughts. Wishing to be sincere in their thoughts, they first tried to acquire knowledge. The acquirement of knowledge lay in the investigation of things. Things being investigated, knowledge would come to them. Knowledge having come to them, their thoughts would become sincere. Their thoughts being sincere, their hearts would then be rectified. Their hearts being rectified, their persons would be cultivated. Their persons being cultivated, their households would be well regulated. Their households being well regulated, their States would be rightly governed. Their States being rightly governed, the whole kingdom would be made tranquil and happy.[35]

Self-cultivation is important, for not only does it give one a great deal of knowledge and makes one gentle and modest, but it also enables one to surpass common people in one's frame of mind. Regulating one's household well is not limited to one's own family, but requires one to gain respect

[35] Zhu Xi. *Collected Annotations on Four Great Books of Confucianism*, Shanghai: Shanghai Bookstore, 1987, pp. 1–2; translation adapted from James Legge, *The Chinese Classics*, vol. 1 (*Confucian Analects*, *The Great Learning*, *The Doctrine of the Mean*). Taipei: SMC Publishing, 1991, pp. 357–359, with some modifications.

from one's extended family and lineage group. Governing the state means managing a large region beyond one's own lineage group, and even different peoples. Making the whole kingdom tranquil and happy implies ability to pacify the people, creating the right conditions so that people can live a life of plenty, be contented with their life and work, and maintain friendly relationships with neighbors so that the land is peaceful.

Fei Xiaotong, an eminent Chinese sociologist in the twentieth century, used a vivid picture as a metaphor for the relationship between the individual, the family, and the state as conceived by the Chinese: "it is like the ripples that appear on the surface of a lake when a rock is thrown into it. Everyone stands at the center of the ripples produced by his or her own social influence."[36] The individual is the piece of rock in Fei's metaphor, while the household, the state, and the whole kingdom are the series of ripples.

This characteristic relationship between the individual on the one hand and the household and the state on the other, as developed in the family instructions, is especially important in traditional China. According to research by a modern scholar, the earliest extant "family instructions" are the admonitions the Duke of Zhou, son of King Wen of Zhou, gave to his son Boqin three millennia ago.[37] After the Han Dynasty, family instructions became more popular, attesting to their long history.

Family instructions have been so important in China because their main aim was to propagate the core values of traditional China, namely, *ren* 仁 (benevolence), *yi* 義 (righteousness), *li* 禮 (courtesy), *zhi* 智 (intelligence), *xin* 信 (trustfulness), *wen* 溫 (temperateness), *liang* 良 (kindness), *gong* 恭 (respectfulness), *jian* 儉 (thrift), and *rang* 讓 (magnanimity). Admonitions in these instructions usually cover the following areas:

1. Respect family rules and laws of the state;
2. Maintain a harmonious relationship with people in one's lineage groups and those in the local community;
3. Show filial piety toward parents and respect to those older than oneself;

[36] Fei Xiaotong 1992. *From the Soil: the foundations of Chinese Society.* (Hamilton, Gary & Wang Zheng, trans.), pp. 62–63.

[37] As the younger son of King Wen, the Duke of Zhou (fl. *c.* 11th century BC) assisted King Wu, his elder brother, in establishing Zhou rule in China. (Sima Qian, *Records of History.* Beijing: Zhonghua Book Company, 1959, p. 1518).

4. Follow requirements of rites and relevant regulations;
5. Worship ancestors, and hold parents' funerals carefully in accordance with rites to show filial piety;
6. Cultivate oneself, and work diligently to further one's learning.

Such family instructions exerted great impact on later generations

The ancient Chinese had a conception of the proper relationship between the individual and his family and the state that was recorded as early as the time when the articles in the *Book of History*, which contains the earliest historical documents in China, were composed. In the chapter "Dayu mo" 大禹謨 ("Strategy of Yu the Great"), the sage king Yao praised Yu (who later became the founder the Xia Dynasty, the first dynasty in Chinese history) thus, "You are able to work diligently for the nation, and practice thrift at home; and you are never self-satisfied. You are indeed a worthy person."[38]

As the founding masters of Confucian thought, both Confucius and Mencius often talked about the relationship between the family and the state. Confucius says, "Bear no resentment whether one is serving the state or staying at home without official positions."[39] And Mencius teaches, "The foundation of world order is in the state; that of the state, in the household, and that of the household, in the individual."[40] For them, the political order of the state, the ethos of the household, and the self-cultivation of the individual all aim at benevolence, which is the basis for social harmony and order.

This cognitive rule of trying to understand others by examining one's own inner world and of starting from what is near oneself and gradually reaching out to ever-larger realms has had tremendous impact not only on the ruling class but also on local communities throughout Chinese history. The Confucians expected to connect the state with the household and make them interdependent through self-cultivation, thus allowing the individual to fulfill his roles in family and in society considered as a community.

[38] Cai Shen. *Collected Annotations for the Book of History*, (multiple authors from the Song and Yuan Dynasties), 1985. Beijing: Zhonghua Book Company, 1985, p. 13.

[39] Zhu Xi. *Collected Annotations on Four Great Books of Confucianism*, Shanghai: Shanghai Bookstore, 1987, p. 133.

[40] Zhu Xi. *Collected Annotations on Four Great Books of Confucianism*, Shanghai: Shanghai Bookstore, 1987, p. 278.

The Confucians reflected on wisdom and human existence centered on life, so the family was seen as the source for life and values for the individual.[41] Family instructions were a kind of textbook used by parents to educate their children. For the common people in an agrarian society, such instructions provided the most important and effective means to manage their free time.

Family instructions include *nüxun* 女訓, or codes of conduct for girls and women. These consist of edification and admonition regarding femininity that was to be internalized as self-conscious control by girls and women. More specifically, *nüxun* are teachings regarding many aspects of social life, including womanly virtues, womanly speech, womanly appearance, womanly work, reading and writing, proper conduct in marriage and family life and in interacting with others, as well as proper manners in speech and conduct. As Jacques Gernet put it, "One thing that is quite certain is that literature played a much less important part in the education of girls than of boys."[42]

The Han Dynasty was a period when Chinese culture reached one of its apogees, and people aimed at higher goals in the cultivation of benevolence, especially with regard to the cultivation of a taste for leisurely activities among women. The great writer Cai Yong (style name Bojie) of the Eastern Han period, who was quite serious with his filial duties and very erudite, possessing broad knowledge in the classics, historical works, phonetics, writing of odes, and calligraphy, had a rather unconventional understanding of the moral sentiments of women. In his *Nüxun*, he discusses the principles for women in cultivating their minds by using the care women devote to their appearance as a metaphor. The entire series of procedures in taking care of one's appearance—looking in the mirror, putting on rouge, putting on powder, oiling the hair, combing the hair, making the hair stand in a coil, putting the sideburns in order—is used metaphorically to instruct the female members of his family that they should purify their mind, keep it in harmony, refresh it, enrich it, smooth it, make it upright, and put it in order. He surely went to great length in coming up with such marvelous metaphors.

[41] Ye Kuangzheng. "Families and country were closely linked," *Hebei Youth Daily*, May 18, 2009.

[42] Gernet, Jacques. *Daily Life in China on the Eve of the Mongol Invasion 1250–1276* (trans. from French by H. M. Wright), Stanford University Press, 1962, p. 157.

It is true that various family instructions and codes for womanly conduct also contained rules that constrained and suppressed the development of women's individuality, but on the whole they were important admonitions conducive to women's self-cultivation.

"Respecting the teacher and emphasizing education" is an important part of the cultural tradition of China, and "getting talented youths from throughout the country and educating them" is considered to be of great value for a teacher.

Industry and Thrift

China has a long history of being an agrarian society. Working industriously and living in thrift, the ancestors of the Chinese created a very successful agrarian culture, which has passed down as a cultural heritage some good principles for maintaining a sound relationship with nature—following the rhythm as set with the solar terms, adapting to local conditions, letting nature run its course, and being united with nature. All of these are still principles and norms governing agricultural activities in the modern world.

In the process of developing intensive farming, where meticulous care has to be taken of the crops, the ancient Chinese invented many rituals to express their gratitude to the heavens, but also to add some entertainment to their lives. Such rituals include praying for rain and for a good harvest, worshiping mountain gods and earth deities, rituals performed before beginning to plough the fields in spring and before harvesting crops with sickles in autumn, festivals to celebrate a bountiful harvest, and various customs associated with the 24 solar terms. These rituals helped to uplift people's spirits, upgrade their ethos and their ideals regarding values, as well as their aesthetic taste, which were all woven into a colorful picture of their leisure life. Thus,

> popular festivals common to everyone, festival and official ceremonies at the court, and festival organized by the religious communities, both Taoist and Buddhist, were all mixed up together. That is why they will be described here in chronological order, without distinction of any other kind, and the account will reveal many aspects of the religious life of the Chinese in particular.[43]

[43] Gernet, Jacques. *Daily Life in China on the Eve of the Mongol Invasion 1250–1276* (trans. from French by H. M. Wright), Stanford University Press, 1962, p. 185.

While working diligently to produce material goods, the Chinese were also immersed in a rich and colorful spiritual life, where they explored the philosophy and wisdom of life.

> There was an aura of magic and religion about arts and about all forms of play: it was on religious occasions that people gave themselves up to play activities, and the aims and character of the games they played went back to very early times when magic had given them a practical or a dramatic function.[44]

Hence, in their hard work, the ancients cultivated faith, strength of character, diligence, and an ability to enjoy life.

With this diligence thus cultivated, the ancient Chinese did not let their free time go by for naught. They abhorred idleness, for it would foster a mentality of disliking hard work and the desire for easy gains. But neither did the ancients want to work like ants who try desperately to move ever more food into their anthills. As the Tang poet Gao Pian comments in his "*Qianxing*" ("Written in Recreation"):

> Those who are always busy like ants in the mundane world
> Should not complain of the snow that keeps on falling.[45]

Zhuangzi also commented, "The tailorbird may build her nest deep in an expansive forest, but the nest occupies but one branch; the mole may drink from the Yellow River, but he can take at most a bellyful. . . . So I have no use for the whole world."[46] Zhuangzi's thinking in this area is very profound, and has had great impact on the practice of thrift. Li Shangyin, another Tang poet, also reminds us,

> Going through what went on in history with households and states,
> One realizes that success came from industry and thrift, and failure, extravagance.[47]

[44] Gernet, Jacques. *Daily Life in China on the Eve of the Mongol Invasion 1250–1276* (trans. from French by H. M. Wright), Stanford University Press, 1962, p. 219.

[45] Sun Tonghai and Wang Haiyan, eds. *Complete Tang Poems.* Beijing Zhonghua Book Company, 1999, p. 6973.

[46] Cao Chuji. *A Simple Annotation of Zhuangzi* (revised ed.). Beijing, Zhonghua Book Company, 2000, p. 8.

[47] Sun Tonghai and Wang Haiyan, eds. *Complete Tang Poems.* Beijing Zhonghua Book Company, 1999, p. 6213.

Thus, only when people embrace a simple life of industry and thrift can the household and the state enjoy lasting prosperity.

Thrift is a good policy for moral cultivation, sound convention for maintaining personal integrity, and wisdom in protecting nature. Industry and thrift also embody the heritage of the "unity of Man and Nature" idea, the reverence for the hermit spirit, the deep understanding of the logic of life, and a subtle understanding of the relationship between work and leisure.

Elegance and Taste in Leisure Life

Elegance and taste in leisure life are the best means for regulating the relationship between work and leisure. In traditional China, the literati were fond of watching flowers and the moon, writing poetry, and painting as activities after work. Even the common people liked to engage in activities similar to what the literati pursued, which nourished their minds, enriched their lives, and made life more enjoyable. Various games that gracefully combined elegance and taste were developed in accordance with nature. These activities not only added an aesthetic dimension to the life of the ancients, but also left rich records of their colorful lives for later generations.

Qingtan

A kind of philosophical discussion, which has been called *qingtan* 清談 ("talk on impractical matters in a leisurely fashion"), flourished from late Han Dynasty to the Jin Dynasty (approximately from the early third to the early fifth century) among the literati, and was considered an activity of elegance and taste. It had its origin in *qingyi* 清議, the examining and ranking of notable people in terms of their virtues, learning, character, talents, and knowledge, which was undertaken by certain individuals who were especially good at evaluating people. Later, a large group of scholar-officials used the form of *qingyi* to appraise people, influence public opinion, and produce political criticism. This kind of activity offended some powerful eunuchs, which led to a move by the latter to restrict the freedom of this group by banning its members from official posts and then to actively persecute them. Many of the former members of the group then began to distance themselves from politics. Lamenting on the changeability of life and sighing for the shortness of life, they indulged in talk about all kinds of impractical matters of the world, especially those concerning the mystical and the metaphysical.[48] The *qingtan* which thus developed became an activity engaged in by many from the aristocratic *shizu* 士族 class,[49] who frequently met to discuss the Taoist ideas of Laozi and Zhuangzi. They deigned not to talk about anything mundane, and considered themselves to be pursuing a spiritual life transcending all mundane concerns, with their meetings being a platform for expressing their noble thoughts and feelings.

The vogue for *qingtan* gave rise to naturalism and individualism in the area of personal life in the Wei-Jin era, and to many concepts and categories used in Chinese aesthetics to explore the source of beauty and to comment on the characters of different people. It brought about the artistic spirit of the Jin people, who found resonance in one another with regard to spiritual freedom and the liberation of human nature, and led to elegant forms of social interaction such as that of the Seven Sages of the Bamboo Grove[50] and the famous gathering at the waterside of Lanting, which is to be described below. *Qingtan* gatherings helped to construct the aesthetics of the time, giving rise to concepts such as *fenggu* 風骨 (strength of character) and *fengyun* 風韻 (charm), and themes for philosophical discussion such as the relationship between words and their meaning, and that between form and spirit. Poems were used to express meanings beyond the literal sense of the words used, music was used to express feelings beyond its sounds, and paintings were used to capture subtle meanings apart from the images. There was much mutual borrowing and interchange among different artistic forms, resulting in the first peak in the history of Chinese literature and art.[51]

[48] Wang Xiaoyang. The implications of Gu Yanwu's essays "Idle talk endangers the nation" and "On the Tao and Its Power," *Studies of Kunshan Culture*, 2013 (1).

[49] *Shizu* 士族 was an aristocratic class which was very powerful during the Six Dynasties. Although they did not have hereditary fiefs as the aristocratic class in Zhou Dynasty had, they did often have hereditary titles and high offices in the government were for the most part monopolized by them.

[50] These were a group of scholars, writers, and musicians of the third century who wished to escape the intrigues, corruption, and stifling atmosphere of court life of their time. They often gathered in a bamboo grove near the house of Ji Kang, one of the seven, where they enjoyed a simple, rustic life and wrote poems about it.

[51] Yuan Xingpei et al., eds. *A History of Chinese Literature*, Beijing: Higher Education Press, vol. 2, 1999, p. 6.

The most vivid recorded scene of such *qingtan* occurred in AD 353, or the ninth year of Emperor Mu's reign in the Jin Dynasty, when the most renowned calligrapher in Chinese history, Wang Xizhi, and 41 others literati gathered at Lanting of Shaoxing. They drank and made merry and composed poems, for which Wang wrote a preface called *Lanting Xu* 蘭亭序 in 324 characters. The preface was written not only in an elegant literary style that expressed well the feelings of those gathered there, but also in a superb calligraphy masterpiece displaying great rhythmic vitality and a perfect coordination of hand and mind on the part of the calligrapher. The gathering was in the name of exorcising some evil spirits at the waterside in accordance with established customs, but according to an article by the modern scholar Zong Baihua, it was actually a great *qingtan* gathering of the *shizu* literati.[52]

Zong, an eminent aesthetician, also commented, "The period from late Han to the end of the Six Dynasties[53] was a time of great political chaos and suffering, but it was also a time in Chinese history when there was much intellectual freedom and a time most abundant in wisdom and passion, and hence in artistic spirit."[54]

In Chinese history, the Seven Scholars of Jian'an, the Seven Sages of the Bamboo Grove, the Eight Tang-Song Essayists, and the Eight Mountain Dwellers were all representative of the *qingtan* spirit.

In his *Xiaochuang Youji* 小窗幽記 (*Notes Written in Seclusion under a Small Window*), the Ming literatus Chen Jiru wrote,

> ......We do not talk about others behind their back, neither are we interested in topics about money or status. We talk at leisure about history and current affairs, and comment on the landscape in the garden. Mild tea and good wine are consumed as befits our interests in this secluded world.[55]

[52] Zong Baihua. "The aesthetics of Jin Dynasty," *Journal of Xuedeng* (Lamp of Learning), 1940.

[53] "Six Dynasties" include Wei, Jin, and the four dynasties (Song, Qi, Liang, and Chen) in the south during the Northern and Southern Dynasties period.

[54] Zong Baihua. "The aesthetics of Jin Dynasty," *Journal of Xuedeng* (Lamp of Learning), 1940.

[55] Chen Jiru. *Notes Written in Seclusion under a Small Window*, (annotated by Chen Qiaosheng). Beijing: Zhonghua Book Company, 2008, p. 190.

This shows what far-reaching influence *qingtan* had had on later generations.

At this, one cannot help but think about the salon, the tavern, the café, *La Rive Gauche*, and afternoon tea in the West, which can also be considered forms and spaces for *qingtan*. It is not clear whether these were influenced by Chinese culture or developed independently in the West, but at any rate, they provided good places for Westerners to get inspiration through leisure activities. The Cambridge Afternoon Tea nurtured close to a hundred Nobel Prize winners, and *La Rive Gauche* produced many a thinker and artist.

However, in contemporary China, *qingtan* seems to have been discarded as a waste of time, and many good places and forms for people to exchange ideas and gain inspiration have been lost, which is quite lamentable. In fact, criticism of *qingtan* was heard throughout Chinese history, with that made by the early Qing thinker Gu Yanwu having perhaps the most profound effect on the modern attitude toward *qingtan*. Gu commented,

> Those who practiced *qingtan* in the past talked about Laozi and Zhuangzi, but now Confucius and Mencius have been made topics for *qingtan*.... Scholars today have substituted empty talks on *mingxin jianxing* 明心見性, or finding one's true self[56] for real learning for self-cultivation and abilities for governing the people. The result is that ministers at court became indolent with their official duties, with no one to attend to important affairs of the state; and officials at lower levels became lazy and disorder spread throughout the whole country. In the end, the divine land of China was turned all over, and the ancestral shrines degenerated into ruins.[57]

Regrettably, views like this led many to misread the *shizu* system and deny the cultural achievements of *shizu* literati, which laid the grounds for the denunciation of the elegance and taste they had represented.

[56] *Mingxin jianxing*, more literally "see clearly one's own mind (through meditation) so as to discover one's true nature," was an idea borrowed by Neo-Confucianists from Zen Buddhism, which supposedly was consistent with the Confucian idea of self-cultivation.

[57] Gu Yanwu. *Knowledge Accumulated Day-by-Day, with collected annotations by Huang Rucheng*. Shanghai Classic Publishing House, 2006, p. 402.

Play

Play is a human instinct, and is also an important leisure behavior. Most of the games of agrarian societies were recreational and sensual, bringing about an experience transcending reality. As Schiller says, "man only plays when in the full meaning of the word he is a man, and he is only completely a man when he plays."[58] Huizinga, likewise, makes clear in his *Homo Ludens*, "Play is never a task. It is done at leisure, during 'free time' ... Here, then, we have the first main characteristic of play: that it is free, is in fact freedom."[59]

A large variety of different games developed in traditional China. For example, according to documentation in historical sources and archaeological findings, soccer has its prototype in the Chinese *cuju* 蹴鞠game which originated five millennia ago in the time of Yellow Emperor. Both *Zhanguo Ce* 戰國策 (*Stratagies of the Warring States*) and *Shiji* 史記 (*Records of History*), two works of history completed more than two millennia ago, contain detailed description of the game. *Zhanguo Ce* describes the popularity of *cuju* in Linzi, the capital city of the State of Qi during the Warring States Period, and *Shiji* states that *cuju* was used in the army of the Han Dynasty as an important means to train soldiers in physical strength and dexterity. After a millennium of development, *cuju* reached its apogee in the Tang and Song Dynasties and continued to be played down to mid-Qing times (i.e., the eighteenth century). On July 15, 2004, Sepp Blatter, president of the FIFA, formally announced to the world that soccer originated in Zibo, Shandong Province of China.[60]

Ice hockey, which many believe to have originated in Canada in the nineteenth century, was played by the Chinese a millennium ago. In the Qing Dynasty, the so-called *bingxi* 冰嬉, or ice-game, caught the attention of the emperor. In 1764, when Emperor Qianlong held a banquet, a large-

[58] Letter XV in *Über die ästhetische Erziehung des Menschen in einer Reihe von Briefen* (On the Aesthetic Education of Man in a Series of Letters), in J. C. Friedrich von Schiller, *Schillers Werke* (Meyers Klassiker-Ausgaben), Leipzig: Bibliographisches Institut, 1895.

[59] Huizinga, Johan, 1949. *Homo Ludens: a study of the play-element in culture*. London, Boston, Henley: Routledge and Kegan Paul.

[60] *Red Star*. "A kick from the Far East: China, birthplace of football." http://www.myredstar.com/a-kick-from-the-far-east-china-birthplace-of-football/, 2004. Accessed March 28, 2016.

scale *bingxi* performance was among the entertainments to amuse the guests. The emperor composed an impromptu poem to commemorate the occasion that contains the following lines,

> Then *bingxi* was tried, with numerous files of soldiers dashing forth on their skates,
> Soon *Heavy Is the Dew* was sung, harmoniously accompanied by many instruments.[61]

A large-sized painting entitled *Bingxitu* 冰嬉圖, jointly painted by two palace painters, can still be seen in the Forbidden City Museum.

Popular games and passtimes were numerous, such as cock-fighting, falconry, aviculture, fish watching, fishing, solving riddles, Chinese couplets, poetic societies, kite flying, shuttlecock kicking, boxing, sword dancing, tea sipping, book market, gardens, Chinese painting, folk music, Chinese opera, calligraphy, bronze and stone inscription, and so on.

Games in traditional China came in many different forms—civil and military, dynamic and tranquil, physically and mentally oriented, vulgar and refined. Often the educative is contained in the amusing, resulting in game forms of good taste and high educational worth. As Zhu Xi puts it, in delving in various arts after one has first grasped the fundamentals of learning,

> (the scholar) comes to be versed with both the root (or the foundations) and the branch tips (or practical applications), with the inner grasp of the fundamentals and the outward expression of technical skills mutually enhancing each other. Thus learning and applying one's knowledge to everyday use, one becomes well-rounded, and, cultivating oneself continuously, one would suddenly reach the realm of sages at some point without knowing it.[62]

With that, the "play" of the ancient Chinese entered the area of culture and education. It is true the ancients also put forth the admonition that "too

[61] Fu Li. *The Social Life of Beijing Residents from Kangxi to Qianlong Reigns*. Beijing Press, 2000, p. 64.

[62] Zhu Xi. *Collected Annotations on Four Great Books of Confucianism*. Beijing: Zhonghua Book Company, 1983, p. 93.

much play would sap one's will," but they never completely denied the playful element in human nature. Furthermore, the "play" of the ancients was guided by those capable of playing with grace and good taste.

Many forms of recreation, such as the diabolo, kite flying, Taiji boxing, cricket fighting, Chinese couplets, poetic societies, opera, and so forth, were well incorporated into the everyday life of the common people, which not only allowed them to give expression to their feelings and interests in leisure, but also helped them to socialize and make friends. Many of these forms of play are still practiced or have been revived recently.

However, in reading Gernet's *Daily Life in China on the Eve of the Mongol Invasion*, we may notice a detail about play in traditional China, "there were also children's games, but unfortunately we know nothing about them."[63] It is this author's opinion that, starting from ancient times, there has been little record of children's play in traditional Chinese sources. Instead, these sources are filled with stories designed to teach children moral behavior and ethical standards, such as a seven-year-old Kong Rong giving his elder brother the larger one of two pears; the young Sima Guang's breaking a big jar of water with a rock to save a playmate who had fallen into it from getting drowned[64]; the 24 stories of filial piety illustrated with pictures, as well as many stories to inspire children to aim high and to achieve more. Stories of the latter kind include the one about Su Qin of the Warring States Period who tied his hair with a string to a beam above and used an awl to prick his thighs in order to stay awake late at night so he could keep on reading books, and the story of the young Che Ying of the Jin Dynasty whose family was too poor to offer a lamp but who caught numerous fireflies and put them in a semi-transparent silk bag for lighting so that he could read books at night. Han Yu's maxim that "one's study is refined with diligence but neglected with sporting was also used to inspire the children. These stories and maxims had profound influence on later generations. In traditional China, people tried to study hard while young in order to pass state examinations and gain official posts in the government, which would not only place them in a privileged status, but was considered a great honor that would bring glory to their lineage groups

[63] Gernet, Jacques. *Daily Life in China on the Eve of the Mongol Invasion 1250–1276* (trans. from French by H. M. Wright), Stanford University Press, 1962, p. 227.

[64] Kong Rong, a descendant of Confucius, was a man of letters in the late Han period. Sima Guang was a scholar-official of the Northern Song Dynasty.

and supposedly even to their deceased ancestors. This tradition has not changed much in the modern era, although the specific forms it takes are different now.

We have noticed another phenomenon related to play—although the Chinese have developed many kinds of games that require rather high intelligence to play, few of them have developed into modern games with clearly defined rules. For example, *mahjong* has been a popular game in China for centuries, but no uniform rules have been developed to this day. The reasons for this would be worth studying.

Womanly Work

In Chinese, there is an idiom "dexterity of the hand comes from the ingenuity of the mind." This idiom is usually used in association with the art and skills demonstrated by women in *nügong* 女紅, which literally means "womanly work," a general term referring to needlework including sewing and embroidery. Such womanly work was an important part of the leisure life of women, a special contribution of those whose lives were primarily devoted to raising children in traditional China.

In many classical Chinese works, there are descriptions of women doing *nügong*. In the "Neize" ("Rules for the Boudoir") chapter of *The Book of Rites*, we find "For ten years, the girl does not go out of the home, but obediently follows the instruction of the governess in handling flax, cultivating silkworms, weaving sleeping mats and silk ribbons. She learns all the work of women so as to be able to provide (the family) with clothes."[65] In the Han poem "Kongque Dongnan Fei" 孔雀東南飛 ("The Peacocks Fly Southeast"), it is said of Jiao Zhongqing's virtuous wife Liu Lanzhi that she "was able to weave white silk at thirteen, and learned to cut out garments at fourteen." In "Mulan Ci" 木蘭辭 ("The Song of Mulan"), we see that Mulan, the girl who was later to disguise herself as a young man in order to join the army in lieu of her aged father, was at the beginning of the poem "weaving while facing the door," with her loom continuing to make a rhythmic sound. And in the *Dream of the Red Chamber*, we have the maid Qing Wen "mending Baoyu's coat made of golden threads from peacocks though she was ill."

[65] Chen Hao. *Collected Commentary on the Book of Rites*. Shanghai Classic Publishing House, 1987, p. 164.

As Gernet commented, "little girls were mainly taught spinning and embroidery: making cloth was traditionally women's work."[66] Though womanly work consists mainly of sewing, weaving, and embroidery, it is by no means limited to these activities. With these core activities as a basis, many elaborate and exquisite artistic forms were developed, such as textile weaving, starching and dyeing, shoe- and hat-making, knot-tying, paper-cutting, food-decorating, toy-making, and so on. For thousands of years, generation after generation of Chinese women have, through their crafts and skills, worked to create art objects, cultivate their minds, and instill truth, goodness, and beauty into the womanly virtues, womanly speech, womanly appearance, and the womanly work required of them.

On the surface, *nügong* is only a system of making things with some unique features, but it potentially can take in many other artistic elements. Women have broad scope in choosing the theme, in designing the pattern and configuration, and in applying colors, all of which have helped to deepen the cultural foundation for the cultivation of feminine virtues.

In the various artifacts and pattern designs created with *nügong*, all things were made lively. There are many auspicious patterns, such as a dragon and a phoenix showing good auspices,[67] a fish jumping over the dragon gate,[68] a pair of mandarin ducks playing in water,[69] cranes under pines symbolizing longevity, and peonies symbolizing riches and honor. All these designs use certain objects to express people's hope for auspiciousness, happiness, and peace, and their desire to exorcise evil spirits. Whether such hopes and desires were expressed directly or in a subtler way, these artworks show women's love for life, diligence, and kindness, feminine virtues that have been sublimated.

Nügong also gives accentuated expression to women's aesthetic tastes. Some of the many forms of nonmaterial cultural heritage produced with *nügong* have profound and rich meanings, while others are exquisite and have a simple charm; some are graceful and splendid, while others are

[66] Gernet, Jacques. *Daily Life in China on the Eve of the Mongol Invasion 1250–1276* (trans. from French by H. M. Wright), Stanford University Press, 1962, p. 158.

[67] The dragon and the phoenix are considered the most auspicious animals in China.

[68] From a legend in which a carp made great effort to jump over a tall gate and became a dragon. The story has since come to be a metaphor for someone from a lowly origin who makes his/her way to great success with tremendous effort.

[69] In Chinese literary and artistic tradition, a pair of mandarin ducks symbolize husband and wife who remain faithful to each other all their lives.

simple, with little decoration. However, all these works are natural and frank expressions of their authors' true nature and sentiments. Like a drizzle or flowers in a peaceful scene, they nourish womanly virtues, womanly speech, womanly appearance, and womanly work.

Nügong was an important part of women's leisure life of elegance and taste. First, it can directly or indirectly foster womanly virtues. Second, it helps to create a spiritual world of goodness and beauty for women, which is then outwardly expressed through their speech, body, posture, actions, and teaching. Third, it has played an important part in forming the role model of the mother for generation after generation of women, especially in their role of giving birth to a later generation, bringing up their children, and inheriting and passing on the feminine virtues through their own earnest practice. Fourth, it was a good guide for leisure life for the family, and helped to enrich cultural and spiritual life in an agrarian society with its general shortage in material goods.

In modern times, *nügong* has diminished among urban residents; but in rural areas, with the rise of the movement to protect nonmaterial cultural heritage in recent years, certain forms of *nügong* are being revived.

The Book and the Zither

Books on the Left

The earliest use of the term *zuoshu youqin* 左書右琴 ("books on the left and a zither on the right") is found in a poem in praise of Zhang Yong that was recorded by Ruan Changling in the early Song Period.[70] Part of the poem reads,

> The governor's room is empty except for a table
> With books on the left and a zither on the right.
> The governor never tried to gather goods for himself,
> Nor was he ever dishonest to other people.
> Those of low statuses or high, he treats them equally,
> Even for small differences, he tries to make it equitable.[71]

[70] Zhang had been quite successful as the governor of Yizhou prefecture and was considered by people there as a good official, but the central government decided to transfer him to another post, on which occasion some people of Yizhou composed this poem.

[71] Ruan Changling. *Lu minci*. In Zhang Yong, *Collected Works of Zhang Yong*. Beijing: Zhonghua Book Company, 2000. 2000: 196–198.

Zuoshu youqin is here used to describe the gentleman's learned and refined demeanor, and is a requisite quality for the gentleman. Hence the saying, "A gentleman's seat must be furnished with books to the left and a zither to the right." Why must the gentleman acquire both learning through books and skills for playing the zither? And what does reading and playing zither have to do with the nurturing of a gentleman? We can take a look at what the ancient Chinese had to say regarding these matters and what they actually did in practice.

Books on the left. Reading was not only an important part of the lifestyle of the ancient Chinese, but also a necessary approach to one's education in rites and proper manners. In the "Baoshi"[72] 保氏chapter of *Zhouli* 周禮 ("Rites of Zhou"), a collection of various rites compiled more than two millennia ago, are these words:

In order to educate the sons of high-ranking aristocratic families with the Tao, Baoshi should teach them arts in six areas, namely, the six types of rites, six dances accompanied by music, five ways of shooting arrows in archery, five skills for chariotry, six scripts for writing (*liushu* 六書),[73] and arithmetic calculations in nine areas.[74]

The "six arts" of rites, music, archery, chariotry, writing, and arithmetic later became the norm for education in traditional China and continued as such for a long time. By the Tang and Song Dynasties, China entered long periods of prosperity and peace, and culture also flourished, with a great abundance of cultural achievements produced by numerous poets and artists. The roots of such achievements lay in the general social ethos in which education, with reading as its most important component, was highly valued. This ethos found expression in many poems in traditional China, such as the following one:

When angry, I become happy through reading,
And when ill, reading helps me recover.

[72] *Baoshi* is the title for the official at the king's court who was responsible both for remonstrating with the king for his mistakes and for educating the sons of high-ranking aristocrats.

[73] The traditional explanation of *liushu* here is that it is the same as the *liushu* theory on the ways Chinese characters are constructed that was explicated by a number of scholars in from late Western Han to the Eastern Han Period (approximated early first to early third century AD). (Xiong Changhua, 2008).

[74] Sun Yirang. *A Rectified Interpretation of the Zhou Rites.* Beijing: Zhonghua Book Company, 1987, p. 1010.

> Books are important to me like my life,
> So I have a big and disorderly pile of them before me.
> —"Ti Shuchu" (On the Bookcase) by Yang Xunji,[75]
> a Ming scholar-official

Even among common people, there was the saying "It is with honesty, kindness, and good education that a family line can long continue." These sayings, or others with similar intent, were often incorporated into family instructions. For people in southern Anhui, which produced many notable merchant houses in history, a Chinese couplet captures well their ideas about household management:

> Houses continue to prosper for centuries because of their good deeds;
> The best thing for later generations to inherit is education.[76]

And in the *Heshi Jiagui* ("House Rules of the He Family") from Yangzhou, we read:

> Revere the Confucian classics, and treasure paper and the writing brush.
> Keep the tables clean, and sincerely prepare your body and mind for reading.[77]

The ancients' understanding of reading is simple and pure, with much attention paid to the relationship between reading and the cultivation of one's character and moral sense. From this reverence for education was developed the social milieu that encouraged people to foster interest in reading—and in reading good books. The reward from such reading is that abundant cultural capital is accumulated for the individual, the family, and the country as a whole, which had tremendous effects on society, far beyond that produced by monetary capital. Thus, in traditional China both society and family encouraged the fostering of self-disciplined gentlemen. For such gentlemen, a life without books or the zither would be quite inconceivable.

[75] Ai Yage, "Poems on Reading," 360doc, http://www.360doc.com/content/11/1110/13/6956316_163294420.shtml. Accessed on January 1, 2017.

[76] Jiang Zhiwei. "Appreciating Chinese couplets in 'Village of Good Family Traditions'." *People's Daily* (overseas edition), April 16, 2014, p. 5.

[77] He Lun. *Ho's Family Rules*, in Ho Family Garden, Yang Zhou, Jiangsu Province, 2010.

Zither on the Right

The zither has been an important part of Chinese culture for thousands of years. Different forms of the zither, *qin* 琴and *se* 瑟,[78] are recorded in several places in the *Book of Poetry*, such as the following lines:

> I play my zither, to befriend
> The gentle and graceful young lady.[79]
>
> Plucking the zither,
> We are full of joy and serenity.[80]

In an essay entitled "On the Zither," Liu Ji, a literatus of the Southern Song Dynasty, commented thus:

> It is beautiful, but not with too much glamour. Its tune has a sadness, but not with excessive sorrow. It is a plain instrument, but is capable of embellishment when necessary; and it can be eloquent without being dishonest. (Jiu Jie, 1988)

> The zither has seven functions, 1) to clarify the Tao and De (laws of Nature); 2) to move the spirits; 3) to reform customs for the better; 4) to make one's heart more sensitive; 5) to create nice tunes; 6) to give expression to refinement; and 7) to aid the teacher's instruction.[81]

Zither-playing is used to stop immorality and maintain moral uprightness. The zither and its music were therefore considered befitting for the sages:

> The zither is an instrument made by sages in order to rectify people's bad intensions, to guide government actions, to harmonize *liuqi* (or six factors in the human body),[82] and to adjust the natural factors of the four seasons to

[78] The *qin* is seven-stringed, while the *se* has 25 strings.

[79] Qu Wanli. The Book of Poetry Annotated, vol. 6 of *Collected Works of Qu Wanli.* Taipei: Lianjing Publishing Company, 1983, p. 4.

[80] Qu Wanli. The Book of Poetry Annotated, vol. 6 of *Collected Works of Qu Wanli.* Taipei: Lianjing Publishing Company, 1983, p. 145.

[81] Jiang Keqian, ed. *Complete Works Related to the Zither.* Beijing: Zhonghua Book Company, 2007, p. 195.

[82] *Liuqi* is a concept derived from the *wuxing* (five elements) theory and used primarily in traditional Chinese medicine. Six factors in Nature, namely, wind, cold, summer heat, humidity, dryness, and fire, are used metaphorically to indicate different conditions in the human body.

> attain the harmonious *yuzhu* (jade candle). It is indeed a miraculous instrument passed down from remote antiquity that was derived from the anima of heaven and earth. Its music is for times of peace and prosperity, and it is an instrument that gentlemen use to help with their self-cultivation.[83]

The zither, then, was an integral part of the daily self-cultivation of the literati, who used it to create an ethereal and limpid spiritual world with a serene and peaceful atmosphere, in which they could keep their minds calm to appreciate and reflect on things. Therefore, the ancients had the saying, "Unless there is some very serious problem preventing him from doing so, the gentleman always keeps a zither at hand." Zither-playing seems to be just the art of playing an instrument, but it represents the Confucian approach to nurturing one's character through music.

Throughout Chinese history, there were many notable figures who kept to the motto, "The gentleman's seat is supplied with books to the left and a zither to the right." For the Warring States Period, there is the often-told story about Zhong Ziqi and Yu Boya as recorded in *Liezi*:

> Boya was good at playing zither, and Zhong Ziqi was good at listening. When Boya played thinking in his mind about high mountains, Zhong exclaimed, "That is wonderful! The music sounds like the towering Mt. Tai!"[84] Boya then played thinking about water flowing in river, Zhong exclaimed, "That is wonderful! The music sounds like water flowing with great strength in rivers!"[85]

The zither tune *Feng Qiu Huang* 鳳求凰 ("The Male Phoenix Courting the Female Phoenix"), composed by Sima Xiangru, a great writer of the Western Han Period better known for his descriptive poems, recorded the story of the passionate and touching love between him and Zhuo Wenjun. As one of the "Ten Great Zither Tunes of China," *Hujia Shibapai* 胡笳十八拍

[83] Zhu Quan. *Miraculous Music with Notation by Quxian*, Beijing: National Library Press, 2013, preface.

[84] Mount Tai, the highest mountain in Shandong Province, was one of the *Wuyue* (five great mountains) in traditional China.

[85] Yang Bojun, *Collected Annotations for Liezi*. Beijing: Zhonghua Book Company, 1979, p. 178.

("Nomad Flute Tunes in Eighteen Stanzas")[86] by Cai Wenji demonstrates her mastery of music in addition to her erudition.

When Ji Kang, one of the Seven Sages of the Bamboo Grove, was about to be executed after having offended those in power, he was very composed. As his last wish before death, he asked for a zither, with which he played his favorite *Guangling San* 廣陵散, which then became a famous zither tune and which is listed among the Ten Great Zither Tunes. The tune expresses the sentiment of "a good warrior is ready to die for a patron who really appreciates him."[87] The tune also transmitted a voice for justice, with defiance of the powerful and indignation at the inequalities of the world.

In his *Yangchuntang Qinjing* 陽春堂琴經, a work completed in the Wanli Reign of the Ming Dynasty, the eminent zither player and researcher Zhang Daming wrote:

> Among the ancients, there were many who passed on the art of zither-playing from generation to generation. Of the most notable ones were ... the three scholars of the Su lineage group of Meishan, Sichuan.[88] All these individuals were able to have their spirit fly up and down freely in refreshing breeze, and never let their family name fall with respect to Yiyang.[89, 90]

Although we have not explored all six arts (rites, music, archery, chariotry, writing, and arithmetic), we can see how profoundly they have influenced the cultural traditions of China.

[86] This famous tune, which has been listed among the Ten Great Zither Tunes, has been attributed to Cai Yan, better known by her style name Wenji, of the late Han Period. Cai, a highly talented daughter of the notable historian Cai Yong, was captured by the Xiongnu, a nomadic people north to the Han Empire, after Yong had died in the midst of the political chaos in the Late Han period, and had to marry a Xiongnu prince, with whom she had two children. After he had restored order in the northern part of China, Cao Cao, who had been a friend of Yong, had Wenji ransomed from the Xiongnu.

[87] The title *Guangling San* means a kind of music in circulation in Guangling (near modern-day Yangzhou), but it originated in the Hejian region in the north.

[88] This refers to Su Xun and his sons Shi and Zhe, all three being among the eight great essayists of the Tang-Song Period.

[89] Yiyang, literally "the south side of Mt. Yi," is a place known for its *tong* trees (of the genus *Paulownia*), the wood from which was superb for making zithers. So "Yiyang" was used as an allusion to the zither.

[90] Zhang Daming. *The Yangchuntang Canon of the Zither*. In Chinese National Academy of Arts and Chinese Association of Zither Research, 2010, vol. 7, p. 329.

From the above, we can see that for the Chinese "books on the left and the zither on the right" is not only a symbol representing the cultural traditions, but also the most important approach to shaping their life in a subtle way. Without books and the zither, one's spirit would be dispersed and scattered around rather than concentrated, and one would be living a dissolute life eating and drinking like an animal, and then becoming worthless after death.

Seven Things for a Life with Refined Taste

Generally speaking, there are seven things that were indispensable for life among the ancient Chinese, and those were: the zither, the game of *go*, books, painting, wine, poetry, and tea. For one thing, these things can help to cultivate one's basic ability for life and to fulfill the three immortalities of leaving one's words (in works that would be long-lasting), leaving one's deeds for later generations to admire, and attaining to a high level of morality that would continue to inspire people. For another, the basic needs for clothes, food, a place to live, and means to move around, reading, play, and interacting with others are also indispensable for the development of the human individual. Thus, the educational goal set by a family for sons was usually to have them become literati and enter the path to become government officials, while that for daughters was for them to be able to cooperate with a husband in the future, taking on the task of assisting their husbands and teaching their sons. According to the tradition developed by the ancients, ability with the seven items listed above were the basic requisites for pursuing a life of refined taste, for "he who is good at playing zither would be understanding and serene, he who is good at playing *go* would be resourceful, he who is good at reading would have good understanding of the nature of things and know courtesy, and he who is good at painting would be intelligent with an ethereal spirit." Having some wine or tea while composing poems would make for a life of refined taste and can be used as a measure of joy in life. Of course, the even more important goal is to practice the "six arts" in one's self-cultivation to reach a high level of morality, to use one's written works as a carrier for the Confucian Tao, and to combine knowledge with action.

Of the four hobbies of zither, *go*, calligraphy, and painting as the literati's artistic accomplishments, zither ranked first. Consequently, the zither was a must among the furnishings in the study of a man of letters, who would "have fun with the zither and books so as to forget his worries," or "be delighted with works written on wooden tablets, and make merry by plucking the seven-stringed zither." The ancients loved the zither not because they wanted to show their zither-playing skills to others, but because through doing so they tried to enter a spiritual realm where they could forget both the world and their own selves. Thus, "wherever the gentleman is seated, there must be books to the left and a zither to the right." Books and a zither were things that were always included among the things placed on his table. It was necessary for the gentleman both to "have knowledge from five carts of books,"[91] and to be proficient with the "six arts." This is because even if he is good at reading books, if he does not know how to play the zither then he is not a complete man. He would be either just a bookworm, or very narrow-minded, and be understood to have some kind of personality disorder. Of course, the "zither" here does not have to be taken literally, but can stand for a healthy attitude toward the leisurely life with elegance and taste and the necessary skills for recreational activities.

The Chinese have been drinking tea for two millennia. Tea is one of the "seven things one has to think of everyday" (the others being firewood, rice, oil, salt, soy sauce, vinegar). It is not just a necessity of life, but also something that can give expression to the quality of one's life, show one's style and taste, and refine one's disposition and intelligence.

Having tea was often associated with moral cultivation. Thus, "friendship can develop between two gentlemen over just a cup of tea," which means people try to have a friendship in which friends can work in concert and weather hard times together.

The entire process of having tea is to be enjoyed. One can watch the tender leaves being put in a cup, and slowly unfold after hot water is poured in, and enjoy a quietude as a foggy vapor slowly rises out of the cup. One can sit at a window and, watching leaves fall or raindrops hit the window lattice, and feel the kind of self-contentment described in *Caigentan* 菜根譚: "Indifferent to honor or humiliation, I only watch the flowers in my courtyard bloom and fade; unconcerned with people coming and leaving,

[91] This is an allusion to the sentence "Hui Shi has many skills, his books being of five cartloads" in *Zhuangzi*. (see Cao Chuji, 2000: 504).

my mind only follows the clouds in the sky folding and unfolding."[92] With such a mindset, how enjoyable life can be!

In his *Xianqing Ouji* 閑情偶寄,[93] the Qing dramatist Li Yu (1610–1680) gave a vivid and exquisite description of the Chinese art of life. For example, the book includes descriptions of the different ways of amusement used by the rich and the poor, different ways of amusement for different seasons, and different ways of amusement when one sleeps, sits, walks, stands, and drinks. Throughout the book, one can feel the wit and philosophical attitude to life of the Chinese. It includes discussions on drama, diet, architecture, horticulture, health, and other topics related to life. For example, in the section on diet, Li advocates the pursuit of refinement along with simplicity with regard to food and drink. His ideas in this section have been summarized in eight phrases, namely, emphasis on vegetable food, thrift, valuing the original taste of things, a diet mainly of light and mild food, avoiding greasy food, trying to make food clean and nice-looking, caution to avoid killing, and care to ensure that food is nutritious.[94] The whole book reflects the Chinese aesthetic conception of being reserved and close to nature, and truthfully records the art of life, the leisurely mood, and the worldly attitude toward life in Qing China in good detail.

An important phenomenon worth explaining is that the modern educational system was developed rather late in history and is still very imperfect to this day. However, that does not mean there is no history of education in China. In traditional China, education took three forms, namely, public schools, private schools, and *jiaxue* 家學, or instruction given by family members at home. Among these, *jiaxue* played a very important role, and skills for playing zither and *go*, for calligraphy, painting, poetry, and appreciating tea and wine were all integral parts of the learning, arts, and cultural values transmitted generation after generation.

[92] Hong Yingming. *Reflections over Vegetable Roots.* Beijing: Zhonghua Book Company, 2008, p. 248.

[93] Li Yu. *Notes Written in Leisurely Mood.* Beijing: Zhonghua Book Company, 2007.

[94] Lin Naishen. *Record on Diet* Vol. 86 in *General Record of Chinese Culture.* Shanghai: Shanghai People's Literature Publishing House, 1998.

Institutional Arrangements for Vacations

Another aspect of the leisure culture in traditional China was the institutional arrangements made by the state for holidays. In pre-Qin times, the government did not make any institutional arrangements specifically for holidays, but there was legislation for regular worship of heaven and earth and of gods and goddesses. The deities worshipped ranged from the greatest ones ruling the world and those corresponding to astronomical entities and phenomena, all the way to minor deities in charge of the watercourses of furrows in the fields, of grasses, trees, insects, and fish, and even deities in charge of food, clothes, houses, and carriages, as well as those who were patrons to farmers, merchants, doctors, and diviners. Government regulations required people to put down their farm work, walk out of their houses and palaces, or halt their official duties to participate in various kinds of religious rites so as to show their reverence for and piety toward Nature, life, ancestral spirits, and the deities. These regulations demonstrate a well-developed political philosophy and administrative skills at controlling the officials, but the real intention for them was the nurturing of the soul, the enrichment of people's spiritual world, the enforcement of the moral order, and the demonstration of the solemnity of social life.

The Period of the Han Dynasty

Official institutional arrangements for holidays started in the Qin-Han Period. From remnants of the *Han Code*, we can see that the government in the Western Han Period had stipulated "government officers are to have one day off every five days to take bath,"[95] which means government officers at that time enjoyed something much like a weekend we have today. In addition to this, the winter and summer solstices in the 24 solar terms were also regular holidays for government officers. In the *Houhan Shu* 後漢書, it is recorded that "around the *lidong*[96] 立冬, a gentleman is supposed to rest peacefully, so all officers are to halt their business. Imperial

[95] Ya Se and Yuan Yu. *Common Knowledge about Ancient China: 1000 questions*. Beijing: New World Press, 2011, p. 272.

[96] *Lidong* (the beginning of winter), also one of the 24 solar terms, is one and half a month prior to the winter solstice.

hearings will not be held until some auspicious day chosen for the hearings to be resumed."[97]

Tang and Song Dynasties

In the Tang-Song Period, traditional China reached its apogee in prosperity and strength, resulting in a society that was politically well governed, economically well developed, and militarily strong. Many countries around China acknowledged her superiority by sending diplomatic missions to her court. Institutional arrangements for holidays also saw further development in this period. Even the Jin Dynasty established by the Jürchens imitated the Chinese dynasties in promulgating a *Jia'ningling*假寧令 (edict on holidays and leaves) with as many as 18 articles covering almost all aspects of life, including weddings, funerals, death anniversaries, and travel to and from official posts to which one was assigned.

The Ming Dynasty

Generally speaking, holidays in the Ming Dynasty were fewer than those in Tang and Song Dynasties, but during the Yongle reign, Zhu Di, the emperor, lengthened the Lantern Festival holidays to ten days, during which time officials could rest at home rather than having to travel to the court to report to the emperor. Commoners also gained more liberty in celebrating the Lantern Festival, including drinking and making merry, since officials were no longer to interfere with their celebratory activities. And these rules were "to be fixed forever." An important feature of the Ming officials' holidays is that many of them enjoyed searching for valuable books and getting their own or others' works printed, to the point where almost everyone who passed the official examinations "is likely to have had a book of his works printed already."[98] "Although the number of holidays for officials had decreased in the Ming Dynasty, the scholar-officials and other literati were engaged in very frequent social interactions that were related to

[97] Fan Ye. *The History of the Later Han Dynasty*. Beijing: Zhonghua Book Company, 1965, p. 3125.

[98] Ye Dehui. *Stories for Bibliophiles*. Beijing: Zhonghua Book Company, 1999, p. 154.

reading and discussion on politics."[99] During the Wanli Reign, a couplet with both a nice poetic touch and a profound meaning came into being:

> The sound of reading, mingled with the sounds of wind and rain, is so sweet to hear;
> The affairs of the world, together with the affairs of the country and of the family, are all within my concern.

The couplet represents not only an embodiment of the cultural heritage of the institutional arrangements for holidays and leaves in the Ming Dynasty, but also left the spirit of "every man is responsible for the rise or decay of his country," which is part of the core value nurtured by the holiday system in traditional China.

Qing Dynasty

The Qing Dynasty largely followed the Ming Dynasty with respect to holidays and leaves.[100] Holidays were extended so that the period from the winter solstice through the Chinese New Year's Day all the way to the Lantern Festival, which is on the 15th day of the first moon, were all days off for officials. Scholar-officials usually used this extended vacation to gather with friends so they could write poems and criticized literary works together. In this respect, both the Kangxi and Qianlong Emperors set an example for their officials. Kangxi spent a great deal of his leisure time studying mathematics and astronomy from Western missionaries at his court, and he made contributions to the propagation of Western mathematical knowledge and thus to the development of mathematics in China. Qianlong reigned as emperor for 60 years, during which time he made as many as six trips to the Jiangnan region south of the Yangtze River. In his *Nanxunji* 南巡記 (*A Record of My Inspection Tour to the South*), which he wrote after completing his last trip to Jiangnan, he said, "In the 5 decades I have reigned, I did only two things that can be called great. One is the military expeditions I ordered

[99] Yue Liangwen. "Holidays and leaves for officials in traditional China." *Study Times*, March 12, 2011.

[100] Lin Yongkuang. *A General History of the Palace Culture of Qing Dynasty*. Shanghai: Shanghai Literature and Art Publishing House, 2014, p. 233.

to the western part, and another is my inspection tours to the South."[101] Qianlong was not only good at writing, but was also fond of archery and collecting things of artistic value. His rule helped to determine the Kangxi-Qianlong period of economic and cultural flourishing in China.

During the Hundred Days' Reform in 1898, it was reported in *Shen Bao* 申報 (*Shanghai News*)[102] that "Kang Youwei founded the Baoguohui 保國會 [Society to Protect China], which attracted more than three hundred members, all of whom were officials."[103] Clearly, a large number of officials had joined Kang's Baoguo Society. This was a modern-type learned society, with the reading of books and newspapers and lectures as its main activities. The society was based on the Western model, to the point that the Western calendar was adopted, with the holiday being set at Sunday. This prepared the way for the Sunday later to be officially adopted by the Chinese government as holiday.

Generally speaking, the institutional arrangements for holidays and leaves for officials in China were started in the Han Period, and "were most lenient in the Tang-Song Period, but were gradually tightened up in the Ming-Qing Period."[104] The tightening up of the arrangement in the Ming-Qing Period was partly because the amount of work that needed to be done had increased as government functions became more complex, but was also a necessary outcome of the need for an increasingly more despotic monarchy to tighten control over the officials. However, it was still quite nice a scene to have the scholar-officials uphold standards of refinement and taste as they delved into classical works and wrote elegant essays and poems when they were off official duty.

In reading through relevant literature, we notice a historical detail that enlightened rulers also tended to show more solicitude for people who had to toil. For example, in the legislations for the city in Zhou Dynasty as recorded in *Guoyu*國語, or "Discourses of the States," we have:

[101] Lin Yongkuang. *A General History of the Palace Culture of Qing Dynasty*. Shanghai: Shanghai Literature and Art Publishing House, 2014, p. 233.

[102] *Shen Bao*, the first newspaper printed in Chinese, was founded by Ernest Major (1841–1908), a British businessman, and was published from April 30, 1872 to May 27, 1949 in Shanghai.

[103] Anonymous. "More News about National Affairs as Reported by a Friend from Beijing." *Shanghai News*, October 2, 1898, p. 1.

[104] Yue Liangwen. "Holidays and leaves for officials in traditional China." *Study Times*, March 12, 2011.

> Do not burden the people with corvée in busy seasons for farm work, and do not take their labor lightly (and use it wantonly). Let them have some free time, keep them well supplied, and do not make them work excessively. Then the construction work in the city will be conducted smoothly, and in the countryside people will also live an orderly life.[105]

In a few sentences, *Guoyu* has given a good account of the ideal governing the relationships between humans and nature, among people, between the individual and the society, between work and leisure, and between urban and rural areas. Another example can be found in an edict issued to *Shangshu Sheng* (the Department of State Affairs) by Emperor Zhang of the Jürchen Dynasty of Jin, which states, "Any project that requires the levying of large numbers of corvée has to be treated with great caution."[106] All these are in accordance with the traditional Confucian teaching that "hard work interspersed with relaxation is the way of King Wen and King Wu."

The general survey of the institutional arrangements for holidays and leaves that has been detailed above reveals the following features: (1) an important aim of holidays is to follow the natural cycle of the seasons, which reflects the principle of "unity between Man and Nature," the typical Chinese outlook on nature and values; and (2) holidays are not for one to give free rein to one's desires for sensual pleasures, but to have time for a spiritual life in which the mind can wander freely and with ease, and to engage in self-cultivation and the nurturing of one's interests. It is true that the institutional arrangements for holidays and leaves in traditional China targeted only the class of the scholar-officials, but that was in accord with the conditions of an agrarian society where common people were responsible for managing their own time.

Conclusion

The concept of the unity between man and nature, self-cultivation, and the pursuit of elegance and taste were the foundations of the ancient Chinese conception of leisure. The concept of the unity between man and nature laid the foundation of the Chinese outlook on life and values, self-

[105] Xu Yuangao. *Collected Annotations for Guoyu.* Beijing Zhonghua Book Company, 2002, p. 66.

[106] Tuotuo. *History of the Jin Dynasty.* Beijing: Zhonghua Book Company, 1975, p. 257.

cultivation was used to shape the basic principles the individual identified with in his conduct, and the pursuit of elegance and taste helped to enrich life in the world.

In history, China was widely known as "a land of courtesy and propriety" and a country marked by its "respect for teachers and emphasis on education." With the Silk Road, that has traversed more than 2,000 years of history, all the way from the pre-Qin era through the Han and Tang Periods to the Song, Yuan, Ming, and Qing Dynasties, China has brought to the rest of the world art objects of elegance and taste as well as items of practical use, which have not only shown to the world exquisite Chinese aesthetics, but also propagated the values of harmonious coexistence. In this whole process, the concept of leisure and the tradition of a rich leisure life in China have played an extremely important role.

The Chinese tradition of leisure culture tells us that the world of leisure has quietly nurtured people's hearts and minds, as well as their moral sense and moral character, and has silently but also with great strength nurtured and guarded the spiritual home of human beings.

This tradition also tells us that leisure is intimately related to philosophy, literature, art, religion, and science, with philosophy being used to study the human mind, and literature to cure our heart,[107] leisure to give quietude to the heart, art to amuse it, religion to give it peace, and science to keep our mind on the right course. Leisure, then, is a prerequisite for creativity in all spheres of culture.

This tradition further tells us that the ancient Chinese understood leisure not simply as a length of free time to be used for recreation, but also a particular state of mind and an opportunity to nurture one's own character and develop healthy hobbies. It is in this state of mind that people can learn that the coming and going of life is always dependent on spiritual activities beyond the physical body and material life.

Leisure can raise one's existence and the quality of one's life to higher levels. It provides a necessary distance between work and life. A quality leisure life allows one's spirit to maintain a state of harmony, and also allows one's body to get repose, with improved blood circulation and relaxed breathing. One's visual and auditory senses, together with one's nervous system, get rest when in a relaxed state, and one's body falls into complete

[107] Both "mind" and "heart" here are translated from the Chinese character *xin* (心), which can mean both.

calm. It is in this kind of state that the human soul can attain freedom and inspiration, thus realizing the freedom, the aesthetic state, and the creativity of the human individual.

The effect leisure has on the human individual cannot be exactly measured, but it is doubtless an important part of human life and of society. Only when sustained by leisure can the dignity of human nature, the richness and interest in life, and the harmony of society advance to ever higher levels.

CHAPTER 3

Leisure in the Modern Cultural Movements of China

While chatting with me, a French friend commented that although both the Chinese and the French like to have revolutions, their revolutionary goals were rather different. Through revolutions, the French overthrew the rule of dictators and won natural human rights, passed on their renowned cultural tradition, and secured liberty, equality, and fraternity. What puzzles the French is that the Chinese revolutions in modern times have done nothing but indiscriminately wreak havoc on China's culture.

His words made me think hard. China's rich and remarkable culture, which accumulated over millennia, and which includes many subcultures, or popular traditions and folklore, has been much mutilated within little more than a century. In this process, three issues have remained unresolved: (1) how are the Chinese to analyze and expound the values of their traditional culture? (2) by what are the values of Chinese culture embodied? and (3) how are the Chinese to re-identify with and endorse their national culture? Over the last hundred years of cultural movements, the Chinese have constantly been grappling with these issues.

Today, China is undergoing many social reforms, and still has to deal with the same issues. At the same time, new issues have been raised: (1) what is the best way to integrate tradition and modernity? (2) how can Chinese culture and Western culture join forces and be fused into a stronger culture? (3) does modernization necessarily imply a farewell to traditional

Huidi Ma, Er Liu, *Traditional Chinese Leisure Culture and Economic Development*, DOI 10.1057/978-1-137-59253-8_3

cultures? A review of the history of modern China may help to address these issues.

The Heyday of Chinese Civilization

Let us first take a look at the so-called Kangxi-Qianlong Era, approximately 1681–1796, which was the last period in history when China enjoyed power and prosperity.

The Prosperous Kangxi-Qianlong Era (康乾盛世)

Economic Prosperity

According to estimates given by the British economist Angus Maddison, in 1820, China's gross domestic product (GDP) accounted for 32.9% of the world total, while all countries in Western Europe together accounted for 23.6%, and the USA and Japan accounted for 1.8% and 3.0%, respectively.[1] The Europeans liked luxury items made in China, such as silk products, tea, porcelain, and various handicrafts. At that time, Europeans were also very interested in Chinese culture and philosophy. The French sinologist Jean-Pierre Abel-Rémusat published a biography of Laozi in 1824,[2] and his student Stanislas Julien, another eminent French sinologist, translated Laozi's *Daodejing* into French in 1842.[3] The German philosophers Hegel, Nietzsche, and Heidegger are all known to have studied the *Daodejing*. Many Western scholars think highly of Laozi.[4] This response to Laozi is just one example of the welcome Chinese culture and thought met with at that time, when they were introduced to the West.

[1] Angus Maddison, *The World Economy*, vol. 2 (Historical Statistics), OECD Publishing, 2006, Table 8b on p. 641.

[2] Jean-Pierre Abel-Rémusat. "Mémoire sur la vie et les opinions de Lao-Tseu, philosophe Chinois du VIe siècle avant notre ère," in *Mémoires de l'Académie Royale des Inscriptions et Belles-Lettres*, vol. VII, 1824.

[3] Stanislas Julien, "Le Livre de la Voie et de la Vertu, composé dans le VIe siècle avant l'ère chrétienne, par le philosophe Lao-Tseu, traduit en français et publié avec le texte chinois et un commentaire perpétuel." Paris, 1842.

[4] James I. Wong, *Chinoiserie and Sinophilism in the 17th- and 18th-Century Europe: examples of cultural symbioses.* Stockton, CA: Koinonia Productions, 1984.

Cultural Flourishing

During the Kangxi-Qianlong Era, China also produced many important works of literature. Such works included literary masterpieces, among which were *Dream of the Red Chamber*, *Strange Stories from a Chinese Studio*, and *The Scholars*, as well as works of less literary renown but nevertheless considered valuable as guides to the art of life in traditional China, such as *Miscellaneous Notes Written in a Leisurely Mood* and Shen Fu's *Six Records of a Floating Life*. From descriptions of scenes of leisure life in these works, one can see the role played by leisure in creating the economic prosperity and cultural flourishing of China at that time.

Dream of the Red Chamber (紅樓夢), ranked among the four masterpieces of classical Chinese novels, is a story about the rise and fall of four aristocratic families, but the book contains a great deal of description of the daily affairs of these families and the leisure activities of the young ladies in their boudoirs, giving a detailed and lively representation of broad social life with the rites, customs, foods, clothes, and mundane daily life of the author's time. A few chapters of the book are devoted to descriptions of the young ladies' activities in their "Haitang Poetry Club,"[5] which are an important part of their leisure life. Both male and female members of the Jia family, known for its emphasis on poetry and rites, were taught to compose poems and Chinese couplets from childhood on, reflecting the taste and style of the wealthy at the time.

Miscellaneous Notes Written in a Leisurely Mood (閑情偶寄), written by Li Yu, an eminent dramatist honored as "the Chinese Shakespeare," has been praised as an encyclopedia of the art of life in traditional China. The book contains notes on a large variety of topics, such as theory of drama, food and drink, architecture, gardening, and health. In the chapter on food and drink, for example, the author advocates the pursuit of refinement in dietary habits while adhering to the principles of plainness and thrift, commenting on how one can have joy in a life of simplicity.

The two examples above reflect only the leisure life of the aristocratic families and men of letters, but the leisure lifestyles of common people were also rich and colorful, including watching plays, drinking tea, guessing riddles, playing *go*, composing poems at poetry clubs, paper-cutting, painting, and making handicrafts. These forms of activity allowed people to enter

[5] Haitang (*Malus spectabilis*) is a species of tree widespread in China that bears white or pink flowers. In ancient mythology, *haitang* is represented by a female immortal and personifies artistic elegance and taste.

a leisurely mood and brought joy, relaxation, and spiritual freedom, allowing them to give individualized expression to their talents and abilities.

Emperors Kangxi and Qianlong

Emperor Kangxi (1654–1722) is known to have taken a strong interest in reading and learning. His diligence in learning is indeed praiseworthy. From the time he was very young, he had acquired the habit of keeping books ready at hand. Although he became very busy with state affairs after his enthronement, he never gave up this habit. He once said, "After finishing the hearings at court, I would peruse my books. I am never tired of doing this, for there are always things of profound meaning we can learn from books."[6] He is known to be the Chinese emperor best versed in mathematics, and is known to have read widely, dabbling in history, different schools of philosophy, music, math and science, Buddhist sutras and works expounding them, Taoist works, and works in many other areas.

Emperor Qianlong (1711–1799) was also a man of broad learning. He practiced calligraphy, painted, collected interesting objects as a hobby, and was fond of traveling. According to *The Complete Biography of Emperor Qianlong*, the Emperor was much captivated by automatic toys from the West, especially by human and animal automata. Besides these, he was interested in many other Western instruments and devices. He was also curious about Western musical instruments, and ordered the Western missionaries serving at his court to teach some young eunuchs to play cello and violin. Indeed, his fancy for Western music was so great that an orchestra including cello, violin, piano, oboe, clarinet, and guitar was organized at his court.[7]

But we also have to keep in mind that with the extravagance of his leisurely pursuits, which became even more serious in his old age, Qianlong squandered away much of the wealth in the national treasury that had been quite full at the beginning of his reign. This extravagance sowed the seed for the decline of the Qing Dynasty. It changed from the prosperous Kangxi-Qianlong Era to the age of decline in the Daoguang-Xianfeng period in the nineteenth and early twentieth century. The latter period was filled with

[6] *Veritable Records of the Reign of Emperor Kangxi of Qing*, chapter 41, p. 9, quoted in Wang Sizhi, *Qingshi Lungao* (*Essays on Qing History*), Chengdu: Bashu Publishing House, 1987, p. 270.

[7] Zhang Hongjie. "Qianlong Huangdi yu Yapian Zhanzheng (Emperor Qianlong and the Opium War)," in Zhang Lixian, ed., *Duku 0904*, Beijing: New Star Press, 2009.

social upheavals and national crises: the Opium War, the Taiping Rebellion, the Muslim Uprising in the Tongzhi period, China's defeat in the Sino-Japanese War in 1894, the Boxer Rebellion, and the ensuing intervention by the Eight-Nation Alliance to suppress the Boxers.

Opium-Smoking as a Fad for the Leisure Class

The prosperous Kangxi-Qianlong Era came to an end at the close of the eighteenth century. When the Opium War started, the Chinese Empire was already very weak although it was still able to present an appearance of strength due to its gigantic size. The earliest record on opium-smoking in China was for 1620, when

> . . .some Formosans were said to have mixed tobacco with opium for smoking, and the practice spread in the 1660s to Fukien and Kwangtung, where the method of smoking was refined: the smoker burned the opium over a lamp and inhaled its fumes through a pipe. It rapidly became a fad with the leisure classes, and before long even the poor took it up. The demand for opium led to increased foreign importation and to native cultivation in Szechwan, Yunnan, Fukien, Chekiang, and Kwangtung.[8]

From 1800 on, opium was imported to China in large quantities, which led to a great outflow of silver from China. Furthermore, since opium is addictive, it caused serious deterioration of the smoker's health, making him essentially a disabled person.[9]

At the same time, Western countries were developing rapidly after having entered the process of industrial revolution. Such development not only improved the life of the Europeans, but also heightened their yearning for and pursuit of refined taste. The gap between China and Europe kept on getting larger.

[8] Immanuel C.Y. Hsü, *The Rise of Modern China*, 6e. Oxford University Press, 2000:168–169.

[9] Immanuel C.Y. Hsü, *The Rise of Modern China*, 6e. Oxford University Press, 2000:171–172.

The Old China

The term "Old China" usually refers to the period between 1840 and 1949, or between the Opium War and the founding of the People's Republic of China. In Old China, The Chinese lived in great hardship, especially in rural areas, where the majority of people lived on the borderline of famine for extended periods of time.

Sun Yat-sen and the "Sick Man of Asia"

In the revolution aimed at democracy, Sun Yat-sen[10] had a grand plan for the future of China, as laid out in his *A General Plan for National Construction*[11] and *Three Principles of the People.*[12] In these works, Sun undertook to design various social institutions based on humanistic principles, with not only long-term plans for economic development for the Chinese society, but also propositions for reforming the national character of the Chinese people.

In view of the national character shown by the Chinese of his time, Sun pointed out that the Chinese had discarded the Confucian tradition of moral cultivation, putting their household in order, and governing the state. He said, "for the last few centuries, the Chinese have not been able to follow this tradition, resulting in their not being able to govern their own country."[13] He also noted that

> when the Chinese first began to arrive in the United States, the Americans treated them equally, with no notion of the Chinese being different from the Americans. But later, the Chinese were refused by all large hotels and restaurants.... Why? It is said the reason was as follows. Once, there was a large banquet in a big restaurant, attended by many gentlemen and ladies.... Suddenly, a Chinese farted loudly, and the Americans went in an uproar and left. The owner of the restaurant drove that Chinese out. From then on, large

[10] Sun Yat-sen (1866–1925), is a great forerunner of the Chinese democratic revolution, and the founder of Republic of China. He was the first to present a thoroughly anti-feudal banner, "from the Republic and end two thousand years of feudal monarchy."

[11] Sun Yat-sen, *A General Plan for National Construction*, Shanghai: Commercial Press, 1923.

[12] Sun Yat-sen, *Three Principles of the People*, Shanghai: Beixin Bookstore, 1927.

[13] Sun Yat-sen, *Three Principles of the People*, Beijing: Beijing Oriental Publishing House, 2014, pp. 68–69.

> restaurants began to refuse the Chinese. Another time, an important Chinese businessman in Shanghai invited some foreigners to a banquet, but when the guests were dining, he, too, farted loudly. Many foreigners blushed, but not this Chinese businessman. He stood up and slapped his trousers, saying, "Excuse me!" Such conduct is really barbarous and vulgar![14]

These are excerpts taken from one of a series of speeches on nationalism, one of his three principles of the people that Sun gave in 1924. He saw the cultural rift between China and the rapidly developing Western world and the gap between them in terms of levels of civilization. From his words, we can also see how the cultural traditions of China had been abandoned at that time.

After the Opium War ended in 1842, "the Sick Man of Asia" came to be a term that stood for the Chinese people.[15] As Liang Qichao said in his *On Rejuvenating the People,* "Since we are known to the world as the Sick Man of Asia, with our hands and legs paralyzed and capacity for self-defense lost, all nations, whether in the West or in the East, are sharpening their knives, ready to put us on their cutting boards as fish and meat."[16]

Chen Duxiu, a leader of the New Culture Movement in the early years of the Republican era, also mentioned this term. In his *The New Youth*, published in 1915, he said, "Other nations call us the 'Sick Man of the East', and of our young people, none can be said not to belong to the rank of sick people. How can a nation like this manage to survive in the world!"[17]

At the 11th Olympic Games held in Berlin in 1936, China entered close to 30 events with a delegation of more than 140 people, but failed to win any medals. When the delegation arrived in Singapore on its way back home, a cartoon appeared in a local newspaper showing a group of emaciated Chinese under the Olympic Rings wearing pigtails and old fashioned gowns and jackets (typical apparel for mandarins in Qing times) and carrying a big "Zero" on a stretcher. The cartoon was entitled "Sick Man of East Asia."[18]

[14] Ibid., pp. 69–70.

[15] The term was first used in *North China Daily News*, October 17, 1896.

[16] Liang Qichao, *On Rejuvenating the People*, Zhengzhou: Zhongzhou Ancient Books Publishing House, 1998.

[17] Chen Duxiu, The New Youth, *Xin Qingnian*, 1916, 2(1).

[18] Xu Min, *Things Absurd from the Republican Era*, Wuhan: Huazhong University of Science and Technology Press, 2014, p. 164.

The New Culture Movement

In 1919, the May Fourth Movement, aimed at "overthrowing Confucianism," was started in Beijing. Young students and intellectuals, the mainstay of the movement, tried to reflect on the obstacles to China's development posed by her traditional culture with its political and moral order, and also to find effective ways to cure the "Sick Man of Asia" of his sickness. However,

> the May Fourth episode did not lead to immediate political results, and there were many in the intellectual stratum, including Lu Hsun, who were not particularly impressed with its significance. There were those such as Hu Shih, Ku Chieh-kang, Fu Ssu-nien and others who were to continue in their belief that the root of China's problem was cultural, and they must therefore "reorganize the national heritage".[19]

"Ku Chieh-kang had himself been touched by the new movement which had emerged among students since 1919 to 'go to the people' and ... his interest in folksongs, temples and festivals gradually took on a more positive aspect."[20] "Another outcome of the May Fourth movement ... was the whole 'neo-traditionalist' reaction against the 'totalistic iconoclasm' of the movement,"[21] which claimed that traditional moral life was still relevant and ought to be encouraged.

In the "Declaration by the People of Beijing" he drafted, Chen Duxiu urged the people to "take direct action so as to transform the society in a fundamental way,"[22] but he also wrote an article advocating a new cultural movement that would encompass "new movements in science, religion, morality, literature, art, music, and so on."[23] Obviously, he did not discard leisure in traditional culture.

[19] Benjamin I. Schwartz, "Themes in Intellectual History: May Fourth and after, in John K. Fairbank," ed., *The Cambridge History of China*, vol. 12 (Republican China 1912–1949, Part I). Cambridge University Press, 2008, p. 435. The names of the figures mentioned in this passage would be spelt Lu Xun, Hu Shi, Gu Jiegang, and Fu Sinian, respectively, in the *pinyin* system.

[20] Ibid., pp. 435–36.

[21] Ibid., p. 437.

[22] Chen Duxiu, A Declaration by the People of Beijing, in Qiang Chonghua, ed., *Sources on the Arrest of Chen Duxiu*, Beijing: Peking University Press, 2010: 447–457.

[23] Chen Duxiu, What Indeed Is the New Culture Movement, *The New Youth*, 1920, 7(5).

Li Dazhao,[24] another leading figure of the New Culture Movement, believed that recreation beneficial to the body and the mind is an important way to balance hard work and to diminish fatigue. He divided recreational facilities into two kinds—commercial facilities such as theatres, and public facilities such as parks, playgrounds, schools, and clubs.[25] He described the life of Beijing people at the time as "dejected, dry, dirty, sluggish, inconvenient, uneconomic, unhygienic, and uninteresting ... So we are in urgent need for a new life."[26] On May 1, 1922, he published an article[27] in which he pointed out, "recreation is not a luxury, but a necessity," and demanded government authorities to build parks, playgrounds, and clubs in neighborhoods where working-class people are concentrated so as to provide facilities for their recreational and sports activities.

Hu Shi,[28] yet another leading figure of the New Culture Movement, promoted a wholesome individualism, and thus placed great emphasis on the value of leisure for the individual's growth. In a speech addressed to college students, he specifically talked about how to make use of one's leisure time, saying:

> One's future is often a function of how one makes use of one's leisure time. If one uses his/her leisure time to play mahjong, he/she becomes a gambler; if you use your leisure time for social service, you may become a social reformer; or if you use your leisure to study history, you may become a historian. The way your leisure is spent often sets the direction of the course of your whole life.[29]

[24] Li Dazhao (1889–1927) was a great Marxist and one of the founders of the Chinese Communist Party. He graduated from Waseda University in Japan, and was a scholar of broad learning and a strong pioneering spirit.

[25] Zhuo Xionghui, "Li Dazhao's scheme for urban development," *Guangming Daily*, June 30, 2009: 12.

[26] Li Dazhao, "The new life which the people of Beijing should demand," *The New Life*, 1919(5).

[27] Li Dazhao, "The significance of the May Day for the labor in China today," *Morning News*, May 1, 1922.

[28] Hu Shih (1891–1962), better known in the West, a graduate of Cornell University, was once the president of Beijing University, ambassador of the Republic of China to the USA, and president of the Central Academy of Taiwan.

[29] Hu Shih, "To students graduating this year," *Independent Review*, 1932, (7).

By focusing on a specific topic, Hu was teaching the youths how to develop themselves as human individuals, and how to grow intellectually and morally. Even today, the message in his speech is worth reflecting on.

Thus, although the purpose of the May Fourth Movement was to fight the old order with its ethical codes and complicated rites and to introduce "Mr. Democracy" and "Mr. Science" to China, it is in this movement that a Chinese intelligentsia, well versed in both traditional Chinese learning and Western knowledge, appeared who were willing to shoulder responsibility for society. In trying to start a Renaissance in China, they became the backbone of society and the cultural elite for the Chinese nation.

The New Life Movement and Life Weekly

Starting from the mid-1930s, Chiang Kai-shek, president of the National Government, put much effort into promoting the New Life Movement. Making the Confucian values of rites, righteousness, integrity, and a sense of shame, the ideological core for this movement, Chiang wanted the people to integrate these values into all aspects of their daily lives. The movement was aimed not only at outward manifestations such as clean cities and orderly behavior, but also at "the reforming of society and the revival of the nation." Chiang idealistically hoped the movement would transform the Chinese people so they would have morality and knowledge befitting citizens, discarding all bad habits. However, the movement came to a "temporary halt" in 1949 when the Nationalist government lost the civil war.

In the late 1920s, *Life Weekly* was launched, jointly sponsored by three bookstores. The purpose of the magazine was embodied in the very names of the three bookstores, Life, Reading, and New Knowledge. Thus, the magazine was intended to address three of the most important issues in human life. First and foremost is life—one should love life and live one's own life well. Then, one should cultivate the habit of reading, a good habit that also represents a kind of attitude toward life. Finally, great value was placed on new knowledge. Coming both from reading and from life, new knowledge in turn make one's reading and life more enjoyable. The purpose of the magazine was also expressed as "to insinuate self-cultivation, to evoke the spirit of serving the society, and thus to contribute to the transformation of society."[30]

[30] Chen Tongxu, *A History of Newspapers and Magazines for Youths in the 20th Century*, Beijing: Xinhua Publishing House, 2014, p. 66.

Recreation in Old China

In Old China, *mahjong* was a popular game.[31] It is unfortunate that this highly interesting and challenging game has been used largely as a means for gambling, with many people indulging in it. During the Republican Era, *mahjong* quickly became the most popular form of recreation. Not only common people, but also those in high positions, men of letters, and even famous scholars are known to have been fond of *mahjong*. In early Republican times, "No less than 1,500 brothels openly provided facilities for gambling in Shanghai. At least two *mahjong* tables or two card tables were used on an average day, which means about 10 people for a brothel, or a total of 15,000 people gambling in those brothels,"[32] with *mahjong* as one of the chief means for gambling. "In Tianjin, some foreigners in the concessions ganged up with local scoundrels to open about 3,000 gambling houses, with *mahjong* as the major traditional means for gambling."[33] Clients frequenting those gambling houses were mainly politicians, bureaucrats, and soldiers, but also included a significant number of middle-class people. With its gambling houses being protected by both the authorities of the concessions and gangster groups, Tianjin quickly followed Shanghai in becoming a gambling center in China.

This phenomenon led to a crusade against *mahjong*. In an article entitled "Thoughts from My Wanderings", Hu Shi devoted a section to *mahjong*, denouncing it as a scourge on the Chinese nation. He did the following calculation, "Four rounds of *mahjong* would take about two hours. For a conservative estimate, let us say there are only a million *mahjong* tables in China, and only eight rounds are played a day. That would yield a total of four million hours, or 167,000 days of time wasted, not to mention the wins and losses at the *mahjong* table, and the waste of people's energy." He then proceeded to write a little sentimentally, "From the whole world, can we find a progressive people or a civilized nation who ever waste so much time while neglecting their work?"[34] *Mahjong* is a reflection of recreation in Old China.

[31] *Mahjong* is a game of skill, strategy, calculation, and chance that was invented in China.

[32] Xie Wuyi, "A glimpse at prostitution in Shanghai in early Republican times," Shanghai Institute of Literature and History, ed., in *Opium, Gambling, and Prostitution in Old Shanghai*, Baijia Publishers, pp. 173–174.

[33] Dong Chunpu, *A History of Police in China*, Jilin People's Publishing House, 2005, p. 39.

[34] Hu Shih, *Collected Works of Hu Shih*, vol. 4, Beijing: Peking University Press 1998, pp. 39–40.

Efforts to Preserve Traditional Culture in Hard Times

In Old China, people frequently had to go through hard times, including severe famines extended over long periods, such as that in Henan Province in the early 1940s. The population of the province dwindled from 30.67 million in 1940 to 24.71 million in 1944, with a decrease of 5.96 million. Taking into account the population outflow and decrease due to the war that was going on, the number of people starved to death is estimated to be over three million.[35]

In the midst of such social upheaval, however, a large number of educators, philosophers, men of letters, and artists well versed in both traditional and modern learning, in both Chinese and Western knowledge, and able to combine science and art, worked steadfastly to preserve the cultural heritage of the nation. Masters in humanistic studies such as Zhu Ziqing, Lin Yutang, Liang Shiqiu, and Feng Youlan not only created another era of literary and artistic splendor, but also helped to perpetuate the leisure values in China's cultural traditions. Lin Yutang and Feng Youlan are representative of these great humanists.

Lin Yutang

Lin Yutang (1895–1976) was an eminent Chinese writer in modern times. In his early years, he studied in the U.S. and in Germany, earning a master's degree in literature from Harvard and a doctorate from Leipzig. He was made the head of the Arts and Letters division of UNESCO in 1954, and was twice a nominee for the Nobel Prize in Literature, in 1940 and 1950, respectively. Through his works, of which *My Country and My People* and *The Importance of Living* are representative, he impressively depicts an ideal lifestyle showing the wisdom, grace, humor, and leisureliness of the Chinese that is worth emulating. In his books, he talks about Confucius' doctrine of the mean, Laozi and Zhuangzi's inclination toward withdrawal and hermitage, and Tao Yuanming's leisureliness, and about how the Chinese drink tea, how they play drinkers' wager games, how they play with water, how they watch clouds flowing, how they appreciate and evaluate rocks, and how they grow flowers, keep birds as pets, watch the snow, listen to the rain, and sing songs of wind and the moon. In a lively and humorous style, he presents the reader with the Chinese people's philosophic way of life, with

[35] Shao Wenjie, ed., *Records of Henan Province*, vol. 9 (population; ethnic groups; religion). Zhengzhou: Henan People's Publishing House, 1994.

its romance, elegance, and taste, leaving a valuable cultural heritage for later generations.

Lin believes that culture has always been the product of leisure, and the art of culture is the art of leisure. From this we can see how profoundly the traditional Chinese outlook on leisure, with its stress on the unity of human beings and nature, had affected Lin's character.

Feng Youlan

Feng Youlan (1895–1990) was an eminent philosopher and educator in modern China. Though he was deeply concerned with the perils China was in during his lifetime, he was confident that the Chinese nation, with her 5,000 years of civilization, would never perish. The distress the nation met with, he believed, was temporary, and the revival of her culture was soon to come. It is with this faith that he devoted himself to the study of the cultural heritage of China. From 1939 to 1946, he published a series of six books, of which one volume, *New Admonitions for the World*, also entitled *A New Theory of the Way of Life*, is the one among his many works that most closely addresses everyday life. The emphasis of the book is to guide people in remolding their moral character and to discuss the individual's social responsibility. In his introduction to the book, he says, "All of us have our human lives, and all human lives more or less follow certain rules."[36] He believes that the human individual has a spiritual life and a social life as well as a biological life. Feng tried to reveal the rules for the new lifestyle he was advocating. His discussion of "interest" is quite penetrating: "In the educational system in the past, it was believed that the individual's interests were for the most part 'improper'. Thus, many were those who could not follow their own interests in deciding what to study, and so their talents were never developed. Candidly speaking, how many gifted individuals had their genius suppressed that way!"[37] Again, "Talent is something one is born with, and thus can be considered part of his nature. Where the individual's interest lies is where his talent is.... When one follows one's

[36] Feng Youlan, *Collected Works from Three Pine Studio*, Zhengzhou: Henan people's Publishing House, 2001, p. 338.

[37] Feng Youlan, *New Admonitions for the World: A New Theory of the Way of Life,* Beijing: Beijing University Press, p. 43.

own interest, that is when he is, in the words of the Taoists, following his own nature."[38]

So, when China was embroiled in the turmoil of war, Feng was still concerned with the "interests" of the individual and how the individual's talents could be developed. From this we can see not only his efforts to interpret the essentials of the cultural tradition of China in the expectation of a revival of that tradition, but also how intellectuals of his generation had inherited the leisure values in it.

In the troubled times when Feng was writing, many people had to keep moving from place to place, often without enough to eat. But great thinkers like Feng, who also went through much hardship, were able to maintain a serenity in which they tried to sort out various elements in traditional culture and reinterpret them in a modern context. They undertook to study the essence of Chinese culture in much depth and in great detail in an effort to use it to help reform deep-rooted bad habits among the Chinese. This shows that Chinese intellectuals were making steadfast efforts to preserve China's cultural traditions. Their thoughts and insights gained through such efforts can still give us much enlightenment today.

The Cheongsam and the Chinese Tunic Suit

The apparel of a people is an objectification of their cultural traditions, sentiments, and pursuits. An ancient saying in China runs thus, "Wearing unsuitable clothes is likely to bring misfortune to oneself."[39] Therefore, people have always paid much attention to what to wear for various occasions.

The Cheongsam

The cheongsam is a traditional dress for Chinese women that emerged in the 1920s. Much of the *shenyi* style (深衣) from the Qin-Han period was absorbed in the design of the cheongsam. After the Republican government determined it was to be one of the formal dresses of the nation, the cheongsam quickly became popular. Combining classical and modern aesthetics, it fully embodies traditional Chinese culture, showing feminine grace and glory through reservedness, restraint, intellectuality, elegance,

[38] Ibid., pp. 45–46.

[39] Yang Bojun, *Zuo's Commentary on the Spring and Autumn Annals Annotated* (revised ed.), Beijing: Zhonghua Book Company, 1990, p. 427.

and charm. When the three Soong sisters went out to conquer the world by frequently visiting various places in China and other countries, Eastern and Western, the cheongsams they wore as well as their own talents contributed to their success.[40]

The cheongsam is considered the embodiment of culture, self-cultivation, and charm. Furthermore, it challenged the moral order that had been in existence for millennia with its many constraints on women and helped greatly to upgrade women's mental and moral character by contributing to a new aesthetics regarding feminine beauty. Although its history is still short, it has already made a deep mark on Chinese cultural tradition.

In the Republican years, wives of the heads of the Chinese state wore the cheongsam on most diplomatic occasions. After the founding of the People's Republic of China in 1949, the cheongsam gradually faded out from the historical stage. During the Cultural Revolution, the cheongsam was considered a symbol of capitalist and revisionist values, and brought misfortune to many who wore it. For example, Madam Wang Guangmei, wife to President Liu Shaoqi, used to wear cheongsam when accompanying her husband on his visits abroad before the Cultural Revolution, but that became one of her "crimes" during the Cultural Revolution.

The Chinese Tunic Suit

The Chinese tunic suit, or *zhongshan zhuang* in mandarin, is a style of male attire named after Sun Yat-sen, who is more widely known in China as Sun Zhongshan.[41] Many prominent figures in modern Chinese history, such as Chiang Kai-shek, Mao Zedong, Zhou Enlai, and Deng Xiaoping, wore it regularly. Because Mao wore it on many official occasions, it came to be called the "Mao suit" in the Western world. It was said that the design of the suit had important cultural connotations, representing republicanism and constitutionalism, but this interpretation has been rejected by scholars.

Even so, attire is not something that can be taken lightly. Liu Mengxi criticizes the extensive "change of attire styles" in China in the 1960s and

[40] Ai-ling (married to Kung Hsiang-his, finance minister of China), Ching-ling (married to Sun Yat-sen), and Mei-ling (married to Chiang Kai-shek), a biography of whom was written by the American journalist Emily Hahn in her *The Soong Sisters* (New York: Open Road Media, 2014 [1941]).

[41] "Yat-sen" was his style name in Cantonese pronunciation, while "Zhongshan" is the mandarin pronunciation of the Japanese name 中山 (pronounced "Nakayama" in Japanese) he adopted while an exile in Japan.

1970s, when all people wore improper clothes, with "women wearing men's clothes; middle school students, those of peasants; intellectuals, those of factory workers; and factory workers, those of soldiers ... the widespread mismatch of attire with social roles reflected severe cultural dislocation.... The damage [from such dislocation] to the cultural character of the Chinese is truly incalculable."[42]

Early New China

On October 1, 1949, the People's Republic of China was founded. This marks the end of the Old China and the beginning of the New China.

The Campaign to Purge China of Drugs and Prostitution

When Mao moved his government to Beiping (later to be renamed "Beijing" again at the founding of the People's Republic) in 1949, the city was in a state of devastation, full of brothels and gangs. At 5:30 p.m., November 21, 1949, the People's Congress of Beijing passed unanimously the decision to close down all the brothels in the city. Right after the decision was passed, Mayor Nie Rongzhen issued a directive to the Beijing Public Security Bureau to take action. A total of 2,400 cadres and policemen of the General Public Security Brigade were mobilized for the task, with Luo Ruiqing, head of the Public Security Bureau, in direct command. By 5:00 a.m. the next day, all 224 brothels in the city were closed down, with a total of 1,268 prostitutes emancipated and a total of 454 procuresses and foremen of the brothels being put under investigation.[43]

Shanghai had been the city with the largest number of prostitutes in the world. In a study by the American sociologist Sidney Gamble, Shanghai is listed to have had one recognized prostitute for every 137 inhabitants, which was the highest ratio among the eight cities on the list (London, Berlin, Paris, Chicago, Nagoya, Tokyo, Peking, and Shanghai).[44] During the period when Shanghai was under Japanese occupation, opium houses,

[42] Liu Mengxi, Attire and Family Ethics, in Liu Mengxi, *Masters of Thought and Tradition*, Guilin: Guangxi Normal University Press, 2015, p. 53.

[43] Yang Jiezeng and He Wannan, eds., *Stories from the History of the Rehabilitation of Prostitutes in Shanghai*. Shanghai: Shanghai Joing Publishing Company, 1988, p. 22.

[44] Sidney D. Gamble, *Peking: A Social Survey*, New York: George H. Doran Company, p. 247.

gambling houses, and brothels were all allowed to operate openly. It was explicitly stipulated that prostitutes could solicit clients on the street, and that the police were not supposed to interfere. According to statistics provided by the Shanghai Police Bureau in 1942 (when Shanghai was under the rule of Wang Jingwei's government backed by the Japanese), there were more than 3,900 brothels in Shanghai, with 39,000 prostitutes.[45] According to the statistics collected by the municipal government of Shanghai in 1947, "there are no fewer than 100,000 prostitutes and singsong girls in Shanghai, and those who make a living out of prostitution indirectly are several times that number."[46]

On October 21, 1949, the Second Plenum of the Congress of the People's Representatives was convened in the Sun Yat-sen Hall of the Sun Yat-sen Park. A resolution was passed to close all the brothels in Beijing. Mayor Nie Rongzhen announced solemnly that the Municipal Government of Beijing would immediately take action to implement the resolution. When Mao learned that the resolution had been passed, he commented, "This is a very good resolution." After that, other cities followed Beijing in waging a general war on brothels.[47]

A Time of Severe Scarcity (1950s–1970s)

In the early years of the People's Republic of China (PRC), there were numerous social problems passed down from the Old China. The scarcity of material goods was one of the main characteristics of the first few decades of the PRC. Indeed, to have enough to eat would be quite a luxury for most Chinese. Wild potherbs, bark, wheat straw, and corncob were all used to feed people, and even sparrows were hunted in massive campaigns throughout China.

[45] Yang Jiezeng and He Wannan, eds, Stories from the History of the Rehabilitation of Prostitutes in Shanghai. Shanghai: Shanghai Joing Publishing Company, 1988, p. 2.

[46] He Yafu, *The Incontrollable Population Control*, Beijing: China Development Press, 2013 p. 58.

[47] Bai Yuntao, House-cleaning: the closing of brothels in the early days of the People's Republic of China, *Journal of Yanhuang Chunqiu*, 1999(10).

A campaign to hunt sparrows was reported in *People's Daily* in 1958: At 5:00 a.m. sharp on April 19 that year, the campaign was started at the order of Wang Kunlun, vice mayor of Beijing and the commander-in-chief of this campaign, and a deafening sound of gongs and drums was heard throughout the 8,700 square kilometers of land in Greater Beijing. People went into action not only in the courtyards, but also on roofs of houses and high up in the trees. From old people with grey hair to children only a few years old, all people, including workers, peasants, cadres, students, and soldiers, had some sort of weapon in their hands, and all made full use of their abilities to hunt the sparrows. According to statistics collected from the whole country, which were by no means complete, more than 210 million sparrows were killed in 1958. The poor birds were almost hunted to extinction.[48] Massive campaigns like this were deemed necessary because sparrows were considered a pest that looted grains from the fields, making the shortage of food even more serious.

The Great Leap Forward

The year 1958 was also the time when the Central Government of China started the massive political campaign espousing "the General Line," "People's Communes," and "the Great Leap Forward," with a plan made to "overtake Great Britain and catch up with the United States." By the end of the 1950s, exaggeration of achievements had become widespread in China. Government officials set very high indices for economic development in the regions under their administration and issued commands without knowing much about the relevant fields. The whole nation was inundated in an extreme egalitarianism in the name of communism, with tremendous damage done to industrial and agricultural production. The proportions of different sectors of the national economy was greatly skewed, bringing severe difficulties to people's lives. The Great Leap Forward was followed by the so-called "Three Years of Natural Disasters," also known as the Great Chinese Famine.

According to official statistics from the government, from 1956 to 1958, there were 60.48 million births and 21.75 million deaths in China. The figures were 42.24 million and 36.02 million for the 1959–1961 period,

[48] Chen Yu, *Memories of Chinese Life: Events related to people's livelihood in the 60 years following the founding of the PRC*, Beijing: China Light Industry Press, 2009, pp. 46–47.

and 81.43 million and 21.52 million for the 1962–1964 period.[49] Deaths during the Three Years of Natural Disasters were mostly related to the famine. The statistics for those years also have to be taken with caution, for, due to interference for political reasons, there is quite some incongruence in statistics from different sources, especially in statistics on deaths.

By the early 1960s, goods could be bought only with coupons the government issued to every family according to a rationing scheme. All goods were produced in planned quantities and sold in rationed amounts. More than a hundred kinds of coupons were in use, covering consumer goods such as grains, coal, cigarettes, cloth, meat, cooking oil, sugar, bean products, matches, soap, eggs, shoes, and bicycles.

Later, Mao realized the severity of the shortages and pointed out that, "We still lack experience in socialist construction"; "Much of our effort to develop socialism has been made haphazardly," and "China is a country with a large population and a weak basis for modernization, making the country rather backward in economic development. It seems at least a century will be needed for us to develop our productive forces to such an extent that we can catch up and then surpass the most advanced of the capitalist countries."[50]

At that time, the "four durable goods" considered to be luxury by the Chinese were the wristwatch, the bicycle, the radio, and the sewing machine. Those were items only a small percentage of Chinese families could afford; and, since they were all rationed, even if a family had managed to save enough money for one of those items, they would not be able to buy it without a coupon. Until the mid-1980s, bicycles were still rationed. Sometimes, when several people wanted to buy a bicycle but there was only one coupon, lottery was used to determine who would get the coupon.

Entertainment and Public Service

Another feature of that time was the lack of entertainment and recreational facilities. The government noticed this problem and thought it was urgent to try to meet people's demands for cultural activities. Mao twice (in 1951

[49] China Population Statistics Yearbook, 1995, Beijing: China Statistics Press, 1995, pp. 355–384.

[50] Mao Zedong, *Collected Works of Mao Zedong*, Beijing: People's Publishing House, p. 300, 302.

and 1953) proposed some basic policies for encouraging cultural productions, and, in 1956, officially stipulated the twin guiding principles of "letting a hundred flowers bloom" and "letting a hundred schools of thought contend to gain hearing" so as to encourage cultural and artistic flourishing to meet the people's demands for entertainment.

Planned construction of recreational facilities in Beijing began in 1950. According to historical records, "The municipal government of Beijing started to plan for the construction of facilities for cultural activities such as cinemas and theatres in the early years following the Liberation.[51] By 1957, Beijing already had more than 20 cinemas, 20 theaters, more than 30 story-telling houses, a few folk art societies, and a few outdoor theaters. In addition, there were workers' clubs in all the districts of Beijing, and the meeting halls of many work units were also used for dramatic performances and film shows. From an issue of *Introduction to Theatrical Pieces*[52] from December 1957, it can be seen that there were 36 famous places where various performances happened." Entertainments like these brought some soothing comfort to people in a generally hard time, opening up a spiritual world for them. However, this situation did not last long.

The problems started in June 1957, when the "Anti-Rightist Campaign" was launched. The Campaign led to more than 550,000 people, including intellectuals, members of non-communist parties, and communist cadres, being labeled "Rightists". These included a large number of celebrities in entertainment circles and famous figures in social science and humanities fields. The vast majority of those labeled "Rightists" had been known to be of noble character and represented the national conscience of the Chinese. But 550,000 was only the number of those labeled during the official Anti-Rightist Campaign. According to the most conservative estimate,

> At that time, the total number of people labeled "Rightists" was 550,000. Adding to these the number of those supposedly "leaked out" during the Campaign but who were not so labeled in 1959, the total number of "Rightists" is estimated to be no fewer than a million, or about 10–20% of the total number of intellectuals at the time. The vast majority of the "Rightists" were punished in rather inhumane ways. Some of them were thrown into prisons,

[51] The word "Liberation" is often used in China to refer to the founding of the People's Republic of China.

[52] Author's collection.

> others were fired from their work units and exiled to remote frontiers regions, to rural areas, or to state-run farms to be "rehabilitated" through hard labor; and still others had their families broken, with family members separated for long years or even persecuted to death.[53]

The Anti-Rightist Campaign was political in nature, but it demolished the spiritual world and beliefs of an entire nation. The Campaign broke the spirit of the elites who had been the backbone of China, resulting in a discontinuation of the cultural traditions that had been passed down for millennia.

But human beings are after all animals with spiritual pursuits. These pursuits, though unlike material necessities, which cannot be dispensed with even for a short time, are nevertheless important, for if one is deprived spiritually for an extended period of time, one is apt to become insane.

A story about an uncle of the author reflects this. At the time of the Anti-Rightist Campaign, my uncle, who was in his twenties, was at the height of his youth and vigor. He was very talented and had many thoughts, and was working in the Municipal Committee of the Communist Youth League of my home city. Embroiled in the many political campaigns that kept on coming one after another, he felt much anguish in his soul and in his life. He began to listen to radio broadcasts from "enemy stations."[54] Such activity could be carried out only clandestinely at night, for there were no earphones at that time, and the listener had to set the volume to the minimum to avoid being discovered by others. Once discovered, such clandestine activity would be punished at least by confiscating the radio set used, suspension from one's duties, and segregation for the purpose of further investigation by the authorities, and could even lead to imprisonment. Influenced by broadcasts from "enemy stations," my uncle often acted impulsively and in a straightforward way to defend people who had been labeled "Rightists," and the result was he himself was also labeled a "Rightist" in the end. As a

[53] Tao Shansheng, *Reflections on the Cultural Revolution by One Who Experienced It in View of the "Anti-Rightist Campaign" in 1957, Utopia* (a leftist website in China), April 23, 2011. It is difficult to find out about the anti-rightist movement in the historical records, including regarding the Cultural Revolution and the 6·4 student movement in the official documents and historical materials.

[54] These included radio broadcasting by stations in all countries and regions of the world politically opposed to the People's Republic of China, such as Voice of America and Voice of the Free China (a station based in Taiwan).

Rightist, he was demoted to the position of a gate-keeper at a construction site and his actions were monitored. That put an end to his freedom and to the days when he could speak up for justice regarding major issues. His love for and talent in literature and art also evaporated, for the circumstances he found himself in no longer allowed for their expression. When he eventually regained his freedom after the Cultural Revolution had ended, he had been much humbled, with the pointedness and courage of his youthful years greatly worn out. Only some of his talent still remained, and that is why he was assigned to a vocational school in civil engineering as the provost. My uncle is but one of the more than a million "Rightists" who had similar fate in those years, and his fortunes were actually far from the worst among them.

The Anti-Rightist Campaign was foreboding of worse things to come. With the "Announcement of the Central Committee of the Communist Party of China" on May 16, 1966, the Cultural Revolution was launched.

The Cultural Revolution

Destroying the "Four Olds" and Cultivating the "Four News"

On June 1, 1966, a *People's Daily* editorial entitled "Sweeping Away All Monsters and Demons" put forth the slogan "Destroy all the old thoughts, old culture, old customs, and old habits created by the ruling classes through millennia in the past to poison the people," which came to be known as "destroying the 'four olds'." Later, "destroying the 'four olds'" and "cultivating the 'four new's'," namely, new thoughts, new culture, new customs, and new habits, were explicitly defined as the major goals of the Cultural Revolution. In the night of August 17, 1966, Red Guards from the Beijing No. 2 Middle School announced they would "smash all old thoughts, old culture, old customs, and old habits." After Mao had given an interview to the Red Guards the next day, numerous Red Guards in Beijing took to the street to "destroy the 'four olds'." Very soon, it became the fashion of the day to change "old-style" names of streets, factories, communes, shops of long-standing fame, and schools into new and revolutionary-sounding ones, and to seize scholars, men of letters, artists, scientists, and the so-called "reactionary bourgeois scholarly authorities," treat them violently, and publicly denounce them.

On August 23, 1966, a *People's Daily* editorial entitled "This Is Wonderful!" pointed out, "There are still many place names, shops names, and outmoded conventions and customs emitting a rotten smell of feudalism and capitalism that poison people's souls. Up, our revolutionary masses! We can no longer tolerate such a state of affairs!" "Thousands and thousands of Red Guards have raised their iron blooms and, within but a few days, have done a general cleaning up of these old names and customs representing the ideology of the exploiting ruling classes."[55]

This tide of revolutionary actions quickly spread to the rest of the country. Imitating the actions of their counterparts in Beijing, Red Guards throughout the country struck at numerous temples and historical sites, including the Confucius Temple and the Confucius Cemetery in Qufu, Shandong Province. Buddhist sculptures, memorial archways, and stela were knocked down, and private libraries were searched for "old books" and calligraphic works and paintings by famous artists, which were then put to the fire. Services such as manicures, beauty treatments, face-massaging, and tooth-cleaning were banned; commodities with a tinge of "bourgeois lifestyles" such as cosmetics and antique handicrafts were taken off the shelves of shops, and numerous cultural relics were destroyed. Let us take Beijing as an example. The first census of cultural relics in Beijing showed 6,843 places of historical and cultural significance had been preserved up to that time. Of those, 4,922 were later destroyed during the "destroying the 'four olds'" campaign. The figure for the whole country is no doubt much larger.

Embroiled in the Cultural Revolution, China was in a lawless state in which people had no liberty. No cultural heritage was protected, nor was any private property or space for private life. There was no protection for individual liberty, either. Absurdity could go to such extremes that the long beards some old men had kept also became an object of the "destroying the 'four olds'" campaign and those old men had to have them sheared.

Intellectuals were persecuted, and lessons were halted in schools. Facilities for cultural activities became desolate, and many research institutes were dissolved. These resulted in a widespread shortage of personnel in cultural and scientific institutions for a whole generation. According to the 1982 census, the number of illiterate or semi-illiterate people in China was more than 230 million, nearly a quarter of the total population of the country.[56] This led to unprecedented ideological chaos for the Chinese nation.

[55] Editorial, "This is Wonderful!" *People's Daily*, August 23, 1966, p. 1.

[56] Guan Haiting, *History of Political Development in Modern China*, Beijing: Peking University Press, 2005, p. 283.

Cultural and recreational life during the Cultural Revolution basically consisted of "reading the *Selected Works of Mao Zedong*", the royalty dance,[57] and the model operas.[58] In the morning and the evening, groups formed everywhere—in workshops, in playgrounds, at the wharfs, in streets, in the field, everywhere—to perform the royalty dance, to read Mao's *Selected Works*, or to sing arias from the model operas. Even today, most people in their sixties (who were in their prime during the Cultural Revolution) can still fluently recite many lines from those operas.

With all of life being enveloped in a revolutionary atmosphere, all other leisure activities were denounced as "bourgeois lifestyle." In those years, even love and marriage were tinged with revolution. Thus, when a young couple were engaged, it was very likely they would each give the other a Mao badge and a copy of *Quotations from Chairman Mao.* During the Cultural Revolution, reciting from *Quotations from Chairman Mao* or shouting slogans was mandatory on many occasions, and everyday life was often infiltrated with such practices. Some stories that have been recorded are as follows:

> (In the grocery store), a customer took up a cucumber and asks the salesclerk, "'Fight selfish thoughts and denounce revisionism!' How much is the cucumber?" The salesclerk replied, "'Long live Chairman Mao!' Fifteen cents a pound!"
>
> Another customer was trying to buy a braised chicken. After he paid the money, the salesclerk took the chicken and was about to pass it to him, but said, "Having been liberated by the Communist Party, we will never forget its kindness!" The customer, apparently absorbed in his thoughts at what a wonderful meal he and his family would be able to have with the braised chicken, failed to reply, and the sales clerk abruptly withdrew the chicken, repeating sharply what she had just said. The customer, alarmed, was quick to say resourcefully, "We will never forget Chairman Mao when eating the chicken!" at which the salesclerk handed the chicken to him.

These stories, which may sound like political jokes now, were actually very realistic and were once very popular. The author has witnessed the history of this period.

[57] Popular dances to demonstrate political loyalty, mainly to Chairman Mao.

[58] Eight operas with revolutionary themes produced mainly under the direction of Jiang Qing, Mao's wife, who had been an actress before she went to Yan'an.

Carrying Out Revolution Deep in the Soul

"Carrying out revolution deep in the soul" was aimed to wipe out the individual's likes and dislikes in his/her personal life. For example, it is human nature to like the beautiful, but in those years, socialist lifestyles were considered to be diametrically opposed to capitalist ones. In normal circumstances, refinement, elegance, emotional appeal, classiness, gentility, fame, learning, education would be causes of admiration and envy, but during the Cultural Revolution, these qualities were looked down upon and became objects of contempt and ridicule, while those who were poor, ignorant, uneducated, and who spoke in loud voices and acted impertinently became models worth imitating.

Tastes in dress, food, residence decoration, or means of transport that were seen as close to bourgeois styles would quickly bring criticism and denunciation from others. In this respect, two things from my personal experience have left deep impressions in my memory. The first is about my mother's younger sister. She entered a dress-designing contest and won a prize, but during the Cultural Revolution she was not only denounced for it, but was sent down to the countryside to be re-educated and rehabilitated through hard labor. Another is about myself: while in middle school, I once wore a pair of trousers made of woolen material with a shepherd check design, after which I was called a "stinky bourgeois girl." In the "down to the countryside" movement in 1968, I was listed among the first group of students in my school who had to go to the countryside to be re-educated, the reason being precisely that I was a "stinky bourgeois girl."

An article published in *Tianjin Evening News* in 1964 voiced the following view:

> I am a young woman worker and I like to dress up a little, with a new perm style or a fashionable dress. Some people make sarcastic comments to my back, saying I look queer and rub them up the wrong way, things like that. But I think having a variety of hairstyles is an indicator that people's life has been improved. I believe everyone likes the beautiful. Especially for us young women, I think it just won't do to make everyone braid her hair into a plait or have her hair cut short.[59]

[59] Dong Chunyan, *Why do people talk so much about my having a new hairstyle?* Tianjin Evening News, May 2, 1964.

But another article published in the same newspaper on the same day and entitled "What kind of beauty do we want?" says the following,

> Some youths in my factory like to slick up their hair in a sparrow-tail style, and some others have grown a little moustache. They dress up in queer ways and conduct themselves in an odd manner.... Although there are only a small number of people like that, but we are still concerned with it.[60]

After the Cultural Revolution began, hairstyles even just a little stylish were denounced as being "feudal-bourgeois-revisionist" or expressions of a "corrupt" lifestyle. If someone with such a hairstyle appeared on the street, Red Guards would come over and forcibly cut off his/her hair. If he/she dared to protest, Red Guards would cut off half of the individual's hair (usually the left half) while sparing the other half, and then paraded the individual on the street. Among the Red Guards themselves, the young men all had their hair cut to about an inch in a plain style, which made them look valorous and powerful, while the young women had their hair a little longer or made into a pair of short plaits, which also made them look valiant and heroic in bearing.

In the early stages of the Cultural Revolution, a big-character poster by "Red Guards of Beijing No. 2 Middle School" declared,

> We are the denunciators of the Old World. We will criticize all old thoughts, old culture, and old customs and smash them to pieces. All hair salons, tailor's shops, photo studios, and stalls for old books that have been serving the bourgeois class are objects of our action. We are rebelling against the entire Old World.
>
> ...
>
> And those shops! You have so many luxury items—perfumes, face creams, lipsticks, necklaces, and Hong Kong style dresses and leather shoes—on your shelves. For whom have you prepared these? Do workers, peasants, and soldiers ever put on perfume and leather shoes? Have you ever thought about this—if things continue like this, then capitalism will be restored in China in a few years or at most in a few decades, and the color of the whole of China will be changed.[61]

[60] Chen Yu, *Memories of Chinese Life: Events related to people's livelihood in the 60 years following the founding of the PRC*, Beijing: China Light Industry Press, 2009, pp. 72–73.

[61] Red Guards from Beijing No. 2 Middle School, "A Declaration of War on the Old World", *People's Daily*, August 26, 1968.

The "Down to the Countryside" Movement: My Experience in a Collective Household

In 1968, Mao Zedong issued a directive saying, "It is absolutely necessary for educated young people to go to the countryside and be reeducated by poor and lower-middle peasants."[62] The greater part of the 16–20 million junior and senior high school students who graduated from 1966 to 1968 answered Mao's call and went to rural areas throughout the country.

Before the above directive of Mao was published, this author had already been sent earlier that year to the No. 4 team of the Huicai Brigade in Qingshan Commune, Yushu County, Jilin Province, and was among the first group of young people to go to the countryside. We arrived at the snowbound county seat of Yushu by train on an October night, and then went to Qingshan Commune in a truck without awnings. From the commune to the team to which we had been assigned there was still a distance of four kilometers, with the road unfit for trucks. But a horse-drawn cart had been waiting for us at the commune, and it was in this cart that our group of a dozen people were sent to our "new home." As the cart went through the wind and snow, we all curled up silently in our heavy coats, resigned, helpless, and hopeless. There was no electricity in those rural areas yet, so the whole place was engulfed in darkness. And most peasants still lived in poverty, with little more than the four walls of their houses. That is the place where for a while I did much planting, weeding, winnowing, and other farm work. The peasants treated us with much kindness, for they felt sorry that a group of tender, youthful students had been brought to a place of great suffering and hardship.

The village where we stayed was located in a region with vast fields of pitch-black soil, allowing for fairly high agricultural production. I still remember a full day's work was worth ten work points, which could be converted to 1 yuan RMB, a fairly good income at that time. However, after staying there for 20 months, I ended up owing my team 63 yuan RMB.

It is true that the whole country was poor at that time. Still, the extent of poverty in the rural area I stayed in went beyond anything I had ever seen before. Every time I returned from visiting my family in the city, I would bring some milk powder, bean powder, medicine, clothes, and other goods and give them to the poorest families in the village. In the village, there was

[62] Mao Zedong, "Quotation from Chairman Mao," *People's Daily*, December 22, 1968, p. 1.

a three-year-old girl who could not sit up because of malnutrition and who eventually died very young, and a woman tormented by illness who, though only 42 years old, looked like a very old woman near her death. And there was a family of four who had only one quilt, and the husband and the wife had to share one pair of trousers. All these things have stayed vividly in my memory. It was then that I began to make observations on society and on life and to think hard about many issues.

Together with the family we stayed with, our group was constituted into a "collective household." The household included 12 middle-school graduates, seven female and five male. The only recreational activities available to us were the royalty dance and the reading of Mao's quotations. In the winter, it was too cold outside, so our daily ritual of the royalty dance had to be performed indoors. However, our rooms were too small, and we had to perform the ritual with several of us dancing on the floor and several others on the large *kang*.[63] Our study consisted of reading and reciting the "Three Articles"[64] and *Quotations from Chairman Mao*. We competed to see who could recite the most from those books and who could do it most fluently. I had taken a "Chinese Language" textbook with me, and would stealthily read some of it when no one else was around.

An important member of our collective household was a large dog. The dog had black hair all over, and we affectionately called him "Blacky." Though kids from cities were likely to be afraid of dogs, peasants needed to have dogs to guard their houses and yards. There was no concept of "pet" at that time in China, but we soon became good friends and companions with Blacky. When we first met him, Blacky was as lean as a rake, but showed a good demeanor and temperament. Very soon, all the 12 middle-school graduates came to be very fond of him. Tending to Blacky and playing with him became something we much enjoyed in our free time. At every meal, we would save some food to feed Blacky. It would be a real treat to have a meal with some meat in our collective household, but every time we did, we were willing to share it with Blacky and he also enjoyed playing with us. When he was excited, he would put his forelegs on our shoulders and kiss us with his pink, slick tongue. Well fed by us, Blacky soon became strong and muscular, and looked very handsome with a luster on his hair. Every day, when we returned from work in the field, Blacky would see

[63] A heatable brick or adobe bed common in North China and Northeast China.

[64] This refers to a booklet of three articles by Mao, including "Serving the People," "In Memory of Norman Bethune," and "The Foolish Old Man Moved the Mountains."

us from a distance and run toward us wagging his tail, which would bring us much joy that took away much of our fatigue from a whole day's labor. Every time we left the village to go home for a visit, Blacky would follow us by running after the cart we were riding. When we switched to the truck after riding the cart for four kilometers, Blacky would run after the truck as well, and we all shouted to him, "Blacky, go home! Go home!" This is a vivid scene that still appears frequently in my mind. Unfortunately, Blacky was sold to a Korean family in a neighboring village by our host for 20 yuan RMB to be slaughtered for his meat. This was a tragedy for Blacky, but also a tragedy of humanity and of that era of Chinese history.

The "down to the countryside" movement severely disrupted education in China. For five years, more than 20 million middle-school graduates were deprived of the opportunity to enter college. This has had serious repercussions on the growth of this generation in terms of their work skills, the perspectives from which they look at and learn about the world, the development of their values, and their inheritance of the spirit of national culture. The negative impacts have been felt not only for these students, but for many others directly or indirectly affected by them. The impertinence and conduct running against public order and well-established customs displayed by many Chinese today is one of the aftereffects of this movement.

The Demolishing of the Ancient City Walls of Beijing

Since it was first made the capital city of China in 1267, Beijing has seen development as the nation's capital for more than seven centuries except for a few short intervals. In this long history, the city has come to have a large number of historical sites and places associated with important historical figures and cultural heritage. In 1948, when the PLA (People's Liberation Army) had besieged Beijing and was preparing to capture it, Mao, after having had a map of Beijing marked for important historical and cultural sites by the eminent architecture historian Liang Sicheng, issued an order to the troops, saying, "Great effort should be made to protect these important cultural sites. When conducting exercises in offensive maneuvers, targets must be accurately calculated!" With Mao's directive, the comprehensive protection of the city was listed as the first item in the top priorities for the impending battle.[65]

[65] Deng Congcong and Zhang Jianwei, "The Twelfth Statue: Liang Sicheng and the City of Beijing," in Zou Zhongzhi, *Caressing Beijing: Beijing as portrayed by contemporary writers*, Beijing: Joint Press, 2012, pp. 52–53.

According to historical records, there were three rings of city walls for Beijing. The inner ring was for the imperial palace, or the Forbidden City, in the center; the middle ring, for the Imperial City; and the outer ring, for the Capital City. In 1924, the Swedish art historian Osvald Siren published *The Walls and Gates of Peking*, in which he gives detailed descriptions of those walls.[66]

Liang Sicheng, a devoted protector of classical Chinese architecture as well as an eminent scholar and educator in architecture history, wrote affectionately of the city walls of Beijing,

> The top of the wall is on average about 10 meters wide. We can build some framed flower beds on it and plant bushes such as of lilacs and roses in them, or cover the wall top with turfs, plant some flowers, and place some round chairs on the turfs. Then we will have a place for hundreds of thousands of people to enjoy the cool and take rest at the dusk in summer. On clear and refreshing autumn days, one could climb up the wall and enjoy looking far into the distance, overlooking the whole city or looking at the grey West Mountain in the northwest or the boundless plain to the southeast. The residents of Beijing would then be able intimately to feel Nature in these ways, which would help make them broad-minded. The gate towers and turrets at the corners can be turned into exhibition rooms, reading rooms, and tea houses. Such a belt of facilities for artistic and recreational activities surrounding the city would make up a three-dimensional park unique in the world.... It would be a 39.75-kilometer-long steric park encircling the city.[67]

Why should the walls of this unique city be demolished? Liang later wrote in his memoirs,

> One day in the early years of the People's Republic, a high official of the municipal government of Beijing said to me on the city gate of Tiananmen, "Chairman Mao said that in the future, when we look south this way, we would see chimneys everywhere!" I was much taken by surprise, for wasn't such a prospect precisely what we needed to avoid? What would a Beijing with "chimneys everywhere" be like? That would be a terrible fate for the city. So I ventured to propose my view in all frankness: I believed that as a capital city,

[66] Osvald Siren, *The Walls and Gates of Peking*, London: John Lane—The Bodley Head, Ltd, 1924.

[67] Liang Sicheng, *Collected Works of Liang Sicheng*, Beijing: China Architecture and Construction Press, 1985, vol. 4, p. 47.

> Washington was a good model from capitalist countries. For Beijing, a city densely populated with historical sites and ancient buildings, emphasis on industrialization would not be a good policy for development. The best approach for Beijing would be the Washington model—it can be a political and cultural center well afforested and with exquisite scenery, and the large number of historical and cultural sites in the city can be put to use to make it a tourist city.[68]

In 1957, when the Anti-Rightist Campaign was in full swing, the demolishing of the walls of Beijing was also being vigorously prosecuted. Should those walls be protected? By addressing this question in an article in the magazine *Xin Jianshe* (*New Construction*), Liang made his last effort to defend for those walls, but in vain. Excerpts from this article, though, can give us a glimpse of the debate regarding this issue at that time. In the following quote, "A" stands for the argument of those for demolishing, while "B" stands for Liang's defense.

A: The walls, as fortifications from the past, are remains of the imperial rule of feudalistic monarchs. Its role in history has been fully played, and it should be demolished now as a matter of course.

B: If so, is not the Forbidden City an imperial palace, or Tiananmen the gate thereof? All these buildings served the emperors and facilitated their rule in the past, but they are also masterpieces created by working people in the past. Today, they have come to belong to the people and are memorials for the Chinese nation.

A: But the walls are limiting and hindering our urban development.

B: To prevent overcrowding of buildings and of people, modern societies have generally adopted methods to divide a large city into smaller districts with strips of park areas. City walls can be put to use this way—to serve as boundaries between districts of large modern cities. And when the need arises in military defense, these walls can also serve as good positions for antiaircraft artillery, which means the fortifications used for defense purposes in the past can still be of use in defense today. What is important is to break the psychological walls. The Greater Beijing being planned by the People's Government is already 21 times

[68] Deng Congcong and Zhang Jianwei, "The Twelfth Statue: Liang Sicheng and the City of Beijing," in Zou Zhongzhi, *Caressing Beijing: Beijing as portrayed by contemporary writers*, Beijing: Joint Press, 2012, p. 54.

the size of the downtown area of the old Beijing. Since this is a set policy, political and economic barriers to the development of Beijing have already been demolished, and we should not be limited or mislead by a wall in our mind.

A: The walls are a hindrance to traffic.

B: This problem can be solved by opening up a few more gates in the walls at carefully selected sites. In the planning for the road system of Beijing, meanwhile, traffic should be controlled and guided so that it will be concentrated onto a few main streets, and the existing gates in the walls can be used to determine the positions and directions of such main streets.

A: By tearing down the walls, we can obtain many bricks to be used for other purposes, and also some extra land areas to be used for building roads. By demolishing the walls no harm is done, while there can be some benefit.

B: Only the outer layer of the walls, which is about a meter thick, is made of bricks. Inside this layer is all dirt and earth, which total 11 million tons. Suppose that everyday a train with 20 cars, each with a capacity for 18 tons, is used to transport the dirt and earth to some other place, it would take 83 years to finish the entire task. And think about how much more useful goods can be transported with this train in 83 years. And the useless earth that needs to be transported amounts to about a dozen Jingshans.[69] Where are we to put it? Beijing being in the middle of a vast plain, there is no lack of land on its outskirts, so why should we spend so much manpower in order to obtain just a strip of extra land from underneath these walls. The tremendous amount of manpower that would be needed to move the earth in the walls could well be put to more fruitful use, producing many products useful for the people. Demolishing the walls with so much manpower while at the same time destroying a relic that is really a national treasure is not just much ado about nothing, but positively a sinful act.[70]

[69] Jingshan is a hill behind the Forbidden City that had been piled up during the Ming Dynasty from coal ash and slag.

[70] Deng Congcong and Zhang Jianwei, "The Twelfth Statue: Liang Sicheng and the City of Beijing", in Zou Zhongzhi, *Caressing Beijing: Beijing as portrayed by contemporary writers*, Beijing: Joint Press, 2012, pp. 57–59.

But the debate was soon ended. History moved forth quickly, with the government making hasty decisions on the matter that completely overwhelmed Liang's proposals and his fairytale-like vision. One day, when Liang had just returned to Tsinghua University, where he had been teaching, from a meeting in the downtown area of Beijing, he told colleagues of what the mayor had said at the meeting—"Whoever still argues against the demolishing of the walls will be expelled from the Party!" From then on, those who had argued against the demolition and given sound suggestions instead had to keep silent.

Thus, the ancient walls of Beijing that had been protected from war on the eve of the founding of the People's Republic were finally destroyed by the very hands that had protected them. They were fated to disappear completely, not due to the bombs and gunfire used to sack the city, but in a time of peace.

Neither was the demolition of the ancient city walls and memorial arches the last move that inflicted major damage to old Beijing. After the reform started in 1980s, reconstruction of the downtown area of old Beijing was accelerated. The greatest change brought about in this new round of destruction was the disappearance of the *hutong* (胡同), or alleys. It was documented that there were more than 1,800 *hutong* in Beijing in Qing Dynasty, more than 1,900 in Republican times, and more than 2,550 in the early years of the People's Republic. In January 1998, a study by Ditu Chubanshe (Atlas Publishing House) revealed there were about 990 *hutong* at that time. By the turn of the century, though, the remaining *hutong* were disappearing at an alarming rate of one every two days.

In 1972, Liang, who had been denounced during the Cultural Revolution, died in poverty and poor health. On his deathbed, he kept on repeating the following: many cities in the world had matured, and China should not repeat the mistakes other countries had made in urban development; one day you will see a Beijing inflicted with serious traffic jams, heavy pollution, and overcrowding.

Liang's prophecies have all come true. Traffic jam, in particular, has become an incurable disease. The government, which went a long way to demolish old Beijing, seems to have realized its mistake and has begun to plan the restoration of certain old buildings, such as Dianmen. However, people devoted to the protection of the cultural heritage of Beijing have voiced the view that it is far more urgent to stop the destruction that is still going on than to rebuild what have already been destroyed.[71]

Now, many insightful people believe that the urbanization effort in Beijing in the last two decades, accompanied by the *Chai!* 拆 ("To be dismantled") signs seen everywhere, has much hollowed the city of its historical sites. A widespread misconception in China is that modernization is a powerful force expressed as the ability to wipe out all that has existed before and thus reach a completely new starting point, from which a new reality can be created and a new miracle can be brought about. However, the new reality and the new miracle have destroyed all that China once had, and all with which its people were familiar.

With the quickening of the pace of modernizing the city, the omnipresent *Chai!* sign has brought keenly felt pain. A decade ago, in order to make preparations for the 2008 Olympic Games, the whole of Beijing was turned into a gigantic construction site. In the name of "reconstructing dilapidated and old buildings," real estate developers mowed down large numbers of old buildings in a sweeping way, with numerous traditional-style buildings being razed to the ground before their historical or artistic value could be duly assessed.

In 2002, Lars Fredén, then counselor of the political section of the Swedish Embassy to China, wrote, "The land area within the old walls of Beijing is only 5.9% that of the entire city. But even so, old buildings in the area are being demolished to make room for nondescript modern constructs such as new buildings and streets. Is it really necessary for Beijing to do so?" He also said, "If so little is left of the old Beijing, then the city ... will be without its own character or any unique charm. The tourists will ask, 'How come a city with so much fame in the world, one that used to be so majestic and kaleidoscopic, has been made so vulgar? And how can a people who are so fond of talking about the grandeur of its culture in history treat itself like this? How come this people seems to have so little respect for its own culture?'"[72]

In 2003, a British observer commented on Beijing's campaign to "demolish and rebuild the city" thus,

[71] Fengsasaxi 2011, *Liang Sicheng's prophecies on Beijing have, one by one, been proven true*, http://bbs.tianya.cn/post-worldlook-1294053-1.shtml, 2014. Accessed on May 16, 2016.

[72] Fu Ruidong, The Woe of Beijing, *Solidarity News*, July 2, 2002. Fu Ruidong was the Chinese name of Lars Fredén at that time. Fredén, who has taken on another Chinese name, Luo Ruide, was serving as the Swedish Ambassador to China.

> China has started another Cultural Revolution. This time, the Chinese are waving not the little red book of Mao's quotations, but the orders by the municipal government to have various areas demolished.... As the capital city of China undergoes the greatest transformation in the history of urban planning, thousands of *siheyuan* (四合院)[73] are being demolished. In order to speed up the modernization of Beijing before the 2008 Olympic Games, developers have been mowing down those *siheyuan* and replacing them with the kind of luxurious high-risers one can find in any large city in the world.... Although the central government has acknowledged that *siheyuan* and the life in this kind of dwellings is an important part of the stock of Beijing's cultural treasure, it can no longer rein in the runaway horse that is the real estate developers.... If the developers do not stop, one can be sure Beijing the historic city will soon cease to exist.[74]

A fallacy that has wide currency among urban planners in China states, "Demolish the old, and what you build anew will become historical buildings in 50 years." This kind of thinking has been dominant in the urban development for the last three decades, and has yet to be critically reviewed.

The Reform and Opening-Up of China

The Cultural Revolution was ended in October 1976. In December 1978, the third plenary session of the 11th Central Committee of the Chinese Communist Party was convened. At this meeting, a strategic decision was made to "carry out reform within and open up the country to the outside." This was the first systematic state policy to open China to the outside world since the founding of the People's Republic, and it basically reversed the tendency toward the increasingly autarkic state of the country since 1949, preparing the way for the rapid development of China's economy.

The Implementation of the "Reform and Opening-Up" Policy

Following the third plenary session of the 11th Central Committee of the CCP, the Chinese government began to implement the policy of reform

[73] Quadrangle dwellings characteristic of Beijing are a courtyard surrounded by houses on all four sides, and is named *siheyuan*.

[74] Report in the British newspaper *Guardian*, the Chinese translation of which was carried in *Reference News*, September 10, 2003.

and opening-up. The first move that helped to improve the recreation of ordinary people was the policy to allow movies and TV programs from other countries to be imported. This move not only helped to make people's daily lives more lively, but also opened a window for the Chinese to learn about the outside world. As the relationship with Japan continued to improve, many Japanese movies and TV programs were imported, of which the TV play series *Akai Giwaku* (*Red Suspicion*) and the movie *Sandakan hachiban shō kan: Bō kyō* (*Sandakan No. 8*) were immensely popular in China. Likewise, the Indian movies *Wanderers of the Desert* and *Caravan* swept the whole of China, and the Mexican movie *Yesenia* captivated numerous Chinese. Critical realist movies and science fiction movies from the West gave much inspiration to the young generation. The sweet songs of the Taiwanese pop singer Teresa Teng, the exquisite *kungfu* of Bruce Lee, rock 'n' roll, and hippie culture all brought new experiences to the Chinese who had long been impoverished in terms of leisure activities.

Attention to Lifestyle

In the last three decades, China's economy has been growing at an astonishing rate. Leisure has emerged as a field that involves consumption, distribution, production, and the transformation of industrial structure, and has also been developing very rapidly.

In the communiqué of the third plenary session of the 12th Central Committee of the CCP convened in 1984, the issue of lifestyle is mentioned three times:

> The reform of the economic institutions will lead not only to important changes in people's economic life, but also to profound changes in lifestyle and mentality of the people.
>
> As the same time as we try to set up vigorous socialist economic institutions, we should also make an effort to ensure a civilized, healthy, and scientific lifestyle that is suited to modern development of productive forces and social progress will be developed in the whole society while backwardness, ignorance, and decadence will be discarded.
>
> Such a lifestyle and mentality are important parts of the development of socialist spiritual civilization and a great force impelling the reform of the economic institutions and the development of material civilization.[75]

[75] Communiqué of the third plenary session of the 12th Central Committee of the Chinese Communist Party, *People's Daily*, October 20, 1984.

Yu Guangyuan, then vice-president of the Chinese Academy of Social Sciences, advocated in many an article that great emphasis should be given to leisure lifestyles. Vehemently against the leftist line, he argued, "Socialist construction, including production and other activities under socialism, is all for the purpose of improving the life of laborers. However, up till now, the issue of laborers' life has seldom entered the agenda of our Party and government agencies."[76] He also said, "We should research the consumption, life, and lifestyles of the people, so as to help them achieve a better, happier, and healthier life under current economic conditions."[77]

Argument for the Policy Decision to "Shorten the Workweek"

As the economy of China grew and Chinese culture became increasingly integrated with world culture, the Chinese government came to realize the necessity of shortening the workweek.

In 1986, a team was formed in the Center for the Development of Science and Technology in China under the National Science Committee specifically to study the possibility of shortening work time. After about eight years of study, the team came up with a feasibility study report entitled "Research Report on Shortening Work Time and Implementing a Five-Day Workweek." In March 1994, China experimented with a system of having a five-day workweek every other week. On March 25, 1995, Premier Li Peng issued Order No. 174 of the State Council "The Decision to Revise 'The State Council Regulations on the Work Time of Employees'," announcing that, starting from 1 May 1, 1995, the five-day workweek was to be implemented, with employees to work for eight hours a day, or 40 hours a week. With Order No. 174, the five-day workweek was officially in force. Recalling the process leading to this decision, Hu Ping, who had directed the team to work on the shortening of work time, said,

> In order to implement a five-day workweek, a series of socioeconomic issues had to be addressed: Was the work time currently invested in the economic activities sufficient? Would the shortening of work time lead to decreases in economic indices? How various social activities were likely to change after work time was shortened? Would our facilities for social services be able to

[76] Yu Guangyuan, *Reform, Management, Life, and Organizational Development*. Changsha: Hunan People's Publishing House, 1986, pp. 346–368.

[77] Ibid., p. 350.

> provide sufficient support for the increased leisure time? Would the increased leisure time be used for acquiring knowledge and activities conducive to better economic and social development? These were the key issues regarding whether a five-day workweek should be implemented in China and also closely connected to the necessary conditions for a successful implementation of the system.... Now the fact is that the service sector has seen tremendous growth after the five-day workweek was implemented. People have been using the two-day weekend not only to relax but also to "recharge" themselves [through various forms of studying], and the tourism sector has also seen vigorous development.[78]

Evolving Meanings of Xiuxian

The evolution of the meaning of *xiuxian* 休閑 (leisure) and leisure thinking associated with it can partly be seen from the way the characters *xiu* and *xian* and the word *xiuxian* have been defined in dictionaries. In the authoritative *Kangxi Zidian* compiled in the Qing Dynasty, *xiu* can be seen to mean "beautiful and nice," and that, pictographically, it means "a person leans against a tree" to "make use of its shadow for rest."[79] *Xian*, on the other hand, means "free time," but is also a phonetic loan for another character meaning "gentility and refinement, with purity of thought and a peaceful mind. Common derivative meanings of the word include morality and law, hence limit and restraint."[80]

After the People's Republic was founded, the government was concerned that all dictionaries published earlier had used classical Chinese as the language to explain Chinese characters and words, and that classical Chinese was quite different from the vernacular spoken by the people, making it difficult of ordinary people to use these dictionaries. In the directive of February 6, 1956, on the popularization of mandarin as the official language of China, the State Council charged the Institute of Linguistics of the Chinese Academy of Science (now the Institute of Linguistics of the

[78] Hu Ping, "The Whole Process of the Introduction of the Five-Day Workweek in China," *Hundred Year Tide*, 2009(12).

[79] Zhang Yushu et al., *Kangxi Dictionary*. Beijing: Beijing Normal University Press, 1997, p. 18.

[80] *A Comprehensive Dictionary of the Chinese Language*, vol. 12, Beijing: Chinese Dictionary Publishing House, 1993, p. 1174.

Chinese Academy of Social Sciences) with the task of compiling a medium-sized dictionary of modern Chinese aimed to set a norm for modern word usage.

In June 1958, the project to compile *Dictionary of Modern Chinese* was officially launched. In 1965, a trial edition of the *Dictionary* was completed. In 1966, while Commercial Press, the publisher which was to publish the dictionary, was doing the final editing work in preparation of its publication, the Cultural Revolution was begun, and the work had to be halted. It was not until 1973 that the trial edition was published for "internal release" on restricted circulation. In 1974, the campaign to denounce Lin Biao[81] and Confucius was launched, and the *Dictionary* met with a great deal of fierce criticism and was labeled "a hodgepodge of feudalism, capitalism, and revisionism."[82]

In December, 1978, the *Dictionary* was at long last officially published. In this edition of the *Dictionary*, *xiuxian* is defined to mean "arable land that is laid fallow for a season or a few years." In the fifth edition of the *Dictionary*, a new item was added as definition of *xiuxian*: "to rest, or to live a life of leisure," with a place for leisure activities given as an example for this usage.[83] Likewise, when *Xinhua Cidian*, another authoritative medium-sized dictionary of the Chinese language, was revised, a new definition of *xiuxian* was added: "to have leisure after work or study," with casual wear and leisure activity given as examples for this usage.[84]

The Soulless State of Leisure in Contemporary China

When the word *xiuxian* re-entered the vocabulary of the Chinese in the 1990s, it was confused with making merry and seeking sensual pleasures through eating, drinking, and so forth. Everywhere in China, be it the city or the countryside, baths, pedicure salons, "farm restaurants", rural home

[81] Lin, who had been the minister of defense and vice-chairman of the CCP, had been designated as Mao's successor, but he later plotted to overthrow Mao's rule and, when the plot was exposed, tried to escape to the Soviet Union but died when his plane crashed in Mongolia on the way.

[82] Han Jingti, "The Crime of the Gang of Four in Suppressing the *Dictionary of Modern Chinese*", in Han Jingti, ed., *Research Papers on the Compilation of the* Dictionary of Modern Chinese. Beijing: Commercial Press, p. 59.

[83] *Dictionary of Modern Chinese*, 5th ed., Beijing: Commercial Press, 2005, p. 1223.

[84] *New China Dictionary of Chinese Characters*, rev. ed., Beijing: Commercial Press, 2001, p. 1106.

inns, real estate development projects, magnificent villas, shopping malls, gourmet banquets have assumed the label of *xiuxian*, and leisure has been reduced to the status of simply a ready source of money.

The "Golden Weeks"?

In 1999, the Chinese government announced new "Stipulations on Leave for National Festivals and Holidays," creating three seven-day vacations by joining the three three-day holidays for the Spring Festival, May Day, and National Day[85] with the preceding and following weekends.[86] These seven-day holidays were named "golden weeks" in the media, and were intended to promote a holiday economy, or to increase domestic demand by instituting long holiday leave. Weekends and holidays had been times when consumption was concentrated to start with, and the seven-day breaks have been occasions when tourism, transport, and commercial activities are even more concentrated, creating marvelous opportunities for businesses to make money.

This author has been questioning whether it is proper to call these seven-day holidays "golden weeks" from the very beginning, and has voiced her disagreement with the term in many articles. These vacations were supposed to be for a festival and two holidays which are very important for the Chinese, and which should be solemn and sacred, while the concept of "golden weeks" leads people to be immersed in excessive consumption to satisfy their desires for material goods. With that, people are likely to take these festival and holidays casually, viewing them as occasions to enjoy mundane pleasures in a boisterous manner.

The "golden weeks" have been castigated for fostering an overly commercial flavor while putting aside the traditional virtues. Not only do the media lack a sense of responsibility to society in failing to maintain a professional integrity in their treatment of the "golden weeks," but government at all levels has also failed to provide proper guidance for the people. The immediate consequence is that these long vacations have not been conducive to enhancing the quality of leisure life.

[85] The Chinese National Day is October 1, in memory of the day on which the People's Republic of China was founded in 1949.

[86] If one or two days of leave fall on a weekend, one or two additional day(s) would be added to the leave to make up for it.

The "golden weeks" have worked to overly concentrate people, money, and goods in time and space, which has led to a lowering of quality in services provided, while putting enormous pressures on various private and public sector resources responsible for the provision of transport, environmental protection, safety, and public administration. In general, the experience of those who have participated in tourism in these long holidays is not very good, and little cultural interaction has taken place on their tours. There are, of course, other forms of concentrated consumption during the "golden weeks," but these have frequently lent opportunities to many businesses to make and sell fake and low quality products and to raise prices disproportionately, while also increasing the costs of administration and necessary safety precautions. A social atmosphere characterized by fickleness, greed, and the desire for quick results and instant benefits has been fostered unwittingly.

In recent years, the negative effects of the "golden weeks" have kept on increasing, and the eroding of cultural values, the low quality of public services, the disorder in social behavior, and the lack of rituals representing the national spirit are all symptoms that lead people to question the value of the superficial "prosperity" brought by these long vacations. What risks are hidden behind this "prosperity" and what costs they entail are issues that have thus far hardly been addressed.

Conclusion

Why was the Chinese Empire, one that had had a long history of cultural splendor, mutilated within a century, resulting in such cultural discontinuity? There are many reasons for that, but one factor of undeniable importance is the discontinuity of education brought about by the Cultural Revolution and the "down to the countryside" movement. In the decade from 1968 to 1978, about 20 million young people were denied the opportunity to enter college, which directly or indirectly wreaked great damage to the growth and development of the next few generations in terms of work skills, perspectives for looking at and learning about the world, development of value systems, and inheritance of the spirit of national culture. The rude behavior and conduct that run against order and established customs displayed by many Chinese are an aftereffect of this damage.

Another reason is that the current understanding of the value of leisure by many Chinese is rather vulgar and shallow. The trap laid by highly commercialized society entices Chinese people with revelry, but that commercialized spirit has actually been cheating society in two ways. First, it appears to provide a general happiness shared by all, since happiness is identified with consumption. Second, consumerism advances a proposition which is actually false—that one would have freedom once he/she has the freedom to consume. Freedom is reduced to consumerism, and free time means endless consumption, as if the individual's self-actualization is attained in his/her consumptive acts. In this respect, the government, the media, and businesses have all been promoters of such "happiness" and "freedom."

Is it that natural disasters, poverty, wars, and corruption among the ruling classes have dissipated the vitality of traditional Chinese culture? Have perpetual sufferings stripped the Chinese of their enthusiasm for exploring the meaning of life and worn out their spirit to pursue a life of true quality? Have the Chinese really become parvenus with much money but little taste? Have they turned into robots which continue to work ceaselessly but are incapable of enjoying life? Are traditional leisure values really incompatible with the modern society?

One cannot help recalling what Hegel said in the inaugural address for his lectures in the history of philosophy at Heidelberg:

> The necessities of the time have accorded to the petty interests of everyday life such overwhelming attention: the deep interests of actuality and the strife respecting these have engrossed all the powers and the forces of the mind—as also the necessary means—to so great an extent, that no place has been left to the higher inward life, the intellectual operations of a purer sort; and the better natures have thus been stunted in their growth, and in great measure sacrificed.[87]

Now the Chinese have at last gained the opportunity to strive for their own material interests, but has that led to the loss of interest in "the higher inward life, the intellectual operations of a purer sort"? Have their "better natures" been "in great measure sacrificed"?

[87] Hegel, Georg W. F., *Lectures on the History of Philosophy* (trans. E. S. Haldane), vol. I, London: Kegan Paul, Trench, Trübner & Co., Ltd., xi.

CHAPTER 4

The Rise of China's Economy and Trends in Leisure Development

What is the China experience? What forces have enabled the 1.3 billion Chinese in only three decades to break away from extreme poverty and to embark on the march toward the goal of becoming a wealthy nation? And what is the significance of this development for the cultural tradition of China? Ronald Coase, Nobel laureate for Economics in 1991, comments thus on the China experience: "due to these achievements, hundreds of millions of Chinese peasants have been raised out of extreme poverty, and an ancient civilization has since been on its way to a great revival... A surprising outcome of China's transition to capitalism is that China has found a way back to its own cultural roots ... China's embrace of both its history and globalization leads us to believe that Chinese capitalism, which just started its long journey, will be different."[1]

Against the background of China's economic rise, what effects has this rise had on people's leisure life and consumption? What improvements have been made in the areas of government policy, system design, public service, and human rights? How should we appraise the trends of the nation's economy in the future?

[1] Ronald Coase and Ning Wang, "How China Become Capitalist," Cato Policy Report, 2013, **35**(1)(January/February).

Huidi Ma, Er Liu, *Traditional Chinese Leisure Culture and Economic Development*, DOI 10.1057/978-1-137-59253-8_4

The Rise of China's Economy

The Economic Situation After the End of the Cultural Revolution

In October 1976, the decade-long Cultural Revolution finally came to an end. Before that, China had been largely closed to the outside world for many years, and the developed countries in the West, on their part, had also put many economic sanctions against China, which made it necessary for China to adopt an autarkic policy for its economy. Relevant data from the period show that, as of 1978, the sector of industry, agriculture, and service output accounted for 28.20%, 47.9%, 23.9%, respectively, of China's GDP.[2]

In the following, we will look at the socioeconomic situation of Chinese society in five areas, namely, dress, diet, housing, means of transport, and recreation.

Dress

At that time, China was able to meet the basic needs of its people in terms of clothing, in that all all, or at least the vast majority of people, had enough to wear, but few could afford to dress fashionably so as to look graceful and dignified. Indeed, it was very common for an article of clothing to be worn for ten years or so. A very small percentage of families could afford to buy ready-made clothes, so most families made their own clothes from cloth. Since cloth was strictly rationed, the quantity of home-made clothes for the typical family was also limited. There was no concept of fashion design, and the style of clothes was much the same for all families, with the colors of clothes mostly blue, grey, green, or white.

Diet

The rationing system for many necessities in life that had been implemented before the reform and opening-up period was continued until the mid-1980s. Under this system, there were many things that one could not buy without coupons, even if one had the money for them. As a result, coupons for grains, edible oil, pastry, and so forth, and booklets for registering a family's purchase of staple and non-staple food products, coal gas, and so on came to be as valuable as money. The diet of ordinary people mainly consisted of products from coarse grains and vegetables, together

[2] State Statistical Bureau of the People's Republic of China, *China Statistical Yearbook 2007*. Beijing: China Statistical Press, 2007.

with small amounts of chicken, duck, fish, and other meat that were strictly rationed. No free market for these products existed.

Housing

In 1978, the average urban resident in China had 6.7 square meters of floor space. Housing was for the most part provided by the government. Although the costs people had to pay for housing was very low, residential buildings were built at very slow rates, so the supply was far less than the demand. One often had to wait for a very long time to get a housing unit through his/her work unit. The population increased very rapidly in the 1950s and 1960s, and it was very common for a couple to have 4–6 children. With many young couples having to wait a very long time to get their own housing, it was not unusual to have a family of three or even four generations living in a housing unit of a dozen or so square meters. The housing units were often worn out and low in height, with toilets, kitchens, and washrooms usually shared by several families. In rural areas, the floor space per capita was about 8.1 square meters, or more than twice the size of urban residents' average space, but the quality of the houses was also very low.[3]

Transportation

As of 1978, China had about 50,000 kilometers of railway and 940,000 kilometers of paved road. Earthen roads built earlier had for the most part been supplanted by asphalt roads. Transport at that time was characterized by a very large population and a small number of vehicles, with privately owned vehicles virtually nonexistent. A small number of taxis existed, serving mostly in diplomatic and other official occasions. As the main means of transportation for ordinary people, a large number of bicycles were running on the streets. Civil aviation was rather backward. Even in 1987, there were only 78 air routes,[4] all belonging to China Air, the sole airline in China at that time. Only cadres of high enough rank could board airplanes upon presenting a document from their work unit proving their identity. In the countryside, people for the most part walked from place to

[3] "Per Capita Housing Area for Residents in Urban and Rural in China (1978–2012)" in the National Bureau of Statistics Report: *Statistical Yearbook of China's Fixed Assets Investment.*

[4] Zhang Xiuhui, "Civil Aviation Memory: The Route Changes of China's Civil Aviation," *China Civil Aviation News*, September 6, 2015.

place. When the distance was too far, people usually rode carts drawn by draft animals, or on farm machines such as tractors.

Recreation

In cities, listening to the radio, playing chess or cards, reading, and watching movies were the main forms of recreation. The wristwatch, the bicycle, the radio, and the sewing machine were called the "four big items," and were the luxury items for that time. In rural areas, film projection teams and troupes of theatrical performers moved regularly from village to village. Entertainments were all supposed to follow the twin principles of "for the people" and "for socialism" set down by Mao. Labor unions were quite effective in organizing various recreational and sport activities at all levels, including work-break exercises in the morning and in the afternoon. Table tennis, volleyball, and badminton had been popular sports since the 1960s.

In late 1970s, the cities' shopping malls began selling 9–12 inch black and white televisions, introducing the Japanese production of tape recorders, as well as color TV and refrigerators from overseas.

From the end of the Cultural Revolution to the mid-1980s, basic needs for food and clothes were the main part of the consumption of citizens. The Engel coefficient for 1978 was close to 60%, at a time when the per capita GDP was only USD 381.[5]

Changes in China's Economic Policy

From the beginning of its reform and opening-up in 1978 to the implementation of a general market economy in 1992, China went through three stages.

The First Stage (1978–1984)

At the third plenary session of the 11th Central Committee of the CCP convened in December 1978, the decision was made to switch the focus of the party and the state to economic development and to carry out reform and open up to the outside world. To break away from the mindset formed

[5] Zhu Jianhong, "35 Years of Reform and Opening-up: a review of the achievements in economic development." *People's Daily*, November 21, 2013.

in the preceding decades, to be practical and realistic were made the basic principles guiding the party's work. The central work of the party was switched from "class struggle" to economic development, and the economic system was to shift from complete public ownership to one with "public ownership as the principal part, but allowing the development of other forms of ownership." The highly centralized and planned economy was to be changed into a market economy, and China would no longer keep its door closed to the outside, but would open up and become integrated with the rest of the world. In 1980, the government set up Shenzhen, Zhuhai, Xiamen, and Shantou as Special Economic Zones, which were to operate completely according to principles of the market economy. This was the greatest turning point for China since the founding of the People's Republic.

The Second Stage (1978–1984)

In 1984, "The Decisions of the Central Committee of the CCP Regarding the Reform of the Economic System" was passed, which stipulated that "the socialist economy is a planned commodity economy, and, as the economy develops, the scope of mandatory planning should be narrowed, while that of directional planning should be broadened." People began to find ways of becoming self-employed entrepreneurs, and the economy began to diversify in terms of ownership.

The Third Stage (1989–1992)

Paying attention to the voices and needs of different forces, the government finally made it explicit at the 14th General Congress of the CCP in October 1992 that the goal of the reform of China's economic system was to set up a socialist market economy.

Deng's Strategic Design for China's Modernization in Three Steps

Deng Xiaoping proposed a strategic plan for the modernization of socialist China in three steps.[6] The first step was for China's gross national product (GNP) to double in ten years starting from 1981, so that the basic needs of

[6] Deng Xiaoping was the chief designer of China's socialist reform, opening up and modernization. His ideas had a great impact on China in the late twentieth century.

the people would be satisfied. The second step was for the nation's GNP to double again in another ten years so that people would become well-to-do. The third step was for China to approach the living standards of developed countries in another 30–50 years, with the country largely modernized. Later, the goal was lowered to match the living standards of moderately developed countries.[7]

The Period of Rapid Economic Growth

From 1992 to 2008, China went through a period of rapid economic development, with its GDP enjoying a double-digit average growth rate. The rate of growth was 14.2% in 1992, 9.10% in 2002, and 10.07% in 2009. According to statistics made public by the IMF, the GDP of China grew by about 10% in 2010, reaching a total of USD 5.75 trillion, which made China the second largest economy in the world.[8]

According to the report made by the State Bureau of Statistics in 2015 about the achievements in China's social and economic development in the course of its 12th "Five-Year Plan", China's economy has maintained a mid- to high-speed rate of growth during these years. It was estimated that the average annual growth of the economy would be close to 8%, which was about 2.5% higher than the annual rate of growth of the world economy for the same period.

In 2014, China's GDP reached 63.6139 trillion RMB, which was equivalent to USD 10.4 trillion, accounting for 13.3% of the world total, up by 4.1 percentage points from the 2010 figure. In 2014, the GDP per capita of China was 46,629 RMB, which represents a 33.6% increase over that of 2010, or an annual increase of 7.5%, after inflation has been taken into account. According to statistics provided by the World Bank, China's gross national income per capita increased from USD 4,300 for 2010 to USD 7,380 for 2014, and its rank among nations with medium gross national income (GNI) levels had continued to improve.[9]

In 2015, the world economy as a whole was in recession, and the new economic policy of China had significantly slowed down the growth rate of

[7] Jin Chongji, "Deng Xiaoping as the Master Designer," *People's Daily*, August 18, 2014.

[8] Lin Qianya, "China Officially Became the Second Largest Economy in the World, with Her GDP Exceeding that of Japan," *World Knowledge*, (5): 8-8, 2011.

[9] Jin Chongji, "Deng Xiaoping as the Master Designer," *People's Daily*, August 18, 2014.

her economy. However, the growth rate of the nation's economy was still nearly 8%.[10]

These figures all come from authoritative sources. They have been questioned by many in China after they were announced, but that is because the statistical means and base figures used can vary greatly among different sources. But whether we believe in these statistics or not, the strong rise of Chinese economy in the last three decades is an irrefutable fact. This continuous growth of the economy has led to an unprecedented increase in the nation's leisure consumption.

Formation and Development of a Market for Leisure Consumption

In the 1990s, large commercial centers integrating sightseeing, shopping, and entertainment began to appear in large cities such as Beijing, Shanghai, Guangzhou, and Shenzhen. Advertisements promoting leisure consumption also came into existence.

The word *xiuxian* ("leisure") became increasingly popular with shops in shopping malls and business districts. New casual clothes were called leisure shirts and leisure trousers. The word *xiuxian* was also attached to words for caps, socks, and shoes. Thus, apart from goods used to meet basic needs in everyday life, there appeared large numbers of products, facilities, and services, called leisure attire, leisure food, facilities for leisure and bodybuilding activities, and leisure parks. Having entered the vocabulary of everyday usage, the word *xiuxian* became widely popular in a short time and is now an important part of people's leisure lifestyles. The primary reason for this development has been the fact that "some sections of the population have become rich first" and a middle-class is on the rise in China.

The Groups That Became Rich First

In the mid-1980s, Deng said on many occasions, "The cat that catches mice is a good cat, be it a white cat or a black cat," and "Let some sections of the population get rich first." With policies made along these lines in effect, some people quickly embarked on the way to make their fortunes.

In the late 1970s and early 1980s, a contract responsibility system was implemented in the countryside in China. Whereas under the commune

[10] State Statistical Bureau of the People's Republic of China: "In the 12th Five-Year Plan, China's economy is expected to grow at an average annual rate of nearly 8%," news.xinhuanet.com, October 13, 2015.

system, peasants worked collectively on land owned by communes according to centralized plans made by the communes (which, in turn, were responsible to authorities at higher levels for meeting certain production quotas) to earn work points which could, at the end of the year, be converted to certain amounts of grain and some cash payments, in the new system, a peasant family "contracted" a certain amount of land from the commune on a long-term basis, and, as long as the family was able to turn in a required amount of grain to the commune, it was largely free to plan what to plant and to work the land in whatever way it saw fit. With the newly gained freedom, peasants who were good at farm work and knew how to manage land quickly became "master hands" in the village and became rich through hard work on their own part or by organizing their families' efforts efficiently. In cities and towns, many firms under collective ownership also had the operation of the whole firm or certain parts contracted and subcontracted to individuals on the distribution principle of "to each according to his work." As a result, more people became entrepreneurs in trade and industrial operations. At that time, to have an annual family income of ten thousand yuan RMB was already a sign of wealth.

In mid- and late 1990s, the standard for being rich was raised to 100,000 yuan, and when China entered the twenty-first century, the standard was "a hundred thousand yuan is only a start, a million yuan is so-so, and only those making tens of millions of yuan can be really counted as rich." The rapid evolution in this respect reflected the profound socioeconomic changes China was experiencing and the great creativity at work in the nation.

But who were those who "got rich first"? It is difficult to obtain a good answer to this question from official data provided by the government. There are some stories circulating among common people which, although a little over-generalized, are perhaps closer to the truth. According to these stories, of those who made their fortunes in the 1990s, a very large proportion were either "second-generation officials" (children of high-ranking government officials) or belonged to the "Red second generation" (children of high-ranking Communist revolutionaries who may have still been alive). With official documents approving their business undertaking, which they obtained by making use of their parents' influence, they would be able to garner great power and wealth overnight. There were also adventurers who, believing that "one's boldness is proportional to the amount what the land would yield" tried to maximize their profits by means fair or foul, not excluding smuggling and tax evasion. Another approach used by entrepreneurial businessmen was to collude with officials to peculate assets formerly under state ownership. The businessmen as well as those who had control of state-owned enterprises both made their fortunes in the contracting of those enterprises or part of their operations. Some officials, in the name of attracting foreign businesses and investment to cities or towns under their administration, made liberal use of state assets by making fraudulent applications for funding and other recourses from higher-level government agencies on the one hand, and receiving bribes from businessmen in exchange for contracts granted to the latter on the other. With such contracts, business magnates proceeded to exploit natural resources or undertake large real estate development projects for short-term gains, often with little attention to sustainability of development. This is the source of the widespread corruption which the government has not been able to root out, although many anti-corruption campaigns, large and small, have been conducted for that purpose.

Of course, there are also a large number of entrepreneurs who have achieved success through their own hard work. With the quickening pace of technological innovation, those who become rich by creating new industries or applying new technologies, such as the founders of the hi-tech corporations Alibaba, Tencent, Huawei, Baidu, and Xiaomi, have kept on setting new records on the Forbes China Rich List.

The Middle Class on the Rise

According to the newest "Global Wealth Report" by Credit Suisse, released on October 13, 2015, the number of China's middle-class adults, defined, per US standard, as individuals having wealth between USD 50,000 and USD 500,000,[11] has reached 109 million, outnumbering that of the USA (92 million) to become the largest in the world. Although the share of the middle class in the adult population of the country is only 10.7%, the absolute number has become the largest.[12]

Ordinary Chinese use rather intuitive criteria here: those who have money and leisure, who own a house and a car, and can take part in tourism often, are middle-class people. To them, middle-class people are those who frequent coffee houses in their free time, are always among the first to watch newly released movies, have a good meal in a Western restaurant almost

[11] Credit Suisse Research Institute, "Global Wealth Report 2015," Zurich: Credit Suisse AG, p. 28.

[12] Ibid., pp. 31–32.

every week, and are never parsimonious in buying clothes—if they see any clothes to their liking, they would buy them right away, in the blink of an eye, even if they cost more than a thousand yuan.

Middle-class people are usually 25–45 years of age and are the pillars of their families, meaning they have to provide financial as well as other support to their parents and bring up their children while working hard at their jobs. The middle class can actually be divided into upper, middle, and lower strata. Financially speaking, there is the saying "a housing unit eliminates one middle-class person," meaning that with the rapid increase in prices for houses and apartments, an individual who used to earn enough income for him/her to be classified as middle class would be turned into a "mortgage slave" after purchasing a house or an apartment. If a formerly middle-class couple have a child, that would incur very high costs for his/her upbringing, education, and healthcare, rendering the couple's income very insufficient, and making it necessary for them to do careful calculations and strict budgeting and to cut down on expenditures on goods and services needed to maintain a middle-class lifestyle. "We have to think of how to provide for our old age, how to provide support for our parents, and how to bring up our child. There are loads of problems to think about regarding education, healthcare, housing, and so on. If life goes on peacefully, then it is still possible to maintain a good quality of life. But such a life is much like a beautiful piece of porcelain, and may go to pieces at the slightest shock." Thus complained a middle-class person.

Who Will Lead the Future Consumer Market?

The experience of China in her economic development has some unique features. Because the economy has developed in large strides, there have been many imbalances—in development, in the sharing of prosperity, in regional development, and in ecological maintenance—which pose challenges for future development. Is it feasible, then, to rely on consumption as the mainstay for the new economic order and for the New Normalcy? And who will lead the future consumer market? We will address the second question later. Here, let us take a look at the first question.

The Configuration of Consumer Groups

In the next few years, those known as the super rich, the rich, the rural rich, the "golden" rural rich, the middle class, the petit bourgeoisie, the millennial generation, the silver-haired, and Chinese Damas will continue to be the major consumer groups in China.

The Super Rich

This term refers to families and individuals who are worth billions of yuan. This group is in possession of 41% of the wealth of the country. They can easily throw thousands and millions of yuan into any fancy they may have, such as piloting airplanes, sailing yachts, hunting, and many other exotic activities, without batting an eyelid.

The Rich, the Rural Rich, and the "Golden" Rural Rich

The rich, the rural rich, and the "golden" rural rich groups all possess great wealth, and tirelessly indulge in purchasing real estate, investment in stocks and bonds, gold, top-grade wristwatches, attire and accessories from famous brands, the collection of valuable and exotic items, and tourism. The rural rich are proud. They lack taste but are willing to spend. The "golden" rural rich are basically *nouveau riche* dripping with gold and silver. The greater part of their money is spent on conspicuous consumption of material goods of a vulgar taste, but which they like to display ostentatiously.

The Middle Class and Petite Bourgeoisie

The middle class and petite bourgeoisie are individuals with stable salaries from decent jobs that give them annual incomes somewhere in the range from 300,000 to 1,000,000 million yuan. They typically have had a good education, and put their emphasis on consumption conducive to self-improvement and self-expression that facilitate their cultural and spiritual pursuits. The cultural market of first- and second-line cities is supported mostly by these groups.

The Millennial Generation

The millennial generation is the generation born in the 1980s, 1990s, and 2000s. Most of them are only children and have ideas about consumption that are rather different from those of earlier generations. In their consumption patterns, they like to "play it cool," to do unconventional and unorthodox things in order to show their individuality. They have had good education, are suave and skillful with the Internet, and lead a life of pleasure. They are willing to spend money for high-quality goods and services. As the sole children of their families, they are the favorites of their parents and even their extended families. Usually their parents would actively save on their behalf so as to be able to help them buy housing units and cars. As a result, they often show strong tendencies for consumption.

The Silver-Haired

This term refers to the elderly who have retired. The younger ones in this group (aged 60–70) have inherited traditional values, but have also been in contact with modern ideas. They are especially enthusiastic with regard to tourism and volunteer activities, but most of them put much value on thrift.

The Chinese Damas

"The Chinese Dama" (中國大媽) as an English expression was coined by the *Wall Street Journal* to refer to the group of Chinese women aged 45–55 who made their fame in April 2013, when they rushed to purchase anything containing gold or silver as the price for gold plunged, and were hailed by the media as having out-maneuvered the big shots in the international financial market. As a group with fairly strong purchasing power, the Chinese Damas make up the main force among tourists on shopping tours. In this group are not only entrepreneurial women and well-educated women intellectuals who have made money themselves, but also some other groups, including wives, mistresses, and clandestine concubines of wealthy men, those who became rich overnight when they were compensated for housing units they owned which had to be pulled down to make way for real estate development projects, and those who made their fortunes through investment in stocks and funds.

What Are They Going to Consume?

In recent years, consumer markets for cruises, motorhomes, accessories for backpacking, jogging, and expeditions have been sharply on the rise. The numbers of Chinese who engage in these activities have been increasing steadily, and are likely to overtake the numbers of those engaged in more traditional leisure activities.

Tourism and the Tourist Industry

According to statistics released by the UNWTO (United Nations World Tourism Organization) in 2015, the number of Chinese taking part in overseas tourism had reached 120 million person-times, while the number for overseas tourism in 2016 for the Chinese Festival season alone is estimated at six million. Extensive shopping has gradually become a prominent feature of overseas tourism undertaken by the Chinese. Statistics from the National Tourism Bureau of China show that the number of 120 million for the person-times of Chinese overseas tourism in 2015, and that the total amount of consumption by overseas tourists as well as their numbers were the highest in the world. Of these, the number of those taking self-service traveling reached 80 million person-times, with a per capita consumption of 11,624 yuan, which represents a 24.1% increase over the previous year. The per capita expenditure of Chinese undertaking overseas tourism during the "Golden Week" of the Spring Festival in 2016 was projected to reach 10,000 yuan.[13]

According to statistics released by the Japan Tourism Agency, in 2015 the amount of consumption by Chinese tourists comprised 40% of the total consumption by foreign tourists in Japan, with a per capita consumption of 283,800 yen (equivalent to 16,000 yuan RMB), which was the highest among all the countries of origin, exceeding the per capita consumption by foreign tourists from other countries by 100,000 yen, or approximately 5,590 yuan RMB.[14]

The major reasons for the large increase of overseas tourism include the loosening of restrictions by foreign countries on visa applications by Chinese nationals, the increase of flights to destination cities, and the improvement of the consumption environment. These factors have stimulated the enthusiasm of the groups of Chinese who have both the money and the time for overseas tourism and consumption in foreign countries. Popular forms of overseas tourism include summer camps, tours by parents with children, excursions to neighboring countries on weekends, short-distance tours on minor long leaves, and medium- and long-distance tours during the National Day long break.

It is somewhat unfortunate that less than 10% of the 1.3 billion Chinese now hold a passport, which means that those who could go on an overseas tour are only a small minority. People who do go on such tours are mainly concentrated in first-line cities and developed coastal regions, rather than spread throughout the country. Also, destinations for such tours are mostly countries and regions geographically close to China, such as Hong Kong, Macao, Taiwan, Japan, South Korea, and southeastern Asian countries.[15] As

[13] Ctrip: "2016 Spring Festival Golden Week Outbound Travel Trends Report." www.199it.com/archives, June 15, 2016.

[14] Ibid.

[15] China Institute on Tourism, "Annual Report on Outbound Tours by the Chinese, 2015."

relevant policies are adjusted and as China as a whole enters the stage when most people are well-to-do in the years to come, the number of people taking overseas tours is likely to keep on increasing.

In 2015, the performance of the Chinese in tourism consumption within the country was remarkable, and the structure of consumption was further upgraded. The numbers of self-service and self-driving tours continued to increase. New tourism packages tailored for individual needs with "light travel" and "tour groups of facilities" characterized by "no getting up early, no harrying, no frequent change of hotels, and enough time for free activities at every stop" became popular. According to the blue book of China's tourism economy published by the China Institute on Tourism, China received over 4.1 billion person-times of domestic foreign tourists in 2015, with the total revenues generated from tourism exceeding 4 trillion yuan. These figures had increased by 10% and 12%, respectively, over those for 2014.[16]

Characterized by a strong pull on other sectors of the economy, a large multiplying effect, and a high employment rate, the tourism industry has become a new locomotive for economic growth. The National Tourism Agency of China has provided the following data: In 2015, investment on tourism was 1.0072 trillion yuan, going over the one trillion mark for the first time in history. The figure represents a 42% increase over the previous year, a growth rate 10% higher than that of 2014. The investment pattern has been summarized by authorities into six areas: (1) a rapid increase in private investment, with investment by private enterprises exceeding 570 billion yuan, which accounts for 57% of the total and represents a 39% increase over the previous year; (2) a rapid increase in investment in Western regions to over 270 billion yuan, which accounts for 27% of the total and represents a 10% increase over the previous year; (3) rural tourism has become a focus for investment, with a total investment of 251.2 billion yuan, which represents a 60% increase over the previous year; (4) online investment in tourism continued to increase, with the process of "combining tourism with the Internet" expedited, generating a total investment of over 77 billion yuan, which represents a 42% increase over the previous year; (5) large corporations not specialized in tourism have accelerated their pace

[16] China Institute on Tourism, "China's Tourism Performance: review & forecast (2015–2016)." www.travel.sohu.com/201601, June 19, 2016.

of entering this sector, with BAT,[17] for example, investing a total of more than 16 billion yuan in tourism in 2015, and the projected investment by the Wanda Group on commercial and cultural tourism projects in the next few years to exceed 700 billion yuan; (6) mergers, recombinations, and expanding abroad of corporations in the tourism industry have quickened, with Beijing Tourism Group acquiring the Home Inns and Hotels Management Inc. for 15 billion yuan, with Jin Jiang International (Holdings) Co. Ltd. making a strategic investment of 10 billion yuan in PLATENO in China and acquiring Louvre Hotels Group abroad for 1.3 billion euros, thus accelerating its of transformation into a globalized corporation, and with HK CTS Hotels Co., Ltd. acquiring Brighton Hotels in Great Britain for 400 million pounds sterling. In the next three years, the National Tourism Agency predicts that direct investment in the tourism industry will exceed three trillion yuan, which will drive over 15 trillion yuan of general investment.[18]

Cruises

Statistics show that, in 2014, 466 tours of cruise ships were provided for tourists from mainland China, which represents a 15% increase over the previous year. The number of person-times for tourists taking those tours was 1.7234 million, which represents a 43% increase over the previous year, a rate 20% higher than that for the Asian-Pacific region. The number of person-times for Chinese tourists taking outbound tours was 1.48 million, which accounts for more than 40% the total for the Asian-Pacific market for cruises. China has already become the eighth-largest source of tourists taking cruise tours.[19]

Motorhomes

With the upgrading of people's consumption levels, the motorhome has come to be a common sight on the roads in China. In the *White Book of Wealth of the Mass Affluent in China* published in the Chinese edition of *Forbes*, it was estimated that China's mass affluent, defined as individuals with 0.6 to 6 million yuan of liquid financial assets, would be 14.01 million

[17] BAT stands for Baidu, Alibaba, and Tencent, three giant Internet corporations in China.

[18] Zheng Bin, "Investment in Tourism Goes over the Trillion Yuan Mark for the First Time in China in 2015," January 17, 2016. http://www.ce.cn/xwzx/gnsz/gdxw/201601/17.

[19] "China is to Become the Second Largest Market for Cruise Tours," October 21, 2015. http://news.xinhuanet.com/fortune/2015-10/21.

strong by the end of 2014. With the continued growth of high-end and middle of the affluent stratum in China, the tourism industry is optimistic about the development of motorhome tourism. It has been predicted that the scale of motorhome tourism industry will catch up with and then surpass that of Europe and the USA.

Statistics released by the Chinese Association of the Automobile Industry show that the annual sales of motorhomes in China was at about 1,000 in 2014, and that motorhome holdings will exceed 20,000 in 2015. A reasonable estimate is that the holdings will increase at a rate of about 30% in the next few years.

Statistics provided by China RV & Camping Association show that, at the end of 2013, there were about 150 campsites in China, mostly in regions where self-drive tours are concentrated, including the Yangtze River Delta, the Pearl River Delta, and the Beijing-Tianjin-Hebei region. Since camping with motorhomes usually takes up relatively large land areas, there are strict standards and requirements for the selection of such campsites and their construction. It has been reported that there are at most ten motorhome campsites in the Greater Beijing area.[20] Besides motorhome tourism, the building and improving of facilities for self-drive tours, such as motels, car camps, gas stations (with auto maintenance capabilities) has also been driving the development of the motorhome industry.

Sports Goods

According to statistics in the 2014 *White Book on the Development of Sports Goods Industry in China*, the value added of the sports goods industry in China reached 241.8 billion yuan, which represents a 15.89% increase over the previous year. This is the eighth year of continuous expansion of the industry, and the first time double-digit growth has been realized since 2011. China's total exports and imports in sports goods this year exceeded the 20-billion-yuan mark for the first time, reaching 20.085 billion. The imports totaled 1.113 billion yuan, 1.81% higher than previous year, while the exports totaled 18.972 billion, 8.29% higher than the year before, generating a trade surplus of 17.859 billion. In terms of sales of different categories of sports goods, the sales of the major listed companies for sneakers totaled 13.254 billion yuan, 11.0% higher than that of the year

[20] "Motorhome Holdings Predicted to Exceed 20,000 in China in 2015," July 23, 2013, http://www.chinanews.com/auto.

before; that of manufacturers of ball sports products totaled 17.435 billion yuan, 9.86% higher than the year before, and the sales–output ratio for the industry was 99.74%; that of manufacturers of training and fitness equipments totaled 32.434 billion yuan, 14.85% higher than the year before; that of the manufacturers of personal sports protective equipments began to grow again, reaching a total of 12.973 billion yuan, 47.07 % higher than the year before; while the growth of the market for outdoor gear slowed down a little.[21]

These figures are corroborated by the continuous increases in the numbers of people participating in various marathons and other long-distance races in recent years. According to figures released at the Chinese Marathon Annual Convention held in Guangzhou in January 2016, as many as 134 marathon races were registered with the Chinese Athletics Association in 2015, which represents a ten-fold increase over the 13 registered in 2010.[22] From January to June 2015, 302 races were organized in China, including 187 road-running races, 109 cross-country races, four ironman triathlons, and two other races. These races helped to drive the consumption of sports equipments and smart wearable devices, such as track shoes, hiking shirts and pants, backpacks, kettles, socks, heart rate monitors, activity trackers, and sports watches, not counting added value generated through registration fees, fees paid by corporations to be allowed to associate the names of these events with their products and to market their products at these events, the use of new media, and so on. The hiring of private coaches, restaurants, transport, accommodation, travel, and shopping in association with these events also add indirectly to the value they generated.[23]

What Has Changed in Consumer Psychology?

The economic development of China shows a temporal and spatial incongruence in relation to that of developed countries in the West, namely, when those countries experienced rapid development, China was closed to the outside world and rather backward, and when the speed of development

[21] Feng Jiajia, "The 2014 White Book on the Development of Sports Goods Industry in China is released," *China Daily* (Chinese Edition), May 8, 2015.

[22] Du Zaocai, "In 2015 Domestic Marathon Held 134 Games and 1.5 Million People Involved," http://www.athletics.org.cn/ January 11, 2016.

[23] Li Haojiao, "In 2015 The Complete Industrial Chain by Marathon Ran out of Tencent Sports," November 24, 2015, http://sports.qq.com/.

slowed down in those countries, China entered her phase of rapid growth. With the economy rapidly growing, conspicuous consumption has been strongly demonstrated among the Chinese, almost as a thing of regularity, particularly in the rather common scenes of shopping sprees on the part of many Chinese consumers, both in China and abroad.

Undoubtedly, the consumer psychology of a large proportion of Chinese includes inclinations to flaunt wealth, to show off, to make invidious comparisons, to follow the crowd, and to nurture vanity. The flaunting of wealth is a rather widespread phenomenon among the rich in China. A celebrity in entertainment circles, for example, is said to have spent a tremendous amount on his wedding, with 5 million yuan spent for hired services and for site use. Adding this to other costs, most of which were covered by sponsors who were eager to have him for celebrity branding, the total would be about 200 million yuan. Such stunning extravagance is likely to have rather bad social effects.

Tourism is part of one's lifestyle, but the sound way of approaching it is to make arrangements for in accordance with the amount of free time and money available. However, many Chinese now seem to think it is necessary for them to do some traveling in order not to lose face before others. As a result, if their means do not allow for a good trip, they would choose to be part of low-price or even "zero group fee" tours, which are hardly enjoyable experiences, of which they are likely later to complain that "if you decide not to go, you would regret for a while, but if you decide to go with it, you would regret for your whole life."

It is also notable that Chinese tourists like very much to take pictures on their travels, and one important reason is that they want to have these pictures to show relatives and friends after they return, so as to satisfy their vanity. A popular joke about the experience of many Chinese tourists traveling abroad has it that these tourists often "doze off or sleep on the bus, and are busy taking pictures and going to the restroom after getting off the bus, but when asked what they have seen upon their return, they cannot really tell you anything." For many, travelling has more to do with vanity rather than rich and enjoyable experiences.

Of course, the situation has been changing in this area. Those who have consumption as a motive for self-improvement and upgrading in taste while balancing work and leisure are concentrated mainly among the rich, the middle class, and the petty bourgeoisie. These groups have paid more and more attention to the location dimension of consumption, for different experiences and feelings can result in different environments for the consumptive act. For example, when a customer dines in an fine restaurant, not only the food, but also the elegant environment and the service provided become objects of consumption. People consume not only material goods, but also added value such as the friendliness, respect, and etiquette that exist in non-material forms.

Individualized and experiential consumption are also on the rise. Although numbers of department stores and shopping centers have mushroomed, the brands and goods in these stores, with their great similarity, no longer arouse much interest. Thus, experience with commodities that fail to offer any novelty or to appeal to individualized interest, together with the shopping malls that seem to have duplicated one another, can no longer satisfy the psychological needs of consumers. Thus, how to transform existing business models into ones designed for individualized and experiential consumption is doubtless a new challenge the commercial world has to face.

M-Shaped Consumption

In 2012, Larry H. P. Lang suggested that China had become an M-shaped society in terms of consumption pattern.[24] According to Lang, the M-shaped consumption pattern had taken shape in the Chinese market of consumer goods. M-shaped consumption means the market shares of high- and low-grade goods are large, while that of middle-grade have shrunk. Lang provided the following statistics: "14% of the population buy only high-grade products, which makes high-grade products very hot; while 85% of the population, who belong to the poor and cannot afford to buy middle-grade products, tend to buy only low-grade products, thus bringing the deterioration of the market for middle-grade products." Using the market for automobiles as an example, he explains, "In the first quarter of 2012, the sales of middle-grade cars made in China dropped by 3.8%, while the sales were increased by 37% for BMW, 20% for Benz, and 41% for Audi. It can be seen that the market for high-grade cars was very hot, while that for middle-grade cars began to deteriorate." In the area of apparel, sales for high-grade garments increased by 31% in 2011, with those for women's clothes priced 2,000 yuan apiece increasing by 65%. On the other hand, Youngor, which

[24] The concept of the M-shaped society was first proposed by the Japanese organizational theorist and management consultant Kenichi Ohmae in his *The Impact of the Lower-Middle Class*, Koudansha, 2006.

specializes in middle-grade men's clothes, laid off 17,000 of its employers, and GAP shops were apparently having a bad time—clothes priced at 599 yuan were reduced to 199 yuan, but still attracted few customers. At the same time, the market for low-grade clothes was also very hot.

In view of the above, Lang believes that an M-shaped consumption pattern will take the lead in China's market for consumer goods, and the fact that the market for high-grade goods is so hot means China's economy has taken a turn for the worse. "If our entrepreneurs all focus on consumption rather than invest for the future, what will the future of the nation be like, with such a large surplus of her productive capacity?"[25] Lang's careful observation reveals two "peaks" of consumption, which is very important. But what is more important, we believe, is that he has asked a very profound question—what effects will the trends in the entrepreneurs' consumption have on China's economy in the future?

Multitudes of Chinese Billionaires and an Outflow of Capital?

According to the *2016 Hurun Global Rich List* announced by the Hurun Institute, as of January 15, 2016, Beijing, had overtaken New York to become the city with the largest number of super wealth creators with people having wealth of one billion USD or more. Five of the top ten cities in the world with the largest number of billionaires, namely, Beijing, Hong Kong, Shanghai, Shenzhen, and Hangzhou, are in China. Manufacturing was the major source of wealth for the billionaires on mainland China, and was followed by real estate development and the IT industry.[26]

China is going through the fastest stratification in wealth in human history. One third of the nation's wealth has been concentrated in the hands of 1% of the nation's population. And in the past decade, China's super-rich "have swept into cities like New York, London, and Los Angeles, snapping up real estate and providing anxieties about inequality and globalized wealth."[27]

[25] Lang Xianping (Larry H. P. Lang) says the M-shaped consumption has become the pattern for the market of consumer goods in China. Stated at the Chinese Bank (China) Spring Forum, at April 20, 2012. http://finance.eastmoney.com/news.

[26] 2016 Hurun Global Rich List: The "over one billion dollars" to hundreds of people in Beijing, February 24, 2016, *Reference News*, http://www.cankaoxiaoxi.com/.

[27] Fan, Jiayang. "The Golden Generation: Why China's super-rich send their children abroad." *The New Yorker*, February 22, 2016.

It is said that China's super-rich are very liberal in spending abroad the money they have made in China. By making investments and purchasing real estate abroad, sending their children abroad for their education, or becoming investment immigrants, the super-rich are moving vast amounts of funds out of China. The "Report on Private Wealth in China 2015" shows that, overall, the HNWIs (high-net-worth individuals) interviewed have differing views on business investment in the next 1–2 years, with about 19% considering increasing investment, about 57% wanting to maintain current levels of investment, and 24% considering decreasing investment. With regard to different areas of business, interest is concentrated in innovative industries and consumer services, with only less than 10% of the HNWIs interviewed considering increasing investment in traditional manufacturing. This is well in accordance with the direction set by the Chinese government to encourage investment in innovative industries. With interest in investment abroad continuing to rise, data show, says the report, that the percentage of HNWIs who have holdings abroad has increased to 37% from the 33% of 2013. With regard to investment abroad, 50% of the HNWIs who already have holdings abroad plan to increase such investment in the future, with about 40% believing they would maintain approximately the same level of holdings abroad.[28]

On the other hand, the super-rich in China appear to be quite parsimonious when it comes to philanthropy. According to a report released by The Roy and Lila Ash Center for Democratic Governance and Innovation of the John F. Kennedy School of Government, Harvard University, both Wang Jianlin, the wealthiest man in China, and Ma Yun, a well-known billionaire, donated less than 0.3% of their personal worth in 2015. The most generous billionaire was Wang Miaotong, a merchant from Zhejiang Province who donated 5.6% of his personal worth, a figure which is not very high either by Western standards.[29]

Data, it is true, provide a kind of basis for using to understand the state of social development. However, simple data can often befuddle and mislead as well. The logical relationship between data and social reality is often unclear. Statistical work in China faces two difficulties—the rapidly

[28] China Merchants Bank and Bain & Company, "2015 China Private Wealth Report," http://news.xinhuanet.com/.

[29] Zuo Maohong, "Chinese Push Charity Law for Offering Mutual Support and Assistance," *Reference News*, March 10, 2016, p. 16.

changing reality that is not so amenable to set statistical procedures and the fact that approaches to data collecting and statistical models used in China often do not conform to international standards. Thus, it is not easy to present a clear and accurate picture of the changing socioeconomic conditions through statistics alone. The proper approach is to remain sober, rational, and objective when faced with contradicting data.

System Design

System design is not just an important field for scholarly research, but also a core issue for the promotion of social reforms. In this respect, China's prosperity today has been much facilitated by system designs on the part of the government that keeps on adapting to changing conditions.

In the area of promoting consumption, important changes in the modern system design in China started with the tourism industry after the Cultural Revolution ended. The reforms of system design to promote consumption in the 13th Five-Year Plan [for the years 2016–2020] for National Economic and Social Development are a recent case of such changes. In the next section, we try to explore through the Chinese experience the purpose of system design and the correlation between system design and the prosperity of society.

Emancipation of People's Minds and the Policy of Reform and Opening-Up

Since 1978, Deng Xiaoping had been thinking about how to develop consumer culture in China as well as how to emancipate people's minds and undertake reform and opening-up to the outside word. Deng's contributions to China include his reforms of the nation's system design, which have brought many benefits to the country. This is one of the reasons why Westerners are interested in studying why China has achieved so much in so short a period of time.

Consumerist Enthusiasm Released by Policy on Tourism

Materials we have collected show that, from October 1978 to July 1979, Deng proposed several times at the meetings of the Politburo of the CCP that there was much that could be done to develop tourism, which should be an emphasis of the government's economic policy and should be carried out quickly. Developing tourism is an important component of his economic thinking.

Adapting to New Demands

At the end of 1979, Han Kehua, the Chinese ambassador to France at the time, was recalled to Beijing on short notice in order to become the first director of China's National Tourism Administration (NTA). At that time, there were only a few hotels in Beijing, such as Beijing Hotel, that were allowed to receive foreign guests. Statistics show that there were only around 150 hotels nationwide, with a total number of beds of about 34,000, that were allowed to receive foreigners.[30] So at that time it was always a headache to take in foreign guests, as it often took a great deal of trouble just to figure out where a clean hotel could be found that would serve genuine Western food and have hygienic toilets.

Mr. Han once told me the following story: After he became the Director of NTA, the first scenic site he investigated was Mount Huang. While on his way up the mountain, he saw a few foreigners shaking their heads after using a restroom, saying in French, "Restrooms here are so horrible!" Hearing such remarks, he felt a great loss of face and thought he was shouldering a very heavy responsibility, for such matters reflected on the honor of the nation. From then on, an important item on his agenda as the NTA director was to build good restrooms at tourist sites.

In order to reduce the incidence of such embarrassment, the government set aside some funds from the very limited budget at the time to support Han's effort to solve the restroom problems at scenic sites in order to promote the development of tourism.

Although the efforts by the Chinese government to develop tourism started in 1978, it was in 1984 that the tourist industry began to gain significant momentum. This development was to a large extent due to four important factors. First, it was in this year that the "Decisions of the Central Committee of the CCP on the Reform of Economic Institutions" were announced, in which it was stressed that the government was to implement further measures according to the principle of stimulating the economy domestically and opening up to the outside world. Second, starting from 1984, the government successively unveiled a series of

[30] Wang Dawu, *China's Tourist Hotel Development White Paper 1979–2000*, China Tourism Publishing House, 2000.

policies, such as arrangements for the people to visit relatives in Hong Kong, Taiwan, and Macao, and those in other countries, which helped greatly to stimulate people's enthusiasm for tourism. Third, material conditions for life gradually improved, as marked by the appearance of the first group of rich people with family incomes of 10,000 yuan RMB or more. Those who had made their fortunes had a strong desire for consumption in cultural and spiritual areas once their material life had great improved. Fourth, large numbers of people began to go abroad for business or to visit relatives, as visiting scholars or students studying in other countries, thus coming into contact with cultures in the world that were rather different from that of China.

At that time, tourism could not yet be counted among the pillar industries of China, but it had advantages not easily matched by other industries in that it could help to propel the development of many other industries and had a great capacity for satisfying people's spiritual needs beyond the basic material comforts of life. Considering those advantages, policy-makers saw that the prospects for tourism were good. For this reason, the central government then promulgated a series of major policies regarding the development of tourism.

A Succession of New Stipulations on Tourism

In 1984, the State Council set out a new policy that made it possible for citizens of the People's Republic of China to travel to Hong Kong and Macau in order to visit relatives.

In 1986, the government initiated a project to conduct research on the feasibility of the five-day workweek. In March, 1994, a system with a five-day workweek every other week was tested.

On May 1, the five-day workweek was officially implemented. Employees were supposed to work for eight hours a day, five days a week.

1997 was the year when travelling abroad at one's own expense really started. The "Provisional Regulations on Self-Supported Travel abroad by Chinese Citizen" was announced in March and put to practice in July of that year.

As mentioned in the last chapter, the new version of "Stipulations on Leave for National Festivals and Holidays" promulgated in 1999 created three seven-day vacations, which gave rise to the "golden weeks" for tourism.

In June 2000, the Office for National Inter-Ministerial Coordination Conference on Holiday Tourism (or National Holiday Office for short) was created and on it was placed the responsibility for adjusting and setting holiday breaks.

In September 2004, the EU became open to Chinese tourists. Towards the end of the year, China signed a memorandum of understanding on tourism with the USA, making a breakthrough in North America with regard to tourist destinations available to Chinese citizens.

In December 2007, the State Council promulgated "Regulations Regarding Paid Leaves during the Year for Employees," stipulating that these regulations were to go into effect on January 1, 2008. The May Day "golden week" was shortened to a three-day "minor long leave," while three more three-day "minor long leaves" were created for Tomb-Sweeping Day (清明), the Dragon Boat Festival (端午), and the Mid-Autumn Festival (仲秋), respectively. Also in that year, group tours for Chinese citizens to the USA were officially launched, and arrangements for tours by residents of mainland China to Taiwan were also officially implemented.

In 2009, the State Council publicized its "Comments on Accelerating the Development of the Tourism Industry," stating that the tourism industry could bring both economic and social benefits, with its low energy consumption, a large coefficient for driving other industries, and its capacity for generating large number of jobs; and that China, with its large territory, had abundant resources for tourism, and that the diversifying consumption needs of the Chinese people had also provided new opportunities for the development of tourism.

In 2012, the American president Barack Obama signed an executive order demanding the simplification and acceleration of the application procedures for non-immigrant visas for citizens from various countries, including China. Chinese citizens entering the USA could now be granted visas for up to ten years by this order.

On February 2, 2013, the State Council issued the "Policy Outline for Tourism and Leisure of Chinese Nationals (2013–2020)," which specifies that institutional arrangements for annual paid leave for employees are to be implemented by 2020.

On October 1, 2013, "The Guide to Civilized Behavior for Chinese Citizens while Travelling Abroad," which was aimed to "upgrade the level of civilized behavior of Chinese citizens and build a good image of them in the world," was officially issued. "The Convention for Civilized Behavior for Chinese Citizens while Travelling in China," issued at the same time, urged people to "help create a civilized and harmonious environment for tourism and be civilized tourists."

By 2015, of the 172 countries which have diplomatic relationships with China, 117, or 68% of the total, provide ADS (Approved Destination Status) visa services for Chinese citizens to enter and leave their countries freely, which has made it possible for the wish of the Chinese to "travel throughout the world" to come true. Chinese citizens can now visit these countries easily. The USA once seemed to be a distant land for many, but now one can obtain a US visa valid for ten years. Britain, Japan, and the EU have followed the example of the USA.

Tourism: A Transformer of Traditional Approaches to Leisure

According to statistics issued by the World Tourism Organization, for every dollar of income for the tourism industry, 4.3 dollars of income is be generated for related industries; and for every job created directly in the tourism industry, 5–7 jobs are created indirectly elsewhere in society. At present, 11 million people are employed directly in the tourism industry in China, while 76 million are employed in tourism-related industries.[31]

Tourism is particularly valuable in two ways. First, it can serve as an engine for Chinese and even world economy. Secondly, it has become one of the most popular leisure activities for many Chinese. In his speech at the Boao Forum in 2013, the number of Chinese participating in outbound tourism in the ensuing five years was estimated to be 400 million person-times. China has been transforming the configuration of the world tourism market.

In April, 2015, a young teacher at the Laboratory Middle School of Henan Province decided to quit her job. The letter of resignation she sent to the headmaster of the school simply said, "The world is so large, and I want to see it." The letter has been widely circulated on the Internet, for it resonates with what many Chinese have felt in their hearts.

For many, "a trip following my heart" is no longer just a phrase used in advertisements, but a dream come true. The new trends in tourism are likely to become clear in the next few years. For example, the source of overseas tourists is likely to expand from first-tier cities to include second- and third-tier ones, while tourists from first-tier cities will turn to high-end and

[31] Speech by Shao Qiwei, Director of the National Tourism Administration, at the 2009 National Tourism Work Conference. www.gov.cn/gzdt/2009.

in-depth tours. Demand for small package tours and individualized tours are to be promoted and highlighted. Package tours for small groups of relatives and friends are going to be the new trend. Travel for business and travel for fun will become more clearly demarcated, and the demand for open-ended free tours will keep on increasing. Group tours to nearby regions for the purpose of shopping will increase in number, and tourists embarking on overseas shopping tours will aim at not only top-grade luxury items, but also at middle-grade cosmetics and even articles for everyday use.

Data released by the National Tourism Administration show that, in 2015, overseas tourists from China reached 120 million person-times, and that China ranked first both in terms of person-times of overseas tourists and in total consumption by these tourists. Of these, the number of people taking open-ended free tours was 80 million person-times, with an average consumption of 11,624 yuan RMB per person-time, which represents a 24.1% increase over the previous year. The number of people expected to take overseas tours in the Chinese New Year season was projected to reach six million person-times, and "buying all" has gradually become the hallmark of the overseas tourists from China, with a projected per capita consumption on overseas tours of 10,000 yuan RMB.[32]

According to data released by the World Travel and Tourism Council (WTTC) in 2015, the consumption by Chinese tourists in places outside mainland China was 215 billion USD, with represents a 53% increase over the 140 billion for 2014. The WTTC also projected that this figure is to increase by 7% a year on average in the decade to follow.[33]

System Design and Consumption Structure

The speed and scale of the transformation of Chinese economy is no doubt unprecedented. However, China's economic growth has gradually slowed down since 2010 to a growth rate of approximately 7%. With this background, voices calling to dampen expectations of Chinese economy are competing with those that encourage it, both in China and abroad. The decision-makers in the national government are no doubt faced with

[32] Ctrip Report: "2016 Spring Festival Golden Week Outbound Travel Trends," www.travel.sohu.com, January 15, 2016.

[33] "Chinese Overseas Consumer Spending Surged by 53% a Year," British *Financial Times* website, March 21, 2016, quoted in *Reference News*, March 23, 2016.

tremendous pressure, which puts requirements on them to change their ways of thinking in system design, which has become the central issue for ensuring stability and continuous economic development for China.

Messages Transmitted Through Top-Level System Design

In 2013, Xi Jinping, with full confidence, spoke thus in his keynote speech at the opening ceremony of the Boao Forum:

> We should abandon the outdated mindset, break away from the old confines that fetter development and unleash all the potential for development. We should redouble efforts to shift the growth model and adjust the economic structure, raise the quality of development and make life better for the people.[34]

This is the voice of a top-level of a system designer in China.

At the National People's Congress in early spring of 2013, the "rate of growth of China's economy" was the focal issue for the media in China and abroad. At the news conference for the Congress, Li Keqiang, the current premier, said the following:

> China is so large, and there are many problems that remain to be solved. But in terms of the major problems, my view is that the first one is still how to continue to develop the economy. In the foreseeable future, the economic environment of China's economy will continue to be severe and complicated. It may be sunny now, but we have to prepare for rainy days. On the other hand, we should also remain calm when faced with sudden challenges to ensure the economy will continue to grow. Measures should be taken to prevent inflation and to control potential risks, so that there will not be great fluctuations for the Chinese economy.[35]

The rapid growth of China's economy has indeed covered up many problems and contradictions and consumed much of the endogenous power of the economy. There are worries both in China and abroad whether China can avoid falling into the "middle income trap." The debate

[34] Xi Jinping, "Working Together Toward a Better Future for Asia and the World" (keynote speech at the opening ceremony of the Boao Forum), April 7, 2013, http://news.xinhuanet.com/china/2013-04/07/c_132290684.htm. Accessed 26 June, 2016.

[35] Li Keqiang, "Talking the talk is not as good as walking the walk," http://www.chinanews.com/gn/2013/03-17.

concerning this issue has continued to this day. The Chinese government has initiated a new cycle of system design, with a shift from investment-driven development to consumption-driven development.

On October 29, 2014, the State Council made arrangements at its executive meeting to promote the expansion and upgrade of consumption, stipulating the triple principles of making the people "able," "fearless," and "willing" to consume in order to create an upgraded consumption pattern. IT, green food, housing, tourism, education and recreation, and health care and housekeeping services for the elderly were stressed as the areas of consumption in which special efforts were to be focused. These six areas have tremendous room and potential and are to play an especially important role in expanding and upgrading people's consumption.[36] Of the traditional troika for pulling the country's economy, export is at an ebb, while investment is experiencing a slump; thus, only consumption remains to serve as the new engine for the economic development of China.

Quick Adjustment in Policy

The shift from a one-sided emphasis on the speed of economic development, as in the catchphrases "unrestrained growth" and "growth at any cost," to a mindset with emphasis on "structural adjustment, transformation of mode of development, and promotion of the upgrading of the economy" has become the most important item on the agenda of the top-level decision-makers of the central government. In real terms, these mean that the transformation of China's industrial structure is to be accelerated.

In two short years since May 2013, the central government issued at least 22 directives regarding the encouragement of entrepreneurship in starting new businesses and for innovation. In March of 2013, the State Council issued "Directives from the General Office of the State Council regarding Policies and Measures to Promote Innovative and Entrepreneurial Undertakings by the Common People." In June of the same year, "Guidelines from the State Council Regarding a Number of Policy Measures to Promote Powerfully Entrepreneurial and Innovative Undertakings by Large Numbers of People" was officially announced. The guiding principles specified in these documents are now being converted to concrete policy measures to promote innovation and entrepreneurship.

[36] Li Keqiang, "Let the Masses Be Able to Consume, Dare to Consume, and Be Willing to Consume," www.news.xinhuanet.com/, October 20, 2014.

In September and October 2013, President Xi Jinping proposed the strategic conceptions of "the New Silk Road Belt of Economic Development" and "the Maritime Silk Road for the 21st Century," respectively. This is intended as an initiative to develop economic partnerships with countries along the historic Silk Road. At the same time, this strategy can also help to promote mass consumption on the part of the Chinese in the form of tourism to regions in China that are on the Silk Road, so as to expand the market space for tourism.[37]

Then, in March 2015, Li Keqiang announced in the annual "Report on the Work of the National Government":

> An "Internet +" action plan will be formulated to drive the integration of the mobile Internet, cloud calculation, big data, and the Internet of things into modern manufacturing, to promote the healthy development of e-commerce, industrial Internet, and online financing, and to encourage IT corporations to open up international markets.

Government measures like this have not only helped to uplift the economic situation that had been heading in the direction of decline, but also encouraged people to help promote economic growth through new forms of consumption.[38]

Because e-commerce has provided a series of attractive options, with items ranging from cosmetics and garments to automobiles and real estate going onto the Web, the consumption power of Chinese consumers has not been greatly affected by the slowing down of economic growth.

How Great Is the Consumption Potential of the Chinese?

There has been widespread worry that the anti-corruption campaign of the CCP was going to impact negatively on the purchasing power of the Chinese. However, according to a survey on 10,150 consumers of luxury items, jointly conducted by the Swiss professional service company KPMG and by Meilihui, a website of a Chinese retailer in luxury items, the average

[37] Xi Jinping's speech at Nazarbayev University, "To carry forward the friendship, To create a better future," www.news.xinhuanet.com/, September 8, 2013.

[38] Wang Mengmeng, "Li Keqiang Promotes Entrepreneurship and Innovation by the Masses, and the State Council Issue 22 Relevent Documents to Implement the Program," *Xinhua News*, August 6, 2015. http://news.xinhuanet.com/politics/2015-08/06/c_1116163454.htm. Accessed Februrary 5, 2017.

expenditure on luxury items for a single purchase by mainland consumers was 2,300 yuan RMB, which represents a 28% increase over the 1,800 yuan RMB from the survey of the previous year. Forty-five percent of the interviewees reported that they purchase most of their luxury items on the Internet. Although only 1% of the interviewees reported they had purchased real estate (both in China and abroad) on the Internet, 50% said they were not against the idea of doing so in the future.[39]

A similar survey conducted on interviewees in 90 Chinese cities by Bain Capital, a strategic consultation company based in Boston, found that the average expenditure on luxury items in most categories by Chinese consumers saw increases in 2015. For example, the average expenditure on bags increased by 109%. The increase was 58% for women's garments, 18% for cosmetics, 126% for wristwatches, and 65% for jewelry. At the same time, Chinese consumers have begun to seek experiences other than just the thrill of shopping. They no longer just own luxury items, but have begun to experience luxury, including dining in high-grade restaurants, tasting expensive wine, privately owned airplanes, hunting tours, luxurious travelling, hydrotherapy, auction of artworks, and increasingly diverse investment services. Aside from luxury items, more and more consumers have been purchasing luxury services online. The most popular form of this is making reservation for hotel and restaurant online, followed by tours in China and abroad booked online.[40]

The rapid rise in online industries has not only greatly facilitated people's lives, but has also provided rare opportunities for raising consumption levels. Data show that the total retail sales in China have maintained a 40% growth rate, and have led to a rapid increase in the consumption of carrier services and information. According to big data statistics released by the State Statistics Bureau of China, 49.3% of users of online purchasing have increased their purchasing after they started going online, and 48.4% of users responded that they would increase the proportion of online purchases in their total expenditures in the future.[41]

[39] "Luxury Online Shopping have been Strong on Average about 2300 yuan each in Mainland," quoted in the finance column of *Reference News*, http://www.cankaoxiaoxi.com/finance. October 7, 2015.

[40] *Ibid.*

[41] National Bureau of Statistics: "2015 Chinese Online Shopping User Survey," www.askci.com/news/cha. September 30, 2015.

What Does All this Mean to GDP Growth?

The upgraded consumption structure has led to an orderly release of people's consumption potential, and consumption has become the main force promoting economic growth. Data show that, from 2011 to 2014, consumption contributed on average 54.8% to economic growth in China, which is 7.8% higher than that contributed by investment. And in the first half of 2015, the contribution of consumption to China's economic growth had increased to 60%.[42]

The service sector has also become a major contributor to government revenues. In 2014, the service sector contributed 53.5% of taxes, with the taxes from the Internet and related services increasing by 24% and those from software and IT service sector increasing 23.7%. With its rapid development, the service sector has also become the major provider of job opportunities. It has been calculated that a 1% growth in GDP would create a million new jobs during the 11th Five-Year Plan Period (2006–2010). But with the increase in the weight of the service sector, a 1% increase in GDP can now provide 1.7 million new jobs.[43]

For the popular Mi-One smartphones, for example, sales amounted to 12.6 billion yuan for 2012 and 31.6 billion for 2013. The sales had the potential to reach 80 billion for 2014 and to exceed 100 billion for 2015.[44] China is really a huge market, and, being clear on this point, the government has kept on developing policies to promote consumption, including the lowering of interest rates for bank loans and the lowering of taxes. At a time when the growth of the economy slowed down, only by encouraging people to use the money in their pockets for consumption can the economy continue to operate in an orderly fashion.

On Bachelors' Day in 2015, the surge of online purchasing in China shocked the world.[45] By 24:00, the total volume of online transactions reached 91.217 billion yuan RMB, which was used to order a total of 760 million parcels to be sent to consumers throughout the world. That

[42] "Achievements of economic and social development in 12th Five-Year," the website of the National Bureau of statistics, www.news.xinhuanet.com, October 13, 2015.

[43] "In 12th Five-Year Plan, Third Industry Accounted for the Proportion of GDP over the First and the Two Industry," *People's Daily*, http://www.chinanews.com. October 14, 2015.

[44] Lei Jun: "Mi-One to sell 100 million cellphones, with total sales probably to exceed 100 billion yuan" www.askci.com/news March 31, 2014.

[45] This holiday was invented on November 11, 2011. The Arabic numeral "1" looks like a "smooth stick," a word that can be used to mean the unmarried "bachelor" in Chinese. The date "the 11th day of the 11th month" was selected because there are four "smooth sticks" in it.

day, 188 million payments were made using PayPal, breaking the record of 158 million set the previous year. The number of payments peaked at 790,000 per minute. PayPal payments made through mobile phones reached 45.18 million, which account for 24.03% of the total number of transactions. The total amount of PayPal payments made through mobile phones exceeded 11.3 billion yuan, setting a world record for mobile phone payments on a single day.[46]

Growing at a fast pace, e-commerce in China still has great potential to be tapped. The upgrading of software automating enterprises and sectors has been proceeding quickly, providing a solid basis for the acceleration of the development of e-commerce.

Public Service

With socioeconomic development and the improvements in the quality of people's lives in recent years, how to provide better public service has become an increasingly urgent issue for governments at all levels in China.

Public Service: A New Challenge for Governments at All Levels

In the past, governments at all levels in China hardly had any idea about public services. For government officials, the function of the government was basically to rule—to set limits, to control, to look suspiciously into people's lives, and to create hindrances. Even the concept of "management" was introduced from other countries only after China had began to reform and to open to the outside world. Common people called government agencies *yamen* (衙門), a term that had been used for the administrative office and residence of local bureaucrats in traditional China. In their experience, very often "it is difficult to gain admission to government offices, the officer show a stiff face with his nose up, and it is especially difficult to get things done." Officials were called "lords."

In 2014, Cao Zhiwei, a member of the CPPCC (Chinese People's Political Consultative Conference), a political body for non-communists to give suggestions to the communist government, took a 3.8-meter-long scroll to the meeting of the CPPCC in Guangzhou. On this scroll, entitled

[46] Tao Duanfang, "China's online shopping boom shocked Europe and the United States," *Global Times*, November 12, 2015, p. 1.

"On the Long March to Obtain Certificates," was diagramed the extraordinarily long and complicated procedures one had to go through to get a typical construction project approved and, upon the completion of the project, to go through the acceptance checks by government agencies. One had to obtain various certificates and documents from 39 departments, centers, teams, and branch offices of 18 different government agencies. More than 100 seals were stamped on the certificates and documents in this process, and numerous fees had to be paid along the way. Later, it was reported that in order to get a certain qualification for an enterprise, it was necessary to obtain certificates and documents requiring more than 200 seal stamps. These reflect the state of public service in China. Since he came into office, Premier Li Keqiang has been trying to simplify government administrative procedures and decentralize government authorities so as to change this situation.

In dealing with government officials, common people had for the most part been resigned and docile, grinning and bearing the arbitrary rule of the government. It is not difficult to understand, then, why so many people want to work in government agencies. Mao had popularized the motto "work for the people," which he intended to be the historical mission for the CCP. On December 21, 2010, however, a silk banner on which was written "Work for RMB" (RMB is the abbreviation for *renmin bi*, or the people's currency) was sent to the Planning Bureau of the City of Zhengzhou, the capital of Henan Province, because an official from the bureau had put it very straightforwardly in a private conversation, "I work for money. If you give me money, I will issue you the certificate. Those who refuse to give me money will not have their projects approved. Once I get the money I ask for, I would approve the project after very casual examination."[47] From such cases we can understand why there are so many government officials, low- or high-ranked, who are corrupt, and get a glimpse of the state of public services in China. For many years now, it has often been the case that dozens or even hundreds of people would compete for one post in government agencies by taking public services examinations.

One may ask, "Didn't the government take care of the food supply, housing, transport, travelling, shopping, and recreation of all the people in the socialist system in the past?" But actually, this was also a means of

[47] "The citizens sent a banner with the words 'Work for RMB' to the Planning Bureau of the City of Zhengzhou," www.news.xinhuanet.com, December 23, 2010.

controlling the people rather than real public services of a civilized society. Theoretically speaking, public services are services provided by authorities using money paid by tax-payers. It is supposed to be that the basic duties of governments of all levels and their performance should be guided by a sound administrative ethic. It is only natural that public services are required to be fair, just, and transparent. Government should be able to gain the trust of the public, and establish its legitimacy through public voting.

In recent years, with the strengthening of the democratic consciousness among the Chinese, people have become less submissive to the "lords" in the government, and incidences of government–citizen conflict have been seen from time to time. There have been a fair number of cases where common people have sued government officials or agencies, and in some of these cases government officials or agencies actually lost in the end. Such conflict has generated a momentum for reform in government functions.

Public Service: An Old Issue and New Developments

Against the background of people's lifestyles becoming increasingly diversified, stratified, and normalized, the government has also been formulating an increasing number of policies on areas related to leisure service, with more humane and humanistic means being adopted to provide services to people in their lives and in their work. For example, for the last two decades, the eight-hour workday has been made a law, and the five-day week has been implemented nationwide. The government has also kept on adjusting the system of leave for national holidays so as to guide the leisure and holiday activities of the people, and has promised to fully implement a system of paid leave by 2020. Governments at different levels have also worked to improve the living conditions and living environment of the people, to encourage the development of facilities for neighborhood cultural life. Investment in urban facilities for public use has been increased, with roads, public transport, afforestation, and park facilities all expanded and improved. As a result, public service has been much improved overall.

Since the material life of the people has been significantly improved, the development of public services to meeting people's needs for cultural and spiritual life has become an increasingly urgent issue. Data released by the National Statistics Bureau show that, by the end of 2014, there were 3,117 public libraries (with an increase of 233 over the end of 2010) and 3,660 museums (with an increase of 1,225); the comprehensive broadcast coverage rate had reached 98.0% of the population (with an increase of 1.2%), and the comprehensive TV coverage rate had reached 98.6% (with an increase of 1.0%). A succession of cultural industries have sprung up.[48]

But we should also note the tremendous deficits that still exist in this area. For example, for a population of 1.3 billion, 3,117 libraries mean one library for every 450,000 people. Furthermore, most of these libraries are located in cities. In comparison, there is on average one public library for every 13,000 people in the USA, about every 10,000 in the UK and Canada, 6,600 in Germany, 4,000 in Austria, and 3,000 in Switzerland. Developed countries, then, are far ahead of China in public services in this area, and China's performance here is not at all compatible with its status as a leading economy in the world. Furthermore, the percentage of public space for sportsgrounds is also very small in China. Many people blame China's football teams for their poor performance and their inability to compete with internationally strong teams, but that may be too harsh, for there are not that many football fields in the 666 large cities in China.

In North America and Europe, special needs of children have been taken into consideration in the planning for public services, with suitable allocation of resources to facilities for children's play in both urban and rural communities. But in China, facilities for children's play are too limited. This author, who lives in Beijing, has done some investigation into such facilities in a number of parks and found that places specifically for children are missing in these parks, not to say adequate facilities to ensure children's safety in their play. It is true that there are a number of commercial amusement parks that attract many children, but the entrance fees to these parks are all very high. This has not only increased the cost ordinary people would have to pay for the upbringing of their children, but it also means people cannot feel the warmth free public services can generate.

China is a country where much emphasis has traditionally been put on filial piety. Now that it has become an aged society, how to care for the elderly is also a challenge posed to the government's capacity in providing public services. Although the government has taken various measures in this area, the real effect of these measures still leaves much to be desired. For example, colleges and universities for the elderly are still a rarity in both rural and urban areas. The generation which has become elderly differs from their parents in that they have a strong desire for cultural pursuits and

[48] State Statistical Bureau of the People's Republic of China: "Review the Achievements of Economic and Social Development in 12th Five-Year," news.xinhuanet.com, October 13, 2015.

opportunities to perfect themselves through self-cultivation. Better educated than their parents, they are more conscious of the leisure ideals of traditional China. This is perhaps an important reason why among classes offered by colleges for the elderly those for calligraphy and painting are the most popular, and why the elderly who have had systematic training in calligraphy seem to be the group who are best able to live a leisurely life and have peace of mind. However, the number of colleges for the elderly is simply too small to meet the demand of the elderly in these areas.

As of 2011, there were only about 40,000 institutions in China, including elderly houses, charity houses, and nursing homes that provide care for the elderly. The total number of beds in these institutions was about 3,150,000, or only 1.77% the population size of the elderly, a percentage that is obviously too low. In recent years, the government has made policy adjustments to encourage private and foreign investment in the building of facilities to serve the elderly in China. Some good facilities have been built, but the cost one has to pay to access such facilities is far beyond the means of ordinary people, while normal facilities fail to meet the needs of the elderly for medical care and continuing education. In 2014, when the National People's Congress and the People's Political Consultative Conference were in session, Proposal No. 1004, submitted by the All-China Federation of Industry and Commerce mentioned the fact that the percentage of people aged 60 or more in the Chinese population had reached 13.26% (or about 178 million), exceeding the baseline of 13% an the aged society. It has been predicted that, by 2050, the percentage of the elderly in the Chinese population will reach one third. With so large a population of elderly people, the government should pay great attention to the issue of how to provide adequate care for them.[49]

An increasingly widespread phenomenon on the social scene in China is the disturbance caused by Chinese old ladies dancing in the streets. Due to the lack of proper recreational grounds, the dancing and singing that they do as recreation for purposes of health and socializing have had to be carried out in residential areas, resulting in disturbances for local residents which sometimes led to quarreling and even fights. This problem has troubled Chinese society for quite some time now. On January 9, 2014, the CCTV (China Central Television) carried the following news report: On the square of a

[49] "Background Analysis: The Status and Development Trend of the Aging Chinese Population," wenku.baidu.com/link, April 14, 2016.

housing estate, a group of people were dancing joyfully to music. Suddenly, they were caught in a heavy "rain" of fecal sewage. Investigation by journalists later uncovered the reason—some families living in the apartment buildings there had long been bothered by the noise from the loud music the dancers had been using, and, after several rounds of fruitless negotiations, took to this act to vent their anger.[50] To be sure, this incident in part reveals the lack of consideration for others on the part of the dancers, but it is also a reflection of the severe shortage of physical space for public life in China.

Whether in London or in New York, in the heart of the city are large and easily accessible parks and greenbelts to be used for recreation and fitness activities. But China has only a few spaces similar to Hyde Park or Central Park; nor is there sufficient land area allocated to greenbelt areas. In the urbanization process of the last three decades, many former greenbelts have been turned over to developers to be built into commercial centers. Thus, recreational space in the cities has been greatly reduced, with a severe shortage of forested areas, parks, and greenbelts, which has in turn rendered it rather difficult for the air to be filtered and cleansed. Lung cancer has become a disease of very high incidence in China. Human needs have been largely ignored in public services, in an atmosphere where planners like to seek quick success and instant benefits in urbanization, and politicians like to undertake vanity projects that would please their superiors and earn credits for them that would help with their future promotion.

The current situation of public services outlined above is an epitome of the larger society in contemporary China. Although there are many constraints in this area, the root cause of the inadequacy is the lack of organization of public life on the part of the government, and the lack of leaders, designers, and executors who are professionally qualified and who can work efficiently toward the goals.

The 13th Five-Year Plan for the National Economy

On October 29, 2015, "The CCP Central Committee's Suggestions for the Formulating of the 13th Five-Year Plan of National Economic and Social Development" was passed. This represents a test for the Chinese leaders on an important decision regarding the most difficult issue defining the

[50] Murong Yixue, "When Can the Chinese Dama Stop Diturbing Other Residents with Their Dancing on the Square?", Ranyan Prose Net, June 19, 2014. http://www.ranyan.com/suibizuowen/32301.html. Accessed January 2, 2017.

economic structure of China at a time when the nation is faced with great challenges from the domestic and international economic situations—the choice is whether to switch from the production-oriented economic structure of the past to a consumption-oriented one for the future.

The Distinguishing Features of the 13th Five-Year Plan

One feature of the 13th Five-Year Plan is that the government has noticed that the old model of development, based on low labor costs and an overuse of natural resources that has led to tremendous damage to environment, while it has helped the nation to accumulate great wealth in the last three decades, is no longer sustainable, and that China should break the dependency of this traditional pathway of development. The latest plan emphasizes a structural rebalance, with a turn toward service and consumption. The third area that received a great deal of attention in the plan is the expansion of the social welfare network, which is seen as a catalyst for China's transformation into a consumption-oriented economy.

However, social welfare has always been a perplexing problem for the Chinese family. This problem has led many families to put their newly increased income into savings rather than use it for consumption, which has for a long time led to a disjunction between the growth of the service sector and the increases in personal income and consumption. If people's worries about social welfare cannot be changed into a faith in it, it will be impossible to realize a consumption-oriented economy in China. With the intensifying of various challenges, the speedy and effective implementation of the 13th Five-Year Plan has become more and more important.

Another feature of the 13th Five-Year Plan is that the attention of the planners has switched from a one-sided emphasis on economic development to a more balanced one on the complementary and mutual promotion between economic development and social progress. The plan insists on progress with stability and an overall plan that encompasses economic, political, cultural, and social development, plus the building of an ecological civilization and the development of the CCP, in order to ensure the goal of transforming China into a moderately prosperous society be reached on schedule. Furthermore, five principles, namely, innovation, coordinated development, green development, openness, and sharing, are put forth, and it is emphasized that the these goals were to be realized with fairness, balance, and effectiveness.[51]

[51] The Communist Party of China in the fifth Plenary Session of the 18th CPC Central Committee Bulletin, http://www.caixin.com, October 29, 2015.

Basic Conditions for Maintaining a Medium to High Speed of Economic Growth

There have been doubts as to what basis the Chinese government has for maintaining a medium to high growth rate for China's economy against a background of a general slowdown of the global economy, what methods will be used to promote growth, what opportunities there are for growth, and what advantages China has in relation to the world economy. We can answer these doubts with the following quote:

> China is in the late stage of industrialization and the stage where urbanization is accelerated. This means the structure of China's economy is undergoing fast changes, and a series of features characteristic of such structural changes are likely to show up. There is no doubt China's economy is going to experience a long-term recession. Being in the acceleration period in industrialization and urbanization is where China's advantage in relation to world economy lies. The base effect ensures China's economy will continue to enjoy a period of medium and high growth, and there is still great untapped potential in the areas of investment and consumption.[52]

It will not be very difficult to reach the binding targets and the prospective targets set in the 13th Five-Year Plan, but there have been some serious worries concerning the targets for institutional reform, including marketization and legalization. If China falls far back in these areas, it could hinder the attainment of the other targets.

Human Rights in China: History and the Current State

In 1946, the *Draft Declaration on Fundamental Human Rights and Freedoms* was adopted during the first session of the United Nations General Assembly. The work to draft an official declaration of human rights was assigned to the Commission on Human Rights established by the UN Economic and Social Council specifically for that purpose. The first draft of the *Universal Declaration of Human Rights* was completed in September 1948.[53] The Confucian idea that "benevolence means love for others" was

[52] Zhongnanhai Think Tank: "Member of the Zhongnanhai Think-Tank Says That the Actual GDP May Indeed Be only 4.5%, but That There Is no Need to Worry," www.money.591hx.com/ November 26, 2015.

[53] Zhu Wenqi, *The Modern International Law*, Beijing: The Commercial Press, 2013, pp. 363–364.

accorded much attention during the discussion leading to this draft. According to the *Memoires* of Eleanor Roosevelt, who headed the Commission on Human Rights, "Dr. Peng-chun Chang was one of the participants."[54]

The History of Human Rights in China

The Spring and Autumn Period and the Warring States Period in China were a time of intellectual flourishing, when great thinkers including Laozi, Confucius, Mozi, Mencius, and Zhuangzi lived. In their thoughts are contained some important ideas about human rights.

Confucius believed *ren* (benevolence) to be a kind of virtue and part of human nature. Differing from the narrowly defined *ren* conceived to be limited to the consanguine family group, Confucius believed benevolence is "overflowing with love for one's fellow men," which means love for all humans, including serfs and slaves. Confucius' idea of benevolence, then, is humanistic in nature.

Advocating the idea of *jian'ai* or universal love, Mozi believed "officials are not always noble, and common people do not necessarily stay in their lowly status through life," and required society ensure "the hungry shall have food to eat, those exposed to cold shall have clothes to wear, and the overworked shall have time to rest." The Mohist idea of universal love includes the ideas of equality and fraternity, and demands mutual love and friendship between the ruler and the subject, between the father and the son, and between older and younger brothers, all on the basis of equality. One is admonished to "love others as you love yourself."

Mencius states that "benevolence means love for others," believing that "the gentleman differs from ordinary people in where he sets his heart—he sets his heart in benevolence and in rites. Benevolence means love for others, while rites means respect for others." He also advocated that "the people are the most important; to be followed by the state, while the ruler is the least important."

[54] Lu Jianping, "Zhang Pengchun and the Universal Declaration of Human Rights," *Southern Weekend*, December 25, 2008.

These ideas not only transcend the traditional interpretation of rights (with its stress on humans' relationships with deities and on a hierarchical social order), but represent the earliest advocation of human rights.

In 1911, Dr. Sun Yat-sen, the leader for China's bourgeois revolution, published his *Three People's Principles.* He gave special emphasis to people's livelihood, defined as "people's life, which has to do with the perpetuation of society, the livelihood of the citizens, and the life of the masses." He was concerned with the lives of ordinary people, and attempted to improve the lives of the hundreds of millions of Chinese by promoting his principle of people's livelihood. In his own words, "the principle of people's livelihood has as its purpose the nurturing of the people," and he interprets this principle as really a "realm of liberty, equality, and fraternity."[55]

However, due to the continuing social upheaval in the Chinese society, these ideas of Sun on human rights have become a thing of the past.

The National Character of the Chinese

Speaking of human rights, a brief discussion of the development the national character of the Chinese in the modern era is in order. Starting from the Opium War of 1840, China was embroiled in domestic strife and troubles with foreign powers. The Sino-Japanese War of 1894–1895, in particular, brought great damage to China. The leisurely, easygoing, and romantic nature of the Chinese was totally subverted. Faced with the distress, poverty, and confusion of that period, the Chinese inclination to appreciate life was also overshadowed by the stringencies of the time.

Toward the end of the nineteenth century, the problem of the Chinese national character caught the attention of Arthur Henderson Smith, an American missionary who is noted for spending more than half a century in China.[56] Based on what he saw and heard in China, he wrote the famous *Chinese Characteristics*,[57] in which he lauded the politeness, thrift, perseverance, respect for the old, and care for the young of the Chinese, but spent more time discussing the more negative features of the Chinese national

[55] Zhao Jing, *An Outline of the History of Chinese Economic Thoughts.* Beijing: Peking University Press, 2003, p. 793, p. 809.

[56] Arthur Henderson Smith (1845–1932) began his missionary work in China in 1872, and retired as a missionary in 1926. His *Chinese Characteristics* was first published in 1894.

[57] Arthur H. Smith, *Chinese Characteristics.* New York, Chicago, Toronto: Fleming H. Revell Company, 1894, p. 318.

character, such as disregard of time, "flexible inflexibility," absence of nerves, absence of public spirit, conservativism, and lack of sincerity. He points out, "Chinese society resembles some of the scenery in China. At a little distance it appears fair and attractive. Upon a nearer approach, however, there is invariably much that is shabby and repulsive, and the air is full of odors which are not fragrant. No photograph does justice to Chinese scenery, for though photography has been described as 'justice without mercy,' this is not true of Chinese photography, in which the dirt and the smallest are omitted."[58]

After being published in 1894, *Chinese Characteristics* caused a worldwide sensation. There was soon heated discussion among Chinese intellectuals as to whether the Chinese indeed had an inferior national character and whether it needed to be transformed. This was a major event in the intellectual history of modern China. In his *Ice-drinking Room Collected Works*,[59] published in 1904, Liang Qichao, a major intellectual figure at the time, responded to *Chinese Characteristics* by summarizing the Chinese national character as including the following: (1) lacking independent and free thinking; (2) servility and egocentrism; (3) lacking public morality; (4) ignorance, cowardice, and deception; and (5) arbitrariness, hypocrisy, and inaction. Lu Xun, another major intellectual figure in modern China, joined in the discussion by raising three questions: (1) what is the ideal human character? (2) what is the most important element that is missing from the Chinese national character? and (3) what is the root cause for that? Only when these questions are properly answered, Lu Xun argued, could one venture to offer a "cure for the malady."

In the century following, intellectuals in China have continued to explore these issues and have had to struggle with the way to modernize in a China that has not changed much since Smith's days in terms of national character.

With the fading of China's traditional culture, the Chinese came to show more self-abasement, more resistance to progress, and a strong tendency to belittle themselves and their countrymen. With the founding of the People's Republic of China, for a while hope seemed to have dawned in China. But with the many political campaigns, one following another with ill-conceived policies, the worse parts of human nature were released and given free rein

[58] Ibid.

[59] Liang Qichao, *Complete Works from the Ice-drinking Room*, collated by Wu Song, Yunnan Education Press, 2001.

in many political campaigns, as seen especially in the inhumane cruelty that arose as people undertook to trick and persecute one another. For the generation born and raised in this period, such political struggle has brought tremendous harm and seriously distorted souls. Against such a historical background, it is not difficult to comprehend that the principles of human rights would not be put into practice.

In the Chinese national character, there is also a hidden megalomania, with people indulging in the country's five millennia of cultural glory. Shocked by the Western civilization with its great power derived from science and technology, however, the Chinese were awakened as if from a long dream of grandeur, and, losing their direction, found themselves in a dilemma. There has always been a great deal of doubt and repulsion among the Chinese in the face of the rise of modern civilization of the West. In such circumstances, an inclination to obstinacy still exists in the Chinese national character, which has worried many people who are more insightful, including many scholars.

At the 120th anniversary of the Sino-Japanese War of 1894, Arthur Smith's *Chinese Characteristics* was again published in a new Chinese translation. The editor's foreword to this new edition tries to persuade the Chinese to give serious consideration to the challenges posed by Smith 120 years before with regard to the Chinese national character. Here are two excerpts from this foreword:

> Arthur Smith, the author of this book, came to China to work as a missionary, and stayed in China for more than five decades. In this long time, he made insightful observation of the Chinese society and gained in-depth experience of it, and the amount of time he devoted to the public good and philanthropic efforts in China far exceeded that he used to speak for God. Thus, we have reason to believe *Chinese Characteristics* is not any shallow description, but much in-depth description of the national character of the Chinese. The author does not directly answer the question whether the Chinese are "beautiful" or "ugly", but keeps on inquiring into the numerous "odd" phenomena in China, whether they pertain to the strengths or the weaknesses of the Chinese, always with interpretation from a Western perspective and suggestions on how to make improvements. It is hard not to applaud the author's objectivity and impartiality.
>
> A hundred and twenty years have passed since the first publication of this book. And this is also the 120th anniversary of the Sino-Japanese War of 1894. Numerous changes have taken place in the space of more than a century. Amidst the seeming prosperity we now experience, do we or do we

> not need to reflect on the question whether the weaknesses in our national character pointed out by someone from a different culture more than a century ago have disappeared, or whether they have actually been intensified. Are not the excessive concern for "face", the overly elaborate formalities that hide much hypocrisy, and the terrible apathy described in this book the very reasons for the rather frequent moral crises in the contemporary Chinese society?[60]

We believe there are many pathogenic factors in the human ecology of contemporary Chinese society. People seldom understand or try to understand the basic principles of the law, and, in order for certain human rights to be widely respected, an upgrading of the humanistic spirit and a revival of civilized conduct among the Chinese will be necessary.

At this point, we return to our narrative of the history and current state of human rights in China.

The Current State of Human Rights in China

An article published in *Beijing Daily* in 1979 states, "Human rights have never been a banner for the proletariat. The rotten weapon of 'human rights', which have long been but something to gloss over the reactionary bourgeois dictatorship [in Western countries], should never be used as a panacea to govern a socialist country."[61]

Is it indeed true that the proletarian class has no need for human rights? After a difficult process of freeing up people's thinking in China, the CCP eventually realized that the problem of human rights had to be confronted. In September of 1997, the idea of "human rights" was for the first time officially recognized by the ruling Communist Party in the keynote report for its 15th National Congress. In Part VI of the report, entitled "Reform of the Political Institutions and Development of Democracy and the Rule of Law," it is clearly stated that "governing the country by the Communist Party consists in guiding and supporting the people to control and manage the power of the state, in implementing democratic elections, democratic decision-making, and supervising of the government by the people, in

[60] Arthur H. Smith, *Chinese Characteristics*, trans. by Zhang Mengyang and Wang Lijuan, China Changan Publishing House, 2014.

[61] "'Human Rights' is not the Slogan of the Proletariat," *Beijing Daily*, March 22, 1979.

ensuring the people would have broad rights and liberties granted by the law, and in respecting and safeguarding human rights."[62]

This was a step forward in the area of human rights that is of great historical significance. It meant the Communist Party would cooperate with intellectuals, scholars, and thinkers in exploring how to promote human rights in China.

Since the 1990s, the Chinese government has made many efforts to ensure the basic human rights to life, to subsistence, to development, to property, to human dignity, to government aid for meeting basic needs, and to equality.

First, the problem of basic needs for food and shelter for the Chinese people has been solved, which has been recognized by the international community as the greatest contribution by the Chinese government to human rights in the world. Second, the rapid economic development in China has helped to create conditions for people of all talents to put their abilities to work, and the notion of "contract" has gradually come to be widely accepted. Third, the cultural and spiritual life of the Chinese has shifted from being closed to being open, from being intolerant to being tolerant of differences, from monotony to a rich variety, and from a unitary frame of mind to a pluralistic one. With much effort, measures to guarantee rights to life, subsistence, and development have been extended to cover the entire country, and additional efforts are now being made to implement measures to guarantee rights to enjoy life, equality, dignity, and government aid to meet basic needs.

In everyday life, values such as openness, tolerance, and respect for law have been incorporated into people's mentality as well as social policy. Free choice in marriage, sexual orientation, divorce, cohabitation, transvestism, and refusal to marry have gained more acceptance. Many Western disciplines, with their associated knowledge, have been introduced with various schools of thought, and for different fields in humanities, social sciences, culture, and art. People have gained much greater freedom in leaving and entering the country, in choosing jobs, in family patterns, and so on. Legislation has been passed to ensure the elderly are treated well, to protect the rights of consumers, to protect Chinese people traveling abroad, and to provide aid from the state in the event of major disasters. The

[62] Bulletin of Communist Party of China in the third Plenary Session of the 15th CPC Central Committee, October 14, 1998.

government has made efforts to improve people's livelihoods and to act on people's concerns, to reform the judiciary system so as to ensure justice, and to improve the relationship between the public and the government and that between people and government officials.

In the face of major natural disasters such as the earthquake in Wenchuan, the government has coordinated relief in such a way as to provide adequate shelter and food for those affected and to undertake reconstruction of the areas hit by the disasters as soon as possible. China has won praise from media in many countries in this respect.

For many years, the international community, especially Western countries, have kept on censuring China for not allowing freedom of speech, of demonstration, of association, and of the press, and there has been much criticism of this kind from some sections of Chinese society itself. The author personally believes that such criticism is in accord with the direction of social progress and with the need for humans to express themselves; the more society and the economy develop, the stronger such appeals are likely to become for a civilized society.

The space allowed by the Chinese government for liberty is still rather limited, but there are also some reasons for it. Why? We actually touched upon the reason when we discussed the national character of the Chinese, namely, the Chinese are still rather narrow-minded when it comes to the understanding of liberty, especially with regard to the idea that a sense of responsibility and duty is the basis for liberty. Furthermore, in the imperial system of China which lasted for two millennia, state control of the people's thinking was the norm, which was started by the Qin Empire and was continued by the later dynasties with the state policy of "banning all other schools of thought while revering Confucianism." With such a tradition, "the need for ideological uniformity" is still much the mindset of the Chinese. Regardless of the many great changes in modern times, history has its own inertia in this respect.

Mill devotes the fifth chapter of his *On Liberty* to the applications of the principle of liberty. He sums the core of his idea in two maxims:

> The maxims are, first, that the individual is not accountable to society for his actions, in so far as these concern the interests of no person but himself. Advice, instruction, persuasion, and avoidance by other people, if thought necessary by them for their own good, are the only measures by which society can justifiably express its dislike or disapprobation of his conduct. Secondly, that for such actions as are prejudicial to the interests of others, the individual

> is accountable, and may be subjected either to social or to legal punishments, if society is of opinion that the one or the other is requisite for its protection.[63]

The author understands Mill's principle of liberty in the following way: a person who gains liberty must be able to shoulder responsibility for society and to perform his/her duty. In other words, in order to be liberated from discipline imposed by others, one has to have sufficient self-discipline. I remember Kant also said in his *Groundwork of the Metaphysic of Morals* that only humans have free will and the right they are born with to liberty, but that in order to have liberty, one has first to respect the liberty of others.[64]

Currently, the Chinese are still mentally and intellectually unprepared in their national character for the implementation of a general right to liberty, with a lack of ability for liberty, among other things. For example, many uncivilized behaviors have been reported of the Chinese in their tourism and other leisure activities, and the nature of such behaviors is a violation of others' right to liberty. The Chinese themselves have been puzzled by the cycle in which initiatives would be stifled when the government tries to tighten up control to achieve ideological unity, at which point the government would then try to loosen control, which, however, would lead to confusion and chaos, making it necessary for the government to tighten up control again. In the last few decades, China has been struggling with precisely this kind of cycle.

China is a society that puts much emphasis on the give-and-take of favors among the people and on maintaining "face," within a rather strict hierarchy. It has been difficult to implement the rule of law or to foster a willingness to adhere to contracts and respect reason. In its attempt to construct a society that reveres human rights, it has been working in a cultural milieu that has not produced great modern thinkers like Montesquieu, Descartes, John Stuart Mill, Kant, Locke, and Spinoza; nor has there been an enlightenment movement like the Renaissance in the West, which would greatly help to instill the modern spirit into its national character. We also have to keep in mind that the political centralization and the stress on ideological unity, which have been prevalent for more than two millennia in

[63] John Stuart Mill, 1859. *On Liberty*. London: John W. Parker and Son, p. 55.

[64] Immanuel Kant, 1785. *Grundlegung zur Metaphysik der Sitten* (*Groundwork of the Metaphysic of Morals*) trans. Mary Gregor, 1997. Cambridge: Cambridge University Press.

China, have also set limits to the speed at which institutional arrangements can be reformed.

As a matter of fact, although there has been discussion on human rights for a long time in the West, many problems have yet to be solved satisfactorily. To be fair, we have to realize that China differs a great deal from the West in this respect, being constrained by many factors, including institutional design, social systems, policy goals, cultural tradition, current level of development, and the general character of the people. Also, human rights have to be implemented gradually. People's rights to have sufficient means of subsistence and to have personal development have to be guaranteed first. Then, in a context of social stability and economic development, the scope of human rights can be expanded to include political rights, rights of liberty, and the right to have the vote. In these areas, it is possible that a rush for quick results would lead to the opposite outcome.

The problem of human rights for a society is related to its social and historical background. It would be difficult to judge whether the demands in this area are sound or not when taken out of their social and historical context, for certain conditions have to be created to meet the requirements of human rights which may seem by nature to be legitimate and reasonable.

The State of China's Economy

Appraisal of the state of China's economy is now a hot topic both in China and abroad. Economists believe that the general economic situation of China is a combination of "macroscopic stability and microscopic inadequacies," with the former term meaning the economy will not continue to fall, but that the possibility of recovery is also slight; and the latter meaning the current growth rate is actually below the potential growth rate, for enterprises are generally experiencing decreased efficiency and having difficulty with their business, a symptom that began to show its face in 2013.[65] From the logic of economics, this combination of "macroscopic stability and microscopic inadequacies" is normal in between two business cycles, and signals the beginning of the new cycle.

[65] Hu Yuexiao, "What are the Combination of Macro Stability and Micro Difference?" *Shanghai Securities News*, November 30, 2015, p. 6.

Thresholds to be Surmounted by China's Economy in the Future

The deep-level problems that now exist in the Chinese economy, according to Hu Yuexiao, the chief macroeconomic analyst of Shanghai Stock Exchange, are "rooted in a lack of true entrepreneurship in the society. What entrepreneurship there is has been played out amidst much concept creation and a strong desire to make quick money by becoming listed on the stock market. Wealth redistribution has gradually replaced actual value creation as the favored means to increase one's share of wealth. It has become an 'empirical rule' for economic activities that operating a company in industry is not as good as speculation in real estate or usury. This kind of situation has not only made economic growth more heavily dependent on investment, but also led to a great deal of short-sighted economic behavior. There is not a strong orientation toward innovation, which has led to increased fluctuation of the economy, resulting in a situation with much 'surplus in productive capacity' and 'great leverage' needed to adjust the economy. An atmosphere is urgently needed for the whole society to focus on real entrepreneurship in order to solve the problems of how to increase momentum for the economy, how to increase the vigor of economic operation, and how to expand the basis of demand."[66]

In 2016, when the world economy as whole was quite weak, China's GDP still grew by 6.5%. However, there are already signs that China's economy, too, lack enough driving force for continued growth. In the past, three forces have been driving the growth of the economy - net export, investment in fixed capital, and consumption, but these have all spent much of their power. The government has been emphasizing innovation as a new driving force, promoting optimal integration of resources, de-capacity, de-stocking, de-leveraging, cost reduction, and improving the weak links of the economy, but it would be a long and painful process to carry these out, and the pull they could exert on the economy in the future is limited. In addition, the loss of the benefits from low labor cost, limited resources, and the damage of over-production on air quality all pose challenges for continued economic development in the future.

Another phenomenon is also worth our attention: some entrepreneurs have been maximizing their gains at the cost of societal values. As another expert points out, "Chinese economy to the mire of low-grade products of poor quality. Chinese entrepreneurs often neglect the development of good

[66] Ibid.

trusted brands, and try to make the last pot of gold before a crisis hits in ways detrimental to the society. . . . Some entrepreneurs have been creating value, but there are also those who are consuming value or even are worms eating up value of the society. This latter kind of entrepreneurship is not likely to get very far."[67]

Why, then, is it possible for enterprises to make money in China in ways detrimental to the values of society? We can look at what Jack Ma had to say on this point. After his Internet giant Alibaba had successfully gone public on the New York Stock Exchange, Ma joined Mary Barra, CEO of General Motors, and others at the Clinton Global Initiative (CGI) on September 23, 2014. At CGI, he talked much about how he felt about his company having gone public. In reply to the question, posed by the Clintons' daughter Chelsea, what he thought of the value that was to be created by Alibaba's going public, Ma said, "Why was Alibaba able to succeed in China? It is because China's trade structure is terribly bad, which has given us great opportunities."[68] This reply really hit at one of the sore spots of Chinese economy.

Innovation Is Better than Replication

In 2015, the concept of "Internet +" descended on China, as if a strong dose of stimulant had been injected into all the entrepreneurs and investors. With that, the existing balance in the world seems to have been broken, and old ways of thinking have been greatly challenged. In addition, there has been a powerful campaign for entrepreneurial and innovative undertakings by large numbers of people. It is still difficult to tell whether this is going to lead to the best or the worst of times.

The massive campaign of entrepreneurial and innovative undertakings promoted by the Chinese government will require many social conditions as its support. In particular, a sufficient supply of talent, funding, and knowledge are the bases for its success. For people trying to start mini-enterprises, the lack of knowledge and funding are the greatest obstacles; and insufficiencies in vocational training and loans are the weaknesses of China's

[67] Ye Tan, "The Entrepreneur of the Price War," *Xin Min Weekly*, 2015, no. 46.

[68] Ma Yun and Clinton's Daughter Talk: "Chinese trade structure is terribly bad which has given the opportunities" at the Clinton Global Initiative Annual Meeting. www.guancha.cn, September 24, 2014.

future economic development. On the one hand, the Chinese economy is experiencing three difficult periods simultaneously, namely, the period of the economy shifting from a high gear to a middle gear, the period it is in the throes of due to structural adjustments, and the period needed to absorb the effects of earlier policies to stimulate the economy; on the other, risks brought about by the slowdown of the economy, such as fluctuations in the real estate market, a surplus in productive capacity, the shadow banking system, and defaults on debt by local governments, have been increasing day by day.

In theory, the massive campaign for entrepreneurial and innovative undertakings can create new room for the Chinese economy to grow by both increasing employment and by promoting social mobility and social justice. However, from what we can see at present, many worrisome problems remain—entrepreneurs are more inclined to replicate the success of others than to pursue originality. Baidu, Alibaba, and Tencent are the major representatives of private enterprises in China, but they have achieved their success largely by taking advantage of the fact that Google, Facebook, and other foreign companies have not been able to have operation in China due to various causes, and it is quite doubtful how much originality these Chinese companies have had in their business models. It has been said, quite aptly, that Chinese entrepreneurs "get started very fast (by imitating others), but are slow in innovating."

The Need for Humanistic Economic Thinking

Some Westerners have also been questioning the future of the Chinese economy, claiming that "China, the world's great growth story, is imploding. Its stock market plummeted ... and its real economy is slowing."[69] However, we have to put these figures in perspective. In the three decades after China began her reform and opening-up to the outside world, the Chinese economy has been growing by leaps and bounds, ridding the country of severe poverty; but the quality of China's economic growth is rather low, with growth from hi-tech being only a small proportion of it, and the country still far from becoming an economically strong nation. Thus, the room for Chinese economic development is still very large.

[69] Yves Herman, "What Wall Street Gets Wrong about China." *Newsweek*, September 11, 2015.

Nevertheless, the Chinese economy has to avoid a "hard landing." With the initiation of the 13th Five-Year Plan, the government has redoubled its efforts at de-stocking, de-leveraging, and reducing productive capacity. At the same time, making up for the weaknesses of the economy and lowering costs are to be the focus of the government's work in the economic sphere for some time to come. Humanistic economic thinking is needed for this process.

This author is a layperson when it comes to economics, but likes to make observations about and reflect on economic issues from a humanistic perspective. In "Inspirations from the History of Economic Thinking," a section of *Leisure Economy: toward humanistic concerns*, published in 2004, this author argues that when economic development has reached a certain stage, the following issues should be considered: (1) economic acts of humans have a moral dimension; (2) emphasis should be given to following the natural order, and the limitations of rationality should be recognized; (3) the civilized world is linked together by a common bond; (4) balance is needed in the world; (5) efficiency is the source of value for economics, and trust is the lubricant for economic transactions; and (6) human beings create surplus value so that they can have free time for scientific, philosophical, and artistic pursuits, which work to uplift human beings from the inside. Ideas such as "small is beautiful," "the limit of growth," and "marginal effect" are also treated in the book.[70] It is my belief that strategic planning should be made for the Chinese economy to shift its emphasis from quantity to quality, from product-centered to human-centered, from material consumption to the uplifting of the inner quality of human beings, from the construction of "hard power" to the enhancement of "soft power," from economic indices to humanistic concerns, and from efforts to seek quick results to those ensuring there is a solid basis for a healthy development. How to make these shifts will be hard questions to be answered for the future development of the Chinese economy.

China has become a society in which leisure is available to all, with leisure life and consumption playing important roles in people's socioeconomic activities. Indeed, the Chinese market is so large and people need so many things! They need numerous automatic rice cookers and toilet covers of good quality at an affordable price, they need a large number of trustworthy

[70] Ma Huidi, *Towards the Leisure Economy of Humanistic Concern*, China Economic Publishing House, 2004, pp. 75–82.

travel agencies, and they need elegant and simple living environments. The Chinese Damas who spend liberally need fitness and nourishing facilities, and the middle class need luxury items with good well-crafted designs. The wealthy class needs gorgeous and posh leisure activities, and common folks need safe grains, vegetables, and fruits. Babies need milk powder that is safe, and the elderly need thickly paddd and comfortable diapers.

Such needs all show that the Chinese economy is in a transition from an investment-driven economy to a supply-side one. People are turning from subsistence needs and many material desires to pursuits of quality life, spiritual enjoyment, and personal tastes, which result in a consumption model centered on the enhancement of the quality of life. Such a historical period may well be one with a great deal of opportunities for humanistic economic theories and for a liberal market of ideas to develop.

Creating an Atmosphere for the "Market of Ideas"

With regard to the future trends of Chinese economy, besides keeping our advantages, it may also be necessary to heed the "ten advices" from Coase:1) privileges for state-owned enterprises must be abolished, so that private enterprises can freely compete with them; 2) government participation in land transactions leads to rampant corruption, so the government must puts itself outside the market; 3) China should undertake to create a free market for land; 4) current systems of education and taxation both tend to increase inequality; 5) the family-planning of China is obviously a wrong prescription and much rethinking is needed to rectify it; 6) "marginal forces" can bring private entrepreneurs and market forces back to China; 7) Chinese economists should go back to the real world from their blackboard economics; 8) political power must be put under the rule of law; 9) China's economy faces an important weakness - the lack of a market of ideas; and 10) China's struggle is the struggle of mankind![71]

One may wonder whether Coase's advices, given from the perspective of his liberalist economics, really apply to the socialist market economy of China, but this author believes that human nature, basic ethical principles, the rule of law, and laws of economics are all commensurate for different societies and follow common laws. In any case, we need to stay away from

[71] The Ifeng News, "Coase's Ten Advices for China: China Is Faced with a Serious Weakness", 2013. finance.ifeng.com/news.

allowing the cold logic of choice in resource allocation primacy for driving the economic development of the world. So, we would do well to hold Coase's ideas in mind and carefully reflect on them.

Conclusion

The rise of the Chinese economy in the last three decades is doubtless the result of the emancipation of thinking, reform, and opening-up, in addition to a series of institutional innovations. This has also benefitted from the "National Power,"[72] which has empowered the nation through its willpower, control, and administrative leadership, as well as through the devotion of its human, financial, and material resources. Although this development model had been receiving frequent questions from Chinese and foreign parties, in reality, at least for the past 30 years, it has been proven that it is the most effective method for an enormous country with a vast population and poor economic foundations like China.

In March 2016, the first year of the 13th Five-Year Plan of China, Premier Li Keqiang spoke thus in his keynote speech at the Boao Forum,

> China has become the world's second largest economy, but its per capita GDP is still at the middle level in the world. There is both a gap to fill and a potential to tap, especially in China's central and western regions, where we see huge space and room for development. China is now in the process of industrialization and urbanization. There is a strong impetus for reform and much space for expanding domestic demand. A resilient development and various ways to boost innovation. The fundamentals of the Chinese economy have stayed unchanged and will remain sound in the long run.[73]

But the Chinese government has been rather objective on this point. While he was premier of China, Wen Jiabao said on several occasions that 1.3 billion is a very large number, and that any tiny problem would become a huge one when multiplied by 1.3 billion, while any resource, when divided by 1.3 billion, would become very small.

[72] "National Power" was a concept proposed by Ma Huidi, in her paper "China's first science and technology plan (1956–1967)", which was later published as "theoretical thinking on China's first science and technology development plan," *Studies in Dialectics of Nature*, 1995, No. 6.

[73] Li Keqiang, "A New Vision for A Dynamic Asia Through Joint Efforts" (Speech at the Opening Plenary of Boao Forum for Asia Annual Conference 2016), *Xinhua New Net.* March 25, 2016. http://news.xinhuanet.com/english/2016-03/26/c_135224412.htm. Accessed February 5, 2017.

Premier Li Keqiang also shared a similar view. When asked what he thought of the view that China had already become the largest economy in the world and was challenging the leadership position of the USA, Li replied,

> I have myself often heard this kind of view, but have always felt someone is trying to swindle me. According to internationally authoritative calculations, China is no more than the second largest economy. More importantly, in terms of per capita GDP, China positions lower than the 80th. Before the Chinese New Year, I visited two families in a rural area in the western part of the country. In one family, it was a mother with a son living together in a worn house with a tiled roof. The son was more than 40 years old, but yet unmarried because of poverty. Another family was fortunate enough to have a son who had become a college student, but in order for him to continue his study in college, his younger sister had to work to earn a meager wage and had not been able to return home for the New Year. My heart twinged on seeing this. And there are many other examples like these. If we go by the standard of the World Bank, there are nearly 200 million people in China who are living in poverty. China is really just a developing country.[74]

The future of Chinese economic development, whether it is to keep up with National Power or differentiate from its original path, it is yet to be explored and adjusted according to the realities of the situation. A successful development model should see an increase in better education, stable employment, satisfactory income, reliable social security, higher standards of living, and an improved medical system, together with good surroundings. Eventually, it ought to provide sensible humanistic care that makes an improved working and living environment for generations to come.

Nevertheless, Chinese economic development has entering a new era, although there are numerous challenges facing it ahead, foremost of which is the speculative bubble; however, China is planning to follow a development concept that is innovative, ecological, open minded, and sharing for the next five years. Adhering itself to deep ointegration into the global economy is what will power China's economic growth in the future, thus delivering further demands for the world's economy.

[74] "Li Keqiang's Reply to the Statement 'China Has Become the Largest Economy of the World'—It Is Swindling," *Xinhua News Net.* March 16, 2015. http://news.youth.cn/gn/201503/t20150316_6527672.htm. Accessed February 5, 2017.

CHAPTER 5

Aspects of Leisure Life in Contemporary China

China has been undergoing profound social transformation for more than three decades. Class struggles have come to an end, but stratification has intensified. Selfless altruism has given way to selfishness, and asceticism has yielded to the unlimited display of desires. People have generally been living with an imbalance of work and leisure and with lives that are in disorder, both mentally and physically. In sum, material wealth has become abundant, but it has been accompanied by poverty in spiritual life.

"Getting rich" and "pursuing wealth" have become the main themes for many Chinese. People do not want to fall behind in the powerfully attractive game of money-making, and all want to try their hands at digging for gold. In terms of material enjoyment, the well-to-do have begun to imitate people in the USA and in Europe. Privately owned gardens, big houses, villas, luxury cars, and expensive tours and holidays are not only for the Americans and Europeans—the Chinese have begun to enjoy them too. Such a mentality has made people short-sighted, with their attention focused only on petty benefits, utterly unable to appreciate any beauty along their way. When objects of aesthetic appreciation, of reverence, and of ethical, philosophical, and religious reflections are far from life and from people's scope, restlessness, confusion, and panic are bound to become the lot of the Chinese.

Huidi Ma, Er Liu, *Traditional Chinese Leisure Culture and Economic Development*, DOI 10.1057/978-1-137-59253-8_5

In this chapter, we will take a close look at the gains and losses the Chinese have had in their lives and work as many people now orient their life toward money.

Three Important Changes in the Social Organism of China

As a super-organism, society is a very complicated system, according to Marx's theory of the constitution of the social organism. In the social transformation of China, three dimensions of change have exerted great influence on the social organism and hence have affected both work and leisure. In the following, we try to analyze each of these changes in turn.

Changes in Family Structure

With the implementation of the one-child policy in China from 1979 to the end of 2015, the traditional family structure, traditional cultural values based in the family, and ethics, which were also based in the family, have been overturned, bringing many uncertainties and instabilities for society as a whole. As a consequence, the following problems have arisen:

(1) Family size has continued to decline. According to *Report on Family Development in China, 2014*, the average family size in China was 3.02.[1]
(2) The pattern for elderly care is undergoing significant changes. Thirty-five years ago, the ratio of the number of adults able to provide for the elderly to the number of elderly people was 6:1, but with the implementation of the one-child policy, after the generation of only children have come of age and with the aging of their parents, they need to provide not only for their parents, but also the parents of their parents, resulting in what demographers call the "4:2:1" structure, which bodes serious social problems to come.
(3) Since the single-child policy was implemented, almost all families in urban areas came to have only one child, but in rural areas, people often managed to get around government policy and have more children. Since rural areas are usually much less developed economically, many

[1] State Health and Family Planning Commission, *China Family Development Report 2014*. China Demography Press, 2014.

families had difficulty keeping their children in school, which gave rise to a new generation of illiterate or semi-illiterate people, making it difficult for them to find jobs after they got out of school. This is an important factor underlying the flourishing of goods "made in China." The general quality of the Chinese labor force was not high to start with, but the demographic pattern has made the situation worse.

(4) In many rural areas, the sex ratio of newborns was thrown off balance, with the maximum reaching 130:92 male to female. At present, there are more than 30 million bachelors unable to find wives. A direct outcome is that a large number of individuals are bedeviled by sexual deprivation, which will continue to produce problems for society.[2]

(5) With rural areas being over-populated, large numbers of young people have migrated out of rural areas seeking employment. For those who are married, this often results in the separation of husband and wife for extended periods of time, which has directly led to increases in the rates of rape and divorce. On the other hand, many young children are deprived of parental care, with many detrimental effects on their physical and psychological development. At present, there are more than 62 million left-behind children 留守兒童 who are separated from their parent/parents.[3]

(6) Some children have followed their parents to urban areas, where, however, they are likely to live a harsh life in bad housing conditions, not infrequently in shanty towns; further, because their household registration is with authorities in rural areas (they do not have registrations needed to go to the better urban schools) they have to go to schools separate from, and with facilities much inferior to, those for children from families with household registration is in the city. A new kind of discrimination has arisen, accompanied by antagonism between such different strata. Many children of migrant workers have low self-esteem, and feel lonely and helpless, which instills in them a motive to take revenge on the urbanites.

[2] Today's Topic, "There Will Be 30 Million Bachelors [in China]. Where is the Way Out?" Netease Women's Forum. September 11, 2015. http://lady.163.com/15/0911/10/B37P5QOT00264IIU.html. Accessed January 2, 2017.

[3] This term refers to children in rural areas one or both of whose parents have left home to find job in urban areas but who remain in rural areas and are placed under the care of their grandparents, other relatives, or friends of the family.

(7) Empty-nest families have seen a rapid increase. Since the 1990s, social transformation in China has led to early retirement or unemployment for many people in their fifties, a large proportion of whom are from social strata with low income, low educational attainment, and few work skills. Many of elderly people are living a life of boredom, spending much of their time watching TV, and are often suffering from multiple geriatric diseases.

(8) The "dink" (Dual Income No Kids) family has come into existence in China. There are an increasing number of families who voluntarily choose not to have children, especially in large cities. As a consequence of this development, the better the family background and the educational attainment of the husband and wife of a family, the lower the birth rate tends to be.

(9) The "single-member household" has also come into existence, unnoticed by many. According to data from the *Annals of National Statistics*, the number of single-member households doubled in the first decade of the twenty-first century, and reached 14.6% of the total number of households in 2013. Among those below 30 years of age, the higher their educational attainment and the better-off they are economically, the more likely are they to choose to remain single. In large cities such as Beijing, Shanghai, and Guangzhou, the average age at which people get married keeps on going up, as does the divorce rate, both of which factors result in larger percentages of the population living as single.[4]

The Unprecedented Generation of Only Children

After the Chinese government loosened its birth control policy, allowing a couple to have more than one child, a *duanzi* (段子)[5] has been circulating in the WeChat groups of the only-child generation that says, "There is some-

[4] Ma Huidi, The Survey on Chinese Family and Marriage in the Era of the One-Child Policy, presented at World Congress of Families, Kuala Lumpur, Malaysia, August 12–14, 2004 (new data is added here).

[5] A *duanzi* is a short story or joke which gives expression to an aspect of common people's lives and their ideas through humor and exaggeration, or which ridicules certain social phenomena.

thing miraculous about me, for I belong to the only-child generation in 5 thousand years of history!" Another *duanzi* goes as follows,

> When we went to primary school, college education was free; but when we went to college, it was primary education that was free. We busted our ass to pass the college entrance examinations and enter college, but when we finished college, it became hard to find a job. When we graduated from college, there were numerous college graduates, who therefore became very cheap on the job market. We entered graduate school to avoid the fierce competition, but upon finishing graduate school, we found there were too many people with master's degrees. When we wanted to find girlfriends, we encountered an unbalanced sex ratio; and when we tried to get married, the price for housing rocketed. When we tried to become white-collared workers, there came the financial crisis.

Though only a *duanzi*, this rather realistically reflects the life experiences and situations of contemporary young people, as well as their sense of helplessness in face of so much frustration and the uncertainty they feel about their future.

In traditional China, a widely shared idea was that "an only child is difficult to educate, just as it would be difficult to make a fire with a single piece of firewood," which is a piece of wisdom summarized from people's experiences with education for the younger generation. The one-child policy imposed on the people by the government led to important changes in people's mentality—the spoiling of only-children was widespread, giving rise to a whole generation of "little emperors" in Chinese families, which led to many problems that troubled the parents in such families.

The generation of only-children were deprived of affection among siblings. Growing up in an environment without siblings as long-term companions, they did not have opportunities to experience such affection, or to learn from and help one another in the family. This represents a great loss of kinship culture. With such a loss, the generation of only-children may well be the loneliest generation in Chinese and even world history.

At present, the generation of only-children have grown up and become the mainstay of the Chinese society. Whether it is for the country and the society or for the family, they must be the pillar and act as the connection between the preceding generations and the generation to follow them. In terms of lifecycle, they are the major force of society, and are the generation who has to shoulder the heaviest burden. In a historical perspective, they are, and are likely to remain, a unique generation, since the only-child policy has now been discontinued.

The aging of the parents of the only-child generation will also lead to changes in the demand for elderly care. The older their parents become, the greater the risks involved with elderly care will become, and the more difficulties there will be for the only-child generation. For them, family responsibilities do not just mean economic burdens and time that needs be devoted to care for their parents, but also ethical burdens and even costs when they are forced to disobey the law. The Chinese government has passed legislation requiring them to pay visits to their parents from time to time.

It is obvious that there would be some weaknesses in the character of this generation as they grew up as only-children. While having too much pride, unable to endure much hardship, lacking in independence, and overly reliant on others. They are often characterized by egocentrism, capriciousness, imperiousness, cowardice, an unsocial inclination, timidity, and a lack of adaptability to new social situations. These characteristics pose great challenges to their life and work, as they need to cooperate and socialize with others.

Some have argued that the Chinese have been undergoing a transformation toward "loneliness." Frequent migration and workplaces separated from one's familial place of residence have contributed to this trend, but the prevalence of indoorsmen and indoorswomen and of men and women past the age when it is easy for them to find partners for marriage has led to rapid increase in the number of people living alone. The "heads bowed down" (to look at cell phones), those obsessed with cell phones, virtual chat, the Internet, and excessive WeChatting, which we see as a phenomenon everywhere, reflect attempts to overcome the loneliness and disinterest this generation feels, and to make up for their empty spiritual world through newly available technologies.

Increase in the Total Amount of Free Time

It can be calculated that at present the Chinese are supposed to have 115 days off work per annum, including the holidays stipulated by the government (11 days) and the weekends (104 days). Some social groups have even more holidays: students and teachers at primary, secondary, and tertiary schools have about 160 days of holidays when winter and summer holidays are taken into account; civil servants, people working in public institutions or state-owned enterprises, and management personnel of overseas-funded enterprises, who enjoy paid leave of about 10–15 days, have a total of about 124 days off work. With the increasing mechanization of farm work, farmers engaged in primary industry now have about half a year when they are free; of the workers engaged in secondary industry, about 40 million are unemployed or "waiting to be re-employed," or have a flexible work schedule, which usually means less than eight hours a day at work, due to governmental measures to adjust the industry structure of the country. And the vast majority of the retired (the age at which people retire from work being currently 50–55 for most enterprises) now stay home rather than find another job. With the diversification of the employment structure and the forms of employment, flexible work schedules for some, and the emergence of freelancers, free time has increased for certain social strata. Ordinary people are able to enjoy free time outside the eight-hour work day. With the prevalence of modern labor-saving domestic appliances, the time people have to devote to housework has declined. Improvements in other areas have also contributed to the increase of free time. The venues through which people obtain more free time have also increased, and the number of holidays available can differ with the nature of one's job.

The Imbalance Between Work and Leisure

China has entered the stage when leisure is available to the common people. For everyone, leisure life has become a matter of fact. Work and leisure are both components of human existence. Labor has created not only human beings, but also opportunities for leisure. Without labor, there would not have been leisure; but, on the other hand, human beings would not have been able to advance to higher forms of labor without leisure. Thus, balancing labor and leisure is of crucial importance for increasing and upgrading people's freedom, aesthetic taste, experience, interest, and creativity. However, in their rush to attain wealth, people too often forget the meaning and value of these relationships. Below we are going to examine the negative impacts the imbalance between work and leisure has had on the Chinese.

Do Not Let A Child Lose at the Starting Line

The slogan "don't let your child lose at the starting line" has been in wide circulation for more than a decade in China. For parents who have very high expectations for their children, this slogan is very attractive and has a great deal of appeal. For a nation that "reveres the teacher and values education," entering a good college is not only a success for the child, but also brings honor to his/her family and ancestors.

With such a mentality, parents believe that the earlier the child is placed on the "starting line" the better. Education begins when the child is still a fetus during the mother's pregnancy. It is common practice to teach to kids in kindergarten knowledge which elementary school students are expected to learn, with math, Chinese language, and foreign languages made into required courses at many kindergartens. According to one parent, when he applied to have his three-year-old son enter a kindergarten, the son had to take an exam that includes the following real-life situation problem:

> Four kids, each wearing a black or a white cap (the cap was put on his/her head when he/she was blindfolded and he/she was not told what color the cap was), were set in a room and told that two of them had black caps and two had white ones. They were not allowed to take off their caps and look at them, neither were they allowed to look at what the other kids were wearing, but each had to figure out what color his/her caps was, and then state the reason for his/her judgment.

It is said that the father, who had a doctorate, was not able to solve the problem, but exclaimed, "This is mental torture for such young kids, who are supposed to be the hope of the nation."

With these kinds of problems, one can easily imagine and understand the reason why Chinese parents have been trying to send their children abroad at younger and younger ages for education in other countries, and why many parents want to have their children born in the USA.

In order that their children do not "lose at the starting line," many parents send their children to a large variety of the so-called "interest classes." These extracurricular classes are supposed to be chosen according to children's own interests, but the actual situation is often quite different—most parents send their children to those classes because they believe their children "cannot afford to lose at the starting line" or to fall back while other children are moving ahead, or out of a mentality of blindly comparing their own children with other children. They do this regardless of whether their children were interested in the subjects or whether they showed gifts for excelling in them. On average, a child goes to —three or four such "interest classes" for any given period of time, and some go to as many as about ten such classes. Parents from well-to-do families have the financial means to send their children to such classes, but even those who are not so well off try their best to send their children, believing "no matter how hard it is for the family, the kid's future should not be allowed to suffer due to the hardship."

A four-year-old girl spoke thus about her experience of going to these "interest classes": "I used to like singing and dancing, to wear colorful skirts, and to be like a little princess, but now I am interested in none of these. I am all the more tired on weekends, for on weekends I have to take so many lessons, in singing, dancing, piano, in playing *go*, ... I feel like crying whenever I hear the word 'class', for I'm too tired." What she has spoken of is actually quite typical of many children, and listening to her words one cannot help feeling sad and helpless for her.

There are a small proportion of parents who are willing to adjust their plans for their children so that they are more adapted to the children's needs, but most parents continue to force their children to accept a great amount of training "for their interests." The admonition they often give their children is, "If you study well, you can become a big official or make a lot of money in the future and rise way above others; and if you don't study well, then you will end up sweeping the dust in the streets, doing hard farm work, or peddling some vegetables on the market to make a living." Some children may understand such admonitions, while some others probably do not, and still others understand it vaguely. But what kinds of values are being instilled into children's minds when they keep on hearing such admonitions? China today has already given an answer to this question.

Relevant government agencies, various organizations, and the schools are also responsible for propagating the slogan "do not let your child lose on the starting line." The whole educational system has gone awry, and every link on the chain of the educational process has become problematic. Public kindergartens as well as private ones compete to organize various kinds of remedial classes, interest classes, and specialty classes, in an effort to cater to the parents' needs in order to attract a large pool of applicants and make more profit. The original motivation and purpose of education has been alienated in the process, resulting in the parents living a tiresome life while their children become completely tired of studying.

There are, however, children who have really lost "on the starting line," and those are the children in underdeveloped rural regions. In those regions, children seem to be left to grow up in a completely natural setting, little bothered by any "interest classes." However, one cannot be optimistic about their case. As numerous peasants in their prime migrated to the cities in search of jobs, many of them left their children with their grandparents. In Chongqing, Sichuan, and Guangxi, this author has seen many rural areas where aged grandparents and small kids live together in a setting where there is little in terms of recreational facilities for kids or for the elderly. Young children are raised like cage-free chickens and ducklings. Such regions are also likely to be affected by many forms of crime, such as rape of teenage girls, the stealing of young children, and abduction and trade of minors, which add to the many accidental deaths of children.

Children are the future of the family—and of the nation. As the parents of individual families struggle to keep their children from "losing at the starting line," perhaps the nation as a whole has already "lost at the starting line."

The Costs to Children of Growing Up in China

The solid background of Chinese primary and secondary school students in basic education seems to have won worldwide recognition. In various international science olympiads, Chinese students have kept on winning gold medals. Many classes have been set up to prepare students for the olympiads, especially the International Mathematical Olympiad. These classes have attracted numerous parents, for many colleges compete with one another in seeking to get top performers in the olympiads to enroll as their students. Authorities of Chinese educational agencies are very happy to see that, for it now seems Chinese education is able to compete internationally.

In August 2015, the BBC covered a week-long program of Chinese-style teaching at Bohunt School in Liphook, Hampshire, UK. The result shows that British students were not able to adapt to the Chinese style of intense teaching, while the Chinese teachers were also quite frustrated by the conduct of the British students. It is reported that at one point a girl burst into tears and ran out of the classroom, simply because her idol, Zayn Malik, the British singer, had announced he would leave One Direction, the band he had been with for five years. "It is quite incomprehensible to me that a student should be so sentimental in class," said Ms. Yang, the Chinese teacher teaching that class. There were even problems in physical education class—two British students cried because they were not able to stand the "intense competitiveness" of the Chinese-style PE class. But the Chinese way of teaching, reported British media, did not seem to have moved Neil Strowger, head teacher of Bohunt, who believed the Chinese way of teaching makes one's mind numb and bored.[6]

Chinese critics commented that this showed the cultural differences between the two countries. They failed to realize that the shortcomings in the educational system of China run against not only the law of biological evolution, but also the law of the progress of culture and civilization. From the perspective of cultural anthropology, we can see that play has always been something indispensable in the development of the human individual, and is particularly important for adolescents. How has education in China come to develop in a direction counter to biological evolution and even to the ethics of life? There are many reasons for that at the deep level, but the immediate cause is the severity of competition in contemporary China.

With intense and cruel competition, tremendous pressure, great imbalance of mind and body, and the lack of regular alternation of hard work and relaxation, most of the extracurricular time of Chinese students has been taken up by education oriented toward various examinations. Parents, the school, and society all focus on fostering student "supermen" who can easily handle all kinds of examinations. In order to get higher scores, the student has to spend a great deal of time on rote memory. In an environment devoid of play, they have become slaves to test scores.

In order for their students to obtain better scores, schools have compressed the hours for physical education, art, and music courses to a minimum. This is especially true when graduation draws near, when these courses are basically taken out in many schools. A survey study has shown that in-class time is greatly extended, with 60% of principals of primary schools and headmasters of secondary schools admitting that their students are burdened with a great deal of homework, and have to have eight or more classes a day, with average in-class hours increasing as we go from primary schools to junior high and then to high schools. In some high schools, students have to have 12 classes a day. In addition, teachers often utilize time for noon break and the few minutes between classes to teach

[6] People's Net, "Chinese Teachers Made British Middle-School Students Weep with Their Austerity, but the British Headmaster Was not Impressed," *People's Net*. http://world.people.com.cn/GB/n/2015/0805/c1002-27412610.html. Accessed February 5, 2017.

whole classes of student's additional things. The amount of homework students have to do is excessive. In the past, students used to compete to earn ten or more points, but now, there is often intense competition for one or even half a point. In such circumstances, children and parents alike have come to believe that test scores are the lifeblood of a student.

When test scores have become the "lifeblood" of the students, vigor and creativity are greatly decreased among the youth. A teacher at an eminent university in Beijing once told me that, when she announced in between two class periods[7] that it was break time to a class of more than 30 students, not a single students left his/her seat. Some bent over their desks; some leaned against the walls, while others were still gazing at their textbooks. Shocked by this scene, the teacher said, "You have had class for 50 minutes; you should leave your seats and stretch your legs a little bit." The students replied, "Teacher, we have long been accustomed to remaining in our seats in between classes." When the teacher asked when they had developed such a habit, the students replied that it was from the time when we had to prepare for the entrance examinations to get into high school. From then on, there had been basically no physical education classes, and during the last year the students were in high school, the students had been immersed in the "sea of problems" to be solved in preparation for the college entrance examinations.

As many schools strive to create their "legends of high scores," the children have to pay dearly. An excerpt from a schedule publicized on the Internet by a high school student runs as follows,

5:30 Rise from bed
5:35 Gather at sports field for a short reading period
...
6:40 Breakfast
7:12 First class period begins (each class period is 45 min, a total of 5 class periods are scheduled for the morning, with some jogging exercise between the 3rd and the 4th class periods)
...
12:15 Lunch
12:40 To be back to dormitory and on bed for siesta.
...

[7] In colleges and universities in China, classes are typically organized in such a way that two class periods, usually 50 minutes each, are held consecutively for one course.

13:45 Rise from bed ... and afternoon classes begin (each class period is 45 min, a total of 5 class periods are scheduled for the afternoon)
17:45 Dinner
17:55 Homework after dinner
18:12 To study together with a classmate[8]

Upon learning about the situation of education in China, Westerners are apt to say things like, "This is not how education is conducted. The innate nature of children should be liberated." When students from the No. 2 Middle School of Hengshui heard about this comment, their response was that for the children of people in the lower social strata, like many of those who attend their school, the college entrance examinations are still the sole venue through which to alter their fate.[9] One may at first be surprised that the students themselves would identify with such an educational system, but with a little more reflection, one comes to appreciate the extent to which they have been hurt by the educational inequalities in China.

The author has made some observations of students who have undergone such a process of struggling to get into college. Although some of them have obtained good positions in promising careers, their lives are far from colorful, and also lack a sense of romance and ease, and their supervisors are too likely to be rigid and overly precise. Their emotional energy level is often insufficient for them to go further and achieve more.

A few years ago, an article entitled "It is after 18 years of striving that I am now able to sit with you to drink coffee" appeared. It says,

> Getting into college was the only way by which I could cast off my status as someone from the countryside and escape the fate of being a peasant for life. I fought a hard battle on the narrow path to college. I did not know whether I, as one who had been winning on the way, should feel glad or sad as I saw the path becoming ever narrower and one group after another of my classmates fell on the way. Faced with fierce competition all the way, I dared not be careless. I had no time to cultivate any hobby besides the courses I had to take,

[8] One day's schedule in No. 2 Hengshui School, http://wenda.so.com/ August 2, 2016.

[9] Located in Hengshui County, Hebei Province, this school is well-known for the military style of school management which makes it possible for large numbers of its students to pass the college entrance examinations and enter college every year.

> neither did my school provide any course for us to develop our own interests. But reality is often even more cruel than this—often when you have finally learned to drink coffee after 18 years of striving, others have already switched to the Japanese tea ceremony.[10]

Indeed, for children from poor families, even when they have come to a campus of a top university after much striving, there is still a strong sense of self-abasement in their hearts.

A direct side-effect of large numbers of children growing up in an environment devoid of play is that a significant number of young people "fall in love" and begin to experiment with sex, totally unguided, while they are still in middle school. It has been reported that among Chinese high school students, who are known to be heavily burdened with homework, stealthy sexual activity is on the rise. Mainland China is undergoing a sexual revolution in a decade that is similar to what the Western world had undergone in half a century. The outcome is the alarming rates of increase in induced abortions among youngsters. A national media reported that the number of induced abortions among girls who are 16 or younger has been increasing by about 7% a year. Official statistics of the government, which are doubtlessly conservative, show that there are 13 million induced abortions a year in China, half of which are performed on women below 25 years of age.[11]

At a deeper level, one reason for this situation is the narrowness and prejudice of the standards used to identify talents. In the past, the Chinese had the saying "Of the 360 vocations, everyone can produce its elite," but now parents all want their children to be famous singers, film stars, or big bosses. Another factor is the strong status awareness among the Chinese. Children have paid a very high price for the distorted values of society.

The Working Population: Walking on the Balance Beam

Of those Chinese who are currently employed, the majority fail to find a balance between work and leisure. Heavily burdened, they live a very hard life, exhausted both physically and mentally.

[10] Maizi, "I've been struggling for 18 years to reach the point where I can sit with you for a cup of coffee." http://www.williamlong.info/story/archives/130.html, accessed August 1, 2016.

[11] Yang Haoting, "China's average annual abortion of 13 million people, an increase of over 7% per year," www.news.qq.com , November 24, 2014.

More than a decade ago, this author did a project entitled "A survey on the state of the leisure life of the Chinese, 2004." Data from that survey show that the young and the old of the working population had relatively more leisure time, while middle-aged people had little time for leisure, and employees of enterprises (three kinds of foreign-funded)[12] and private enterprises had the least leisure time.

A decade later, a similar survey conducted by researchers at Sun Yat-sen University showed that from 2012 to 2014, the three kinds of work units with the highest percentages of employees reporting their having worked overtime are enterprises totally or partially invested with foreign funds (52.66%), state-owned enterprises (39.39%), and party and government agencies (37.52%).[13] The average leisure time of the working population remained fairly constant over the decade between the two surveys, but the leisure time possessed by younger employees saw a significant difference. Overall, the patterns revealed by these surveys are quite consistent with the real situation.

The Ant Tribe

The situation of the working population is best exemplified by the so-called "ant tribe" that has been on the rise in recent years. The term refers not to any specific group in terms of age or specialty, but to broad socioeconomic strata that have low income and insecure jobs, including ordinary city dwellers and migrant workers from rural areas who live in crowded residential areas in the cities, and recent graduates of colleges and technical schools who have yet to find stable jobs.

Many belonging to the "ant tribe" come from rural areas. In terms of educational attainments of parents, 49.2% of those interviewed had both parents with educational attainment below junior high, and most of their parents were peasants, who were thus not in a good position to provide the interviewees with adequate financial assistance or social resources to help them along in their career. What is more worth noting is that the majority (81.4%) of those in the "ant tribe" are poor graduates of colleges or junior colleges, with an average monthly income of just more than 4,000 yuan and

[12] The three kinds being foreign-funded enterprises, foreign-invested enterprises, and enterprises with part of their investment from foreign sources.

[13] Cai He, ed., *2015 Report: Chinese Labor Force Survey*, Social Sciences Academic Press (China), 2015, p. 218.

an average size of 6.4 square meters for their residences. Individuals in the "ant tribe" are in an important stage of their life, and according to traditional ideas of China, they are supposed to establish themselves in society. Buying an apartment is the foremost task most of them have to complete in trying to establish themselves, but it places a very heavy burden on them. The forbiddingly high prices for housing have made them afraid to spend, and their emotional energy level is often insufficient for them to go further and achieve more.

Indeed, ownership of housing unit(s) is replacing occupation as the most important factor for social stratification and even solidification of social statuses. A survey has shown that affordable housing is the most urgent need for individuals of the "ant tribe,"[14] who cannot do anything for recreation except equipping their cell phones with WiFi and gaining access to the Internet. Thus it is only these technological devices which are available to meet the need for recreation.

Another survey shows that the four largest cities in China—Beijing, Shanghai, Guangzhou, and Shenzhen—rank among the ten cities where people spend the greatest amounts of time commuting. Beijing led all the other cities with an average commuting distance of 19.20 kilometers and an average of 52 minutes spent on commuting one way. Salarymen tend to live far from the city center, and they are the group that has to endure the most hardship in commuting, with an average commuting distance exceeding 50 kilometers, and an average of 4–5 hours spent on the way to and from their workplaces.[15]

Yanjiao, as an example is a town on the border between the Municipality of Beijing and Hebei Province, where there live hundreds of thousands of people who commute to Beijing to work. Here, dramas of familial affection and bitterness are played out every day. For example,

> Zhang Hongying's family lives in Yanjiao, Hebei. Zhang's daughter works near Beijing Town of World Trade Center. Every day, the 54-year old Zhang would get up at 5:30 and go to line up for her daughter at the station for the morning bus to the center of Beijing. She said, "My daughter is too tired. She was able to find a job in Beijing, but didn't know it would be so hard to work

[14] Lian Si, "Research on the Phenomenon of 'Ant Tribe'," *Administrative Reform*, 2012, No. 1.

[15] Chen Yixin, "Survey in 50 Cities: Commuters on the Road," *China News Net*, January 26, 2015, www.chinanews.com.

at this job. I just take it to be a kind of exercise for me to get up early, and by doing so I can let my daughter sleep half an hour more.[16]

According to statistics by some observers, one may have to wait for up to 40 minutes in order to get onto a bus. It is not difficult to imagine how crowded the buses are.

Most of those in the "ant tribe" have unstable jobs and meager means, but at least they have dreams for the future, for if they had chosen to stay in their hometowns, they would be only bystanders of an age that is undergoing rapid changes. The rule of commercial society is survival of the fittest, but such a society certainly puts one's endurance to the test. Just because it is a test, many of the "ant tribe" chooses to persist. The sentence "Hometown is too small for my dream" reflects well what they have in mind. Thus, the "ant tribe" has the potential to become the major driving force for innovation and entrepreneurship in China as well as for its economic development—but without a leisure life, it would be difficult for them to continue their existence in the biological sense, not to mention finding new inspiration for their entrepreneurship and innovation. The government should pay attention to this problem.

The Middle Class and the Petty Bourgeoisie

The middle class and the petite bourgeoisie, by definition and from what they appear to be, give people the impression that they live a glamorous and fun life. They typically have a good salary and are well-dressed. Most of them are from a good family background and in possession of houses and cars, able to enjoy coffee or tea as part of their daily life, and have holidays and paid leave when they do much traveling. But if we go deep into their spiritual world and see through the appearances, we can have a better and more realistic sense of their real lives. In their own words, they have paid a dear price, shedding many tears and much sweat on the way, to get to where they are today.

Middle-class individuals often have jobs involving office work in technology-related fields. They work as engineers, designers, IT technicians, and medical professionals. Their jobs involve work of a managerial nature, such as finance and accounting, human resource management,

[16] "Mother Queues Up on Behalf of Commuting Daughter so that She Can Have More Time for Sleep," www.news.xinhuanet.com, April 30, 2014.

corporate administration, or assistance to a CEO or a general manager; or work involving writing and designing, such as journalism and editing, translation, copywriting, advertising planning, or general planning. It should be mentioned here that, because the idea of liberal education has been little emphasized, students specializing in these areas have mostly learned only the technical aspects of the work needed in these fields, but generally lack a sound background in the humanities and social sciences. Usually they do not have a good understanding of human nature, of the different personalities of different people, of different interests, or of styles. In order to be able to show to others that they are "successful," they choose to work overtime whenever they can so as to make as much money as possible. Given their means, it is no wonder that they should often talk about the necessity of making money—"By purchasing a housing unit I would have spend all my savings and fall into poverty"; "If just one member in my family has some serious health problem, all the effort I have made to make money would be naught"; "I do not lack money, What I lack is sleep"; "I have no time to get a girl/boyfriend, for all of my time is spent on making money"; "Our lives are like vases that look very pretty, but would fall to pieces upon a single touch"; . . .

In their hearts, they experience much anguish and uncertainty; so, although they have no need to worry about the necessities of life, there is not much color in their lives, which are gloomy in a way, without much that is interesting going on.

Such uneventful and prosaic "middle-class" lives have made middle-class people feel lonely, uninterested in life, and bored. Sometimes they complain a lot about society—for its failing to recognize and appreciate their talents and abilities. They may find it difficult to give vent and expression to their feelings, and thus come to doubt the meaning of their striving. With such a state of mind, there can be little in their life in terms of grace and taste.

Many middle-class people are wary of marriage. They prefer to remain single, which has led, in recent years, to interesting phenomena such as parents urging their son or daughter to get married and parents arranging "blind dates in the park." To cope with their nagging parents, many unmarried young men and young women resort to "renting a girlfriend/boyfriend"[17] when they have to go to see their parents. In the Spring

[17] That is, to pay someone, preferably a stranger, who would pretend to be one's girlfriend/boyfriend so as to give some assurance to one's own parents that "I'm on my way to getting married."

Festival season, the traditional time for family reunion, the amount of girl/boyfriend rental business skyrockets. Prior to the Spring Festival in 2016, the author searched for "girlfriend rental" on Baidu, the largest search engine in China, and obtained more than 9,750,000 results, with a large variety of price tags, such as "20,000 yuan for 7 days" and "1,200 yuan a day, no sharing of bed." The search for "boyfriend rental" yielded about 5,570,000 results. One ad for such rental business read as the following,

> Male, 32, unmarried, high school graduate, 178 cm, 70 kg; residence: Chengdu, Sichuan; honest and upright, no bad habit or addiction; available for rental in the Spring Festival season; you set the price, but you are to bear travel expenses and purchase suitable attire for me. If you are interested, please send a photograph of your resident ID card as proof. Willing to do whatever you want, but no improper thoughts on my part. Being still a virgin, I will not take initiative to cross the boundary. Do not contact unless you are serious.[18]

This ad was viewed by 172,473 people and attracted 1,710,572 replies.

According to the "Report on the Current State of Young People being Urged to Marry" by The Health and Physical Education Development Centre, China National Working Committee for the Care of Children, the survey conducted for the report shows that more than 70% of those interviewed had experienced being urged by parents to get married. The 25–35 age cohort had the greatest pressure in this respect, with 86% of them having had such experience.[19]

The middle class is not a static concept, but one used by people to conceptualize such things as social forces, lifestyles, policy proposals, and economic power, and one that can serve as an indicator of ideological innovation, social stability, and trends of development of culture and civilization. People in the middle class not only have the capacity to generate wealth for society, and to create and enjoy a decent life, but middle-class people can raise themselves to a higher level of existence in the process. They should lead the way to a balanced life with both material and spiritual elements and become the carriers of morality and social justice. Regrettably,

[18] "Is there anyone who would like to rent a boyfriend to go home for the Chinese New Year of 2016?", http://www.kktie.com/article.php?id=4067771&pd=feeling&see=1. Accessed August 5, 2016.

[19] Report on the Current State of Young People being Urged to Marry, *NetEase News*, http://news.163.com/16/0215/03/.

however, the differentiation and fragility of the middle class have diminished the space in which they can play these roles. This leads directly to the depression and dispiritedness felt by many individuals in this class, and indirectly to the lack of innovation and passion for progress in society as a whole.

According to the standard used in China, the country currently has a middle class of about 300 million people, with the middle and upper strata within that class being close to 100 million people, most of whom are higher-level managerial personnel, owners of various enterprises, those who have worked in financial circles for 2–3 years, inventers in the IT industry, film and TV stars, singers, sports stars, undiscovered corrupt officials, real estate speculators, owners of large numbers of stocks, children of the newly rich, and so on. These middle-class, and especially upper-middle-class, people account for the greater part of the leisure consumption of China, such as in the growing number of tours abroad and the purchase of luxury items, luxury cars, mansions, deluxe wristwatches, expensive dresses, and so on. Only about 5% of Chinese hold passports, and most of those who do belong to this social group.

One cannot be very optimistic about the middle class of China, for there is a long way for them to go before they can reach a point where they are able both to balance their own material lives and spiritual lives, and to act as the bearers of morality and social justice. It is this author's opinion that China should try not just to avoid the "middle-income trap," where there will not be enough driving force for economic growth because the transformation of the mode of economic development fails, leading to stagnation of the economy, but also to prevent the lower stratum of the middle class from falling into a mood of gloom, decadence, and frailness, and its middle and upper strata from acquiring the habits of ostentatious display of wealth and of wastefulness, extravagance, presumption and an overbearing attitude, which would lead to the subversion of the social structure and social values.

Employees of Non-Governmental and Private Enterprises

The "Annual Review of Chinese Economy, 2012" provides five sets of data showing: (1) non-governmental enterprises (including small businesses owned by individuals, private enterprises, and collectively owned enterprises) had come to account for more than 90% of the business entities in the country; (2) non-governmental enterprises were employing 85% of the non-agricultural labor force; (3) capital of non-governmental enterprises had come to account for more than 60% of the total capital of enterprises;

(4) non-governmental investment had come to account for more than 60% of the total investment in the country; and (5) the non-governmental economy had also come to account for more than 60% of the total tax revenues of the country.[20] From this, we can see that non-governmental enterprises are a very important force in the development of the Chinese economy. This sector of the economy has played an indispensable role in providing jobs to those who had become unemployed in the reform of state-owned enterprises and in absorbing the surplus labor of the countryside that had migrated to the cities. In the 13th Five-Year Plan, the development of non-governmental enterprises is still a very important part of China's economic strategy.

But unfortunately, the "paid leave" system promulgated by the government can hardly be implemented for the massive number of people employed by the non-governmental sector. When interviewed, people working in this sector said that "paid leave" could hardly be real for them, but were no more than "flowers in the mirror" and "moon in the water." Few enterprises in this sector are so generous as to be willing to grant paid leave to their employees, nor has the government passed any legislation to guarantee their rights to enjoy such leave. They often say self-mockingly, "The law is the law, and rights are rights, but none of them can be turned into money for a family waiting to be fed." In fact, the balance of life and work has always been seriously tilted toward work for this group.

A few years ago, a series of 14 incidents of employees of Foxconn Technology Group jumping off tall buildings to commit suicide attracted the attention of the nation and even of the news media of many other countries.

Within a zone of three square kilometers in the city of Shenzhen, Foxconn employs about 400,000 people, most of who were born in the 1980s and the 1990s. The youngest employees are 16–18 and can be asked to work overtime.

> They must subject themselves to very precise management on assembly lines. They get only one day off a month, and have to work 12 hours a day, with 1 hour in total for their meals. Hours worked in excess of 8 hours are considered overtime. According to investigators, the remuneration the employees get is fairly good, but they all have to work under great pressure.

[20] Chen Yongjie, "The Proportion of China's Private Economy Continues to Rise," www.finance.qq.com, May 18, 2012.

> Roommates do not get to know one another. They are not allowed to talk while working, and the number of welding spots one completes is timed to seconds. A few cadres roam around in the workplace monitoring their work and can choose to test any worker by asking difficult questions or asking them to perform very difficult tasks. Any errors at such tests would entail a deduction in their bonus and other penalties, such as having to write a self-criticizing report confessing one's own mistakes.[21]

Thus, the large number of young people, mostly in their late teens and twenties, seem to be just so many nuts and bolts on the huge machine that is Foxconn. Making money has become the only thing that counts for their status as human agents, their interests, and their vitality, and even the only driving force for their human existence. In order to maintain a life with bare necessities that are devoid of colorful and refreshing qualities, they have to pay not only the price with their youth, but also with alienation of their body and soul. Such alienation, furthermore, is by no means limited to the employees of Foxconn. We can look at a few more cases of the life and work of people in several other vocations.

We all know that taxi drivers spend the greater part of the day in a narrow space of just a little over one square meter, and that this is the case for years on end. It is not difficult to see the state of their work and life—fatigue is their normal lot.

According to a survey of taxi drivers in Beijing, drivers work on average of 14 hours a day, 427 hours a month. The total hours they work a year is equivalent to that for 585, eight-hour workdays, about 2.5 times the work days stipulated by law. A sample of the physical examinations performed on 233 taxi drivers by the Pujing Hospital of Beijing show that 40% of the drivers suffer from prostatomegaly, 38% from hypertension, 32% from obesity, and 31% from hyperlipidemia. Less than 20% of the examination reports show good health in the subjects. From these results, it can be inferred that at least 80% of taxi drivers are in sub-healthy states or keep on working with health problems.[22] Unfortunately, this situation has not been changed in many years.

[21] Pan Yi and Xu Yi, "Monopoly Capital and Chinese Workers: A Case Study of the Employees of Foxconn," BCR (*Cultural Review*), 2012 (2): 48–54.

[22] "The Miserable Life of Taxi Drivers", *Tianya Forum*. bbs.tianya.cn/post-dev, December 8, 2005.

In many private and non-governmental enterprises, the owners and managers, in setting demands on their employees, often do not care about their physical and biological limits. If there are laws or other regulations against their practices, they find many ways to avoid the penalty by bypassing them. Of course, one factor for this situation is that Chinese laws often are not strictly enforced, and labor unions are very weak, often unable really to safeguard the workers' legal rights.

The right to have rest from work is a right citizens should be able to enjoy, but most private enterprises and small businesses hiring small numbers of people have not fully implemented paid leave. The reason for that is not just that there is too much work to allow the employees to have leave, but that in most of these enterprises, the organizational pattern is that only one person is recruited for one post, or even one person for multiple posts. In such cases, even if an employee applies to have a paid leave, his/her boss is likely to reject his/her application using all kinds of pretexts. If the employee insists on going on leave, it is very likely that he/she would lose his/her job. This kind of situation is very common in private enterprises and organizations, as well as in labor-intensive industries.

It has been difficult to implement the system of paid leave mainly among private and non-governmental enterprises. More than 80% of the labor force in China are employed by these enterprises, and because the operation of these enterprises tends to be unstable, there is relatively high risk for their employees to be laid off. Employees of these enterprises have to work very hard to keep their jobs. Although there are laws and governmental rules stipulating fines and other penalties for enterprises that have failed to implement the paid leave system, employees of these enterprises are unwilling to risk losing their jobs by asking for legally granted leave or actively defending their right to have such leave.

For the numerous enterprises distributed on China's land, whether in urban or in rural areas, and whether in the service sector or in industry, employees usually come to the workplace early and leave late, typically working 10–12 hours a day. There are several reasons for this pattern. First, the Chinese people have a cultural tradition of working hard. Secondly, they all hope to make more money to support their families. Third, the enterprises, heavily burdened with various taxes and fees, try to generate more profit by having their employees work long hours so as to offset their expenses. In fact, an important step that should be taken to protect the rights to vacations and leave of those working in non-governmental enterprises would be to reduce the burden of the enterprises by lowering the taxes and fees they have to pay. With such a step, the current situation would be gradually improved. Also, vocational training should be strengthened so as to raise the professional caliber of the employees. Although some effort has been made in that direction, agencies responsible for such training have often made short shrift of it, with their main purpose being to make more profit. There are some governmental agencies engaged in vocational training, but, though they are less bent on profit-making, they are able to provide only a small proportion of the training needed.

Civil Servants

Civil servants are workers in various agencies of governments at all levels. The number of civil servants in China is very large, though the precise number can vary depending on different criteria used. Statistics provided by the government usually cover all those working in public institutions,[23] which number more than 30 million. But some non-governmental agencies have estimated the figure to be as great as 71 million.

Rather than trying to come to an accurate calculation of the number of civil servants in China, the author is more concerned with the physical and mental health of the leaders, administrators, policy-makers, and the "public servants" of the people in the Chinese system, where society is dominated by the state. Proper balance between work and leisure among this group would result in greater efficiency in their work and better public services for society, allowing government officers to be models for the people, as they are expected to be in Chinese culture.

This author would love to see news report of China's national leaders going off on vacation, for such acts of theirs would help government officials of all levels, people from all walks of life, and enterprises of all kinds to realize the importance of leisure, with the common people trying to imitate the leaders. If fact, a few years ago, this author already advocated that China's national leaders should learn from presidents and heads of state in capitalist countries in adhering to the principle "annual leave of absence should never be changed under any circumstances." Although different countries have different cultural traditions and different systems, humans as a species have

[23] Public institution in China means organizations set up by the government and supported with government-controlled resources in fields such as education, science and technology, culture, health, sports, and publishing.

one thing in common—rest, vacation, and leisure are of vital importance for sustaining the body and the mind.

Earlier we mentioned that, in China, a job with the government has been the dream of the vast majority since very early times in history, and this pattern has continued to this day. Today, government officials profess to be "public servants of the people," but in fact they are high above common people in social status. Why are they able to enjoy such high status? First, they have a great deal of power. An official just one rank above another would enjoy overwhelming power over the latter. Secondly, a government job makes one feel dignified. Thirdly, government jobs come with very good benefits. Fourthly, government jobs entail a steady income. Fifthly, if but one member of a family enters the officialdom, the whole family would be raised high above others. Although paid leave may not be available every year because civil servants can also be rather busy, nevertheless they are often able to go on tours to nice places in the name of conducting some kind of official business. And there are also some civil servants who are able to "muddle along for a day with a cup of tea and a pack of cigarettes." Cadres and leaders of government agencies at all levels are likely to entertain or be entertained at banquets on a daily basis. Some of them take advantage of their positions to trade power for monetary gains or sexual favors, to cultivate their own cliques, or to build various "connections" that can be utilized for their own personal gain when needed. This kind of conduct on the part of the cadres and leaders not only works to corrupt the ethos of the government and the CCP, but has greatly contributed to the rent-seeking, speculation, and frivolity that permeate the whole society, resulting in the decrease in the public trust of government and resistance to the implementation of government decrees. In the most scenic sites in a given region of the country, there are likely to be mansions, villas, golf courses, and so forth, which provide occasions for the exchanges between government officials, with their power, and merchants, with their money, in the course of the "leisure" and "recreation" enjoyed by government leaders and cadres. The vast majority of officials who have been found guilty of corruption have had extramarital affairs: some of their mistresses are partially or fully supported by the officials, and others may even be clandestinely kept as a second wife. Some officials have had not just one or a few, but rather have had a large number of mistresses, and they pursue their pleasures with their mistresses not only in their free time, but even when they are supposed to be at work.

High officials have great power, and petty officials have lesser power, but even those who do not have official positions can manage to garner significant benefits for themselves. Individuals as low as a village head or a director of a neighborhood committee, positions with the lowest ranks in the giant administrative machine, have been found to have embezzled or receive as bribes tens, or even hundreds, of millions of yuan. An important consequence of the rampant corruption in officialdom is its misguidance of leisure life. As the saying goes, "When those high above act in a crooked way, those in lower positions would follow suit." Corruption among government officials has led to corruption of the ethos of society, to misguidance provided by the news media and the entertainment circles on values, and to the distortion of attitudes with respect to values among the younger and more inexperienced generation.

It is against such a background that, from the very beginning of his administration, President Xi Jinping has been warning officials that "a thing has to be rotten first before worms can eat their way into it" and stressing that "if corruption is allowed to go unchecked and become more and more serious, the end result must be the demise of the Party and of the socialist state of China."[24]

Now, with Xi's anti-corruption campaign in full swing, officials in large cities have been restrained to some degree under the great pressure it has generated, but in many remote regions, the effect of the campaign is rather limited. In late 2015, two years after the campaign was launched, about 300,000 party and government officials, in positions high and low, were found guilty of infringing on the disciplinary requirements with regard to "four unhealthy ways," namely: formalism, bureaucratism, hedonism, and wasteful extravagance.

After the stringent anti-corruption campaign was launched, hidden benefits for civil servants in China were decreased, and the "iron rice bowl"[25] they have had is being changed into a "clay rice bowl." The central government has set forth the requirements that work efficiency has to be raised, that civil servants should not forget that they are there to be "servants to the people," that the number of personnel in various government agencies are to be reduced; the scope of government power is to be narrowed, and so

[24] Xi Jinping: "If corruption is allowed to become more and more serious, it will eventually lead to the demise of the Chinese Communist Party and the Chinese State," www.news.hexun.com/2012-11-29.

[25] This terms refers to the job security of people employed by government agencies, state-owned enterprises, or public institutions supported with government funds, for it is very rare for these employees to lose their jobs.

on. The central government also requires that civil servants should spend their free time with their family or in reading, rather than frequenting expensive clubs or going to banquets.

Common people have enthusiastically applauded the anti-corruption efforts of the Xi administration. Officials at various levels of the government, on the other hand, have very mixed feelings about it, for it has become more and more difficult for them to lord it over others or to use their power for personal gain. They have been using many strategies to cope with the implications of the campaign. In many places, officials who have been restrained from garnering benefits for themselves by exercising their power, have now chosen to behave in ways that make things difficult for other people instead. Government functioning is now less affected by favoritism and "face," but nonfeasance has become more widespread. Some leading cadres have professed loudly that they take the anti-corruption campaign seriously, but have nevertheless continued to delay taking real action. These phenomena have unfortunately lowered people's expectations of what can be achieved through the campaign and thus greatly weakened its positive effects.

In 2014, the magazine *People's Forum* organized surveys centered on two questions: (1) what do officials worry about, what are they unhappy about, and what are they afraid of when they try to do things? (2) With the anti-corruption campaign undertaken with great determination by the government, what conduct of officials should be tolerated, and what should never be? A total of 12,156 people responded to the questionnaires, and the results can set us thinking: 64.4% of the respondents believed that currently officials were most afraid of "anything unusual happening in their work," and they believed officials had a widespread mentality of wanting to "act in ways that would allow them to ride out the campaign while maintaining stability." In other words, the overwhelming spirit is: "do not upset the apple-cart." This attitude has obviously limited the initiative of officialdom. Further, 78.8% of the respondents believed that the greatest worry officials had was that "someone's interest would be touched if I try to do things, and it is very easy for me to offend others"; and 73.1% of respondents believed officials did not have enough motivation for doing things.[26]

[26] "A Survey on the Mentality of Government Officials", *People's Forum*, 2014, No. 19.

However, it is no easy matter to change in a short time the age old ideas of "the primacy of the officials" and "the administrative dominance model" that have been built up through millennia.

Doctors

Doctors have been seen as angelic and as saviors for the patients. But in recent years, there has been a great deal of tension between doctors and hospitals on the one hand, and patients and their families on the other. There have been many incidents of doctors being injured or even killed by patients or their relatives. How have doctors, who are supposed to be the patients' saviors, become targets of the wrath of patients and their relatives? After working in a hospital for a few years, a graduate from the surgery department of an eminent medical school decided to abandon medicine and go into some other field. Before he did that, he posted an article on the Internet, in which he explaines:

> A doctor of a key section of a major hospital sees more than 100 patients on a single morning. So for how many minutes can a patient get the doctor's attention? How can the quality of the doctor's diagnosis be ensured? . . . On holidays, a doctor in China is likely to become all the busier. Even if he really does have the day off, he has to make the rounds of the wards. For surgeons, the work schedule is even more irregular. For key sections of a relatively large hospital, doctors often have to go for many years without much rest. Besides their medical work, they have to apply for funding for various research projects, write papers, do research, teach courses, make all sorts of preparation for promotion opportunities, go to conferences, write books, translate articles, and so on. Perhaps the only kind of time when they can relax a little is to tour some nearby places when they are at a conference.[27]

From this description, we come to see the extremely busy work schedules of these doctors, who are supposed to be decent, noble, and respectable. Being so busy with their work, how can they have enough time to have rest and thus to have enough physical and mental energy to do their work properly, or to really do worthwhile research in their field?

This author once had some experience with this kind of problem. I went to a large hospital and, seeing that there were too many patients there, I

[27] Han Xiaotian, "The Present Situation in China the Doctor–Patient Relationship," October 5, 2011, http://club.china.com/data.

registered to see a famous doctor as someone in need of special attention. The registration fee was a hundred times that for regular registration, but I was willing to pay it, hoping I would have a better environment in which to seek medical help. However, the situation of the consulting room of that doctor was actually very bad. The corridor outside the room was very disorderly, filled with people who were waiting to see the doctor, and in the room itself, which was about 20 square meters, the doctor was surrounded by more than ten patients and their relatives who accompanied them. In such a situation, there was neither much respect for the doctor, nor any protection for the patients' privacy. When my number was called, I saw how bad the situation was and asked to have my registration cancelled. Some patients around me tried to persuade me to stay, saying, "It's not easy to be able to get registered to see the director of the hospital, so it is better that make do with it. As veteran patients, we are used to this kind of situation." I glanced toward the director-doctor and saw he was answering the patient's questions succinctly, diagnosing one patient's problem in less than five minutes. I felt clearly that he was very tired and trying to restrain himself so as not to show his fatigue. Suddenly, I felt very sorry for him. Later, I learned that he was not only an associate director of the hospital, but also an academician. It pains one's heart that a doctor with his status had to work under such conditions. Of course, this is not an exceptional case, but the "normal" state of affairs at all large hospitals. Small wonder then that many of those Chinese who can afford it would choose to go to countries where medical care is more developed, such as the USA, Great Britain, Germany, Singapore, and South Korea, to get treatment, spending on average around 150,000 USD per person. About 70% of those who go abroad for medical care suffer from some kind of tumor.[28]

Take pediatricians as an example. According to statistics, in China there are only 0.34 pediatricians per thousand children. On the one hand, there are the parents complaining about their having to stay in line for four or five hours in order to get three minutes' attention for their children; on the other hand, many interns from medical schools who have had clinical experience try to "escape the pediatrics section" because of the high risk involved in working there while the return is low for pediatricians.

[28] "Why more and more Chinese people choose to go abroad for health care?" http://www.jrzj.com/, June 6, 2015.

In recent years, students who want to study medicine in college often find their parents, relatives, and friends are opposed to their idea. This phenomenon is quite widespread. Many medical school students change to other professions once they graduate, because in the medical profession people have to work very hard in bad environments, while the income one can get is rather limited.

Educational Professionals

Important cultural features of the Chinese people have traditionally included "veneration for teachers and emphasis on education" and exhibiting China to be "a land of decorum." From ancient times there are many examples of records noting these cultural traits. The ancient Chinese said, "Each human being has three kinds of people whom he is to venerate—his ruler, his father, and his teacher(s)."[29] And as the Tang Confucian Han Yu put it, the role of the teacher is to pass on knowledge about the Way to the student, to help the student learn a profession, and to dispel the student's doubt and confusion. Teachers are revered because they are "well learned and thus can serve as models for others to emulate." But since the 1990s, changes have taken place quietly among teachers as a group. In a greatly commercialized society, they face great challenges both in trying to remain well-learned and in trying to maintain their uprightness. Here, we will dwell neither on the increasingly disharmonious relationships among teachers and the students and their parents, nor on the extent, which leaves much to be desired, to which teachers are able to play their role as the mainstay in an educational system helping to enhance the abilities of the people and make the nation cultured. Instead, we will focus on the current state of teachers' life and work out of our concern for these "engineers of human souls."

In real life, most teachers in colleges and universities are heavily burdened with teaching, research, doing projects, writing papers for publication, and translating books. Insufficient achievement in any of these areas would mean one cannot be promoted to associate professor or full professor, or even be able to keep one's job as a teacher. If one cannot be promoted to associate professor or full professor, one would not only have low salary and

[29] The "Feng Gongjue" chapter of *Bai Hu Tong* (*Discourse on General Virtues at the White Tiger Hall*) explains the phenomena of nature, society, ethics, life and daily life, has a certain influence on the human nature theories. The text was written by Ban Gu in the Eastern Han Dynasty.

benefits, making it difficult for one to provide for one's family, but one would also lose "face" among colleagues and friends. Most college and university teachers are deeply concerned with their professional rank, and that is why they can hardly have any rest under the heavy pressure in those five areas.

Those who have been promoted to professors or have made their name in some academic field are likely to be in a hurry all the time, going to different places to give talks, both to increase their fame and to earn extra money, both of which are quite enticing for most teachers.

Teachers who are from the older generation usually do not have doctorates, which makes it difficult for them to become full professors. In order to become full professors, a doctorate is a must. So, quite a large number of these teachers have to apply to programs of graduate study when they are well into their forties. Unfortunately, they have to do their graduate studies at the same time as keeping up with their own teaching duties and family responsibilities. It is not hard to imagine what strains they are working under, both physically and mentally.

According to the "Report Based on a Survey on Young Teachers at Institutes of Higher Learning,"[30] young teachers at colleges and universities, although a group with the highest educational attainment, with almost 90% of them having doctoral degrees, are also a group under heavy pressure. Of the respondents, 72.3% confessed they are under "heavy pressure," with 36.3% believing they are under "very heavy pressure." According to the respondents, the pressure comes mainly from three areas—the demanding research tasks, the heavy workload in teaching, and the low income level. "Research tasks are the greatest source of pressure."

Because most institutes of higher learning have linked promotion in professional rank to quantified indices such as number of papers published, number of books published, and number of research grants, 78.1% of the young teachers responded that they "did not have enough time" for their research tasks.

Many of the young teachers surveyed had not been long at their jobs in colleges and universities and have relatively low income and professional ranks. It is difficult for them to get grants, partly due to their low ranks, but nevertheless expenses for a wedding, for the purchase of a housing unit and

[30] "The First Survey Report on the Life Situation Young Faculty Members in Colleges and Universities Has Been Released," *China Youth Daily*, September 14, 2012.

car, for the education of their children, and for supporting their parents are also concentrated in this stage of their life. Many of them have had to undertake a second job, teaching courses at some other institutions or at some special training programs, or accepting various projects, in order to make ends meet. In this survey, 14.2% of the respondents reported that remuneration from their second jobs was actually their major source of income. In addition, colleges and universities of all kinds are not transforming into a system of having contracts signed between their faculty members and the school, and if the performance of a faculty member fails to meet the requirements of the school, he/she can be fired.

Data from the *Report on the Social Progress of Beijing* show that the number of young teachers below 40 years of age in colleges and universities in China exceeds 860,000, and accounts for 63.3% of the total number of teachers in these institutes of higher learning. Differences in income are very large in this group. In 2010, the lowest total income for professors was 49,500 yuan, while the highest was 797,000 yuan; and the lowest for associate professors was 28,000 yuan, while the highest was 570,000 yuan. The commercialization of the profession of teaching has to some extent negatively impacted the enthusiasm young teachers may have had for their teaching and research work, for much of their attention is now focused on the market.[31]

One may ask why there is so much difference in the income of college and university teachers. We can find part of the answer by looking at one case:

> A few days ago, Song Chang, who is currently a professor at the business school of People's University of China but who also serves as an independent director for 4 listed corporations, became suspect of inside trading and short-swing trading, and China Securities Regulatory Commission (CSRC) has put his case on file for investigation. *BEIH-Property Financial Report* shows that Song receives a salary of 60,000 *yuan* from BEIH. In addition, he is also independent director for K-bird and Feilihua, with annual salaries of 180,000 and 100,000 *yuan*, respectively.[32]

[31] Zhang Xiaohong & Li Qi, "A Survey Shows Young Teachers in Colleges and Universities Have High Pressure but Low Income," *Jinghua Times*, June 29, 2013.

[32] Zou Wei, "Song Chang, a Professor of the People's University of China, is Suspect of Inside Trading, Having Purchased BEIH Stocks through Irregular Channels," *Phoenix Finance*, January 25, 2016. http://finance.ifeng.com/a/20160125/14187638_0.shtml. Accessed September 18, 2016.

Of course, this is only the tip of the iceberg for the phenomenon of "high-salary professors."

The situation for primary and secondary school teachers is similar. In particular, with the great emphasis placed on test scores by the whole society, teachers in primary and secondary schools have to lead their students through the immense difficulties of test preparation, with the teachers for the graduating class having the worst lot, having to work their students hard all day long. These teachers have to work under tremendous pressure, for the percentage of their students enrolling in the higher level of schools and that of their students earning high scores are hard indices used to measure their performance. If they fail to meet the requirements of the school, their professional rank, opportunities for promotion and salary increase would all be affected. Some teachers who are less than conscientious have been found to refrain from teaching certain knowledge or methods to their students but ask them to pay an extra fee to go to tutorials after their classes at school. In doing that, such teachers have not just made money from the students in a very problematic way, but, by having the students spend much of their time on those classes and on the way to and from those classes, they have deprived the students of leisure time that could be used to develop their own interests. The worst effect such conduct has is the doubt it casts on the students' young hearts.

Migrant Workers

In one sense, migrant workers are also employees, but they are distinctive enough as a group that it is worth discussing their situation separately. In China, most migrant workers come from rural areas, and hold jobs that are relatively flexible. Some of them seasonally alternate between a job in the city and farm work at home. Another set of migrant workers keeps moving from city to city. A small number of migrant workers come from abroad.

In this section, we focus on one kind of the migrant labor force in China, namely, the migrant "peasant workers." In 2010, this author conducted a "Survey on the State of the Leisure Life of Peasant Workers." In the following I will describe what I found at that time; and then try to analyze how conditions have changed in the five years since then.

As is well-known, China has benefited greatly from the rise of the tremendous labor force of peasant workers in her modernization and urbanization during the last three decades. According to statistics provided by government authorities, there are currently about 270 million peasant workers in China, who are an important part of the industrial labor force, making up the greater part of the human power that drives the engine for "Made in China." But how much time do they have for rest and recreation after their hard work? My survey yielded "Eight Zeroes" as the results characterizing the state of their leisure life, as shown below[33]:

(1) The leisure time of peasant workers in their daily life is almost zero. When they saw the theme of our survey was "leisure life," almost all of them replied in a similar way, "If we are to have leisure, how can we make enough money?" This is especially true for those who worked on lower-end jobs, such as those who sell vegetables, those who clean the streets and collect garbage, and those who deliver take-outs for restaurants. These groups often have to get up very early in the morning and work until about midnight; sometimes they do not even have enough time for their biological needs, such as sleep. During holiday seasons, they become all the busier. It would be very unrealistic to expect that they would have time to cultivate their interests and tastes.

(2) Of the little time peasant workers have for leisure life, the amount devoted to cultural pursuits and spiritual life is almost zero. Most respondents reported that they had never bought any books. Some young peasant workers do go to theaters once in a while to enjoy drama, music, or singing and dancing. Some respondents said they, too, would like to go to theaters to see those performances, but have to save money and time. In recent years, college graduates have been having difficulty finding jobs, and a new version of the view that "education is useless" has had a quite negative effect on the children of peasant workers. When asked whether they would like to continue their education, the vast majority of these children gave a negative reply. When asked what they would do in their free time, they would say joyfully, "Oh, we like to read gossip in the media to while away the time."

(3) Peasant workers have almost zero understanding of the concept of cultural pursuits in leisure life. The word "leisure" has come to be widely used in rural as well as in urban areas of China, but in the

[33] Ma Huidi, "'Eight Zeros': The Worry on the Leisure Life of Migrant Workers in China," *Studies on Mao Zedong and Deng Xiaoping's Theories*, 2010, No. 12.

understanding of the peasant workers the term basically means "to eat, drink, and make merry," an understanding which is similar to that of the common run of urban residents. They thought it was something quite novel when we tried to explain that leisure has to do with the cultivation of one's own interests and tastes, the discovery of one's own potential, and the upgrading of one's attainments in cultural spheres. When we mentioned that in the past people in rural areas also adhered to ancestral admonitions that it should be made a family tradition to have children well educated and to have them read books alongside farm work, the older people among the peasant workers would have a wry smile and say, "Well, everyone knows it would be nice to have a good education, but education is expensive. As it is, leisure is not important to us. What is important is to make more money." And the younger ones would say, "Regardless, it is a nice thing that the society has now provided us with the opportunity to come to the city to work and make some money." Complacency seems to be widespread among peasant workers.

(4) There is nearly zero participation in community activities. Many peasant workers have lived in a neighborhood for quite a few years, but few of them are actively taking part in community activities. They reported, "First we don't have time for it. Then we are rarely taken into account in the planning of community activities." They are largely estranged from their communities. The peasant workers seem hardly connected to the community except when they have to deal with neighborhood committees in matters of family planning and education for their children. On their part, they generally tend to have low self-esteem and feel estranged from urban residents; but it is indeed a fact that they are marginalized for the planning of community work, and seldom taken into consideration when it comes to the allocation of resources for public service.

(5) The degree to which they are integrated into the city is almost zero. Peasant workers have been trying, through hard work, to earn an income higher than what they can have in the countryside, so they have entered the city, often bringing their families with them. They believe that the lifestyle, the quality of the people, and the level of civilization of the cities are all superior to that in the countryside. Although they have come to the city aiming to make more money and improve their lives, they have failed really to understand and to appreciate urban life and to integrate into urban culture, due to limitations in their knowledge, ability, skills, and habits of thinking.

It is very common for their living environments to be found dirty and disorderly, and they often live in rooms with very little space. Those who have managed to be on good terms with their landlords may have some interaction with them, but most of the peasant workers believed that "in their heart city-dwellers look down upon us."

(6) The peasant workers have basically zero concept that they need to have rest and recuperate after hard work. Many respondents said, "When we have work to do, that means we can make money. The worst thing for us is to be without work to do." Many of them have very little time for rest, to the extent that they are going against the laws of biology. One gets the feeling that they are ready to give anything to make money. We conducted some in-depth interviews with people who were selling vegetables on the market. They told us that they have to get up at 2:00 or 3:00 a.m. to go to the distant wholesale market for vegetables. They go to the wholesale market, which is far away from the retail market in order to get fresher and nicer looking produce which they can sell at slightly higher prices. The retail vegetables market is open for 12 hours a day, running from 7:00 a.m. to 7:00 p.m. The stalls at the market are operated mainly by families, so the family members have to work at least 12 hours a day, with the one responsible for procuring vegetables from the wholesale market having to work more than 15 hours. And it is not that they work such long hours only occasionally; they typically go on like this for months or even the whole year on end.

(7) The amount of free time spent with children is nearly zero. Many young and middle-aged peasant workers have brought their children to the city to be brought up while the parents continue to work. A small percentage of the peasant workers are able to send their children to day-care centers, but the children are left to themselves after they return from the centers, and on weekends. Usually they play with older children of the neighbors, without any parental attention. Some parents take their children to where they work. Many parents say, "How can we have any time to play with the kids? It's true that we are spending a great deal of time working, but aren't we trying to make more money so that they can get a better education?" From our survey, we learnt that some peasant workers have two children to a family, but few of them have both children with them in the city. Typically, they would leave one child at their

home in the countryside, and with that child the major means of communication is the telephone.

(8) There are basically zero channels for them to appeal to the government with their needs. Many a respondent said, "The fee for the stall is too high. We rise early and go to bed late and work long hours in between, but more than half of what we earn goes to the various fees collected by the government." The rent for a stall of about ten square meters is about 40,000 yuan a year, and after a whole year of hard work, the net income they can earn from a stall is only 20,000 to 30,000 yuan. Some peasant workers work at stations for garbage recycling, which helps to protect the environment of the neighborhood. But not only do they get no help or support from the neighborhood, they also have to pay 5,000 yuan a year as an "administrative fee." "The taxes and fees are too high, but there is no one to speak on our behalf," complained these peasant workers. It is true that there were three representatives from peasant workers in the 11th National Congress of the People, but that is too small a number relative to the more than 200 million peasant workers.[34]

How much has the leisure life of the peasant workers changed since our survey was conducted five years ago? Data from the most recent survey shows that the only change is that the average monthly wage has increased to 3,100 yuan,[35] while the situation has remained essentially unchanged. Toward the end of each year, we still see many news reports of peasant workers undertaking to demand payment of the wages their employers owe them. The large number of peasant workers full of complaints has greatly challenged the government's credibility and capacity for law enforcement.

Although the central government has kept on stressing the importance of problems related to rural areas, to agriculture, or to peasants by having them as the issues for the very first directive it promulgates every year, and has been giving subsidies to peasants for planting crops for many years now, peasants are still getting meager incomes after a year of hard labor. Because of that, there are still many peasants who are willing to leave their family and

[34] A total of 2,987 Representatives were elected to the Eleventh National Congress of the People in January 2008.

[35] "Income Increase Slowed Down for Migrant Workers," www.news.xinhuanet.com, February 28, 2015.

their land in the countryside to go into the cities. However, as China undertakes to adjust its industrial structure, the peasant workers say "It is becoming more and more difficult to find jobs and make money."

The gap between the harsh reality in the countryside and the dreams they have about life in the city has created a unique dilemma for the peasant workers in China—the cost to live in the city is too high, while the countryside is becoming ever more distant and unfamiliar to them.

Whatever the case, free time is an important component of human life and as a category belongs to the same level as that of work. Without leisure there would be no work, for without high quality leisure it would be impossible to foster high quality workers for society or to let the cultural strength of a nation accumulate.

China has been urbanizing for three decades, and a total of close to 300 million peasants have come to the city in search of jobs. In the years to come, a few hundred million peasants are going to become city dwellers. Enabling them to get integrated into city life and to live decent lives with dignity will raise new issues and pose new challenges for the structure, the organization, the management, and the welfare system of urban society, and will also present challenges for the psychology of the nation.

The Elderly

The most recent statistics provided by the national government show that by the end of 2014, there were 212.42 million Chinese, or 15.5% the total population of the country, who were above 60 years of age; 137.55 million, or 10.1% the total population, who were above 65; and 21.32 million, or 12.25% the total number of the elderly, who were above 80. It is projected that by 2020, the number of elderly people in China will exceed 200 million, and by 2050 it will exceed 400 million.[36] Here, it is necessary to give a demographic analysis of the elderly population.

Rural Elderly

China has a history of being an agrarian society for millennia, which gave birth to an agrarian cultural tradition that espoused "learning and honesty as

[36] Kou Jiangze, "Megadata Show that the Number of China's Elderly 60 Years of Age or Older Reached 212 Million, or 15.5% or the Total Population, in 2014," *People's Daily*, June 17, 2015.

qualities that would help perpetuate the family." The basic agrarian lifestyle was "starting work at sunrise, ending work at sunset, cooking meals using water from a well, and obtaining food by plowing the fields." This is also an accurate description of the "unity of humans and nature" of the agrarian society—people not only become partners with Mother Earth in their hard work aimed to ensure abundance in foot and clothes, but have evolved a unique agrarian leisure lifestyle, with family schools, womanly work, and various aspects of worship incorporated into it that both help to comfort the soul and expand one's knowledge and to make life enriched and joyful.

In traditional China, due to the underdeveloped material life, classical works passed down from the ancestors were the best comic relief and spiritual nourishment. The maxims in short, pithy books of wisdom, together with the extensive body of books in Confucian classics, history, philosophy of different non-Confucian schools, and collections of works by individual authors became an important part of people's lives, helping them to cultivate themselves and to practice in accordance with the moral admonitions they had received. The wisdom and knowledge of the ancients were also condensed into textbooks for children, such as *the Book of Family* Names (《百家姓》), *Three character primer* (《三字經》), and *The Thousand Character Classic* (《千字文》), which were widely circulated because the contents were in simple language, easy to read, understand, and recite. These books also provided a kind of moral education, and putting into practice what they have learned from these books became an important part of the leisure life experience of most families.

This tradition was gradually in decline until after the founding of New China. At present, most people of the older generation (60 or above in age) grew up in a milieu of traditional culture, but they have also experienced the tremendous changes of modern times. In the last three decades, the massive flow of peasant workers into the city has brought great changes to the temporal-spatial structure of most families in rural areas, and thus important changes in their family structure and life structure.

With the rise of rural enterprises in the 1990s and the "New Countryside Movement"[37] that started later, most local governments, in order to raise the areas under their administration out of poverty, have been promoting development programs that would bring rapid and great changes. With the rise of

[37] A similar formulation has been used many times since the 1950s, like the New Countryside Movement, which aimed at changing the backwardness of rural areas.

wave after wave of wealthy families, leisure lifestyles have also been modernized. Public baths, saunas, *mahjong* parlors, and sex-toy shops are seen everywhere, and many scenic sites have been developed for tourism. In recent years, some elderly people have learned to use cell phones in order to keep in contact with children who have left their hometown in search of jobs, but there are very few elderly people who are good at using computers and the Internet. Currently, the Chinese government has been promoting the "Internet +" policy in an attempt to stimulate economic development in rural areas. People in rural areas, mostly the young and middle-aged who have returned to their hometown from the city, are encouraged to learn skills for using the Internet.

President Xi Jinping, in talking about the direction for future rural development, said, "We have to retain the green mountains and clear waters in rural areas so that people from these areas will always long to return to their beautiful hometown." Most of the elderly who are in the early stage of their life in old are caring for their grandchildren whose parents have gone into the city as migrant workers. They still enjoy a life with grandchildren around, an ideal for people in their old age in traditional China. But for most such rural families, there are only grandparents and grandchildren, with the generation in between having left home for the city. Therefore, it is necessary to have a look at *the left-behind children*[38] mentioned earlier in this chapter.

According to government statistics, there are 61 million *the left-behind children*. Research has shown that children with both parents absent are the largest group, accounting for 51.7% the total; those with only the father absent are the second largest group, accounting for 40.2% the total; and those with only the mother absent are the smallest group, accounting for 8.1% the total. There are nine million children who get to see their parents less frequently than once a year.[39]

The consequence of this is that, because the children are taken care of by their grandparents and because parental care is missing, these children tend to show apathy, have low self-esteem, feel lonely, and close their inner world to others. Some of them become delinquent at a young age. At the same time, the elderly women among the grandparents are burdened with great pressure because the labor intensity involved in taking care of their grandchildren is

[38] Left-behind children, refers to the parents or one party to go out to work, they are generally left with other relatives and friends, and even parents of other relatives, friends living together.

[39] Gui Jie: "Whitebook on the Mental State of Left-Behind Children in China Released," www.news.cyol.com/content, June 18, 2015.

high, the psychological burden is heavy, and they lack a sense of security. The author of a blog post reported seeing such a set of data that gave details that "of the elderly people, who stay home, more than 82% have to continue to work in the field, 90% have to take care of their grandchildren, 89% do not have any savings, and there are no family members to care for them when they are sick."[40] And, "in a family in Shuangfeng County, Hunan Province, there was only an old woman with a granddaughter less than two years old, since the little girl's parents had both gone to the city to work. The old woman died, and for 7 days, only the little girl was around guarding her body."[41] Such scenes of misery are by no means a rarity, and incidents of suicide, of rape, and of women or children being abducted to be sold elsewhere by criminals do occur from time to time for such families.

Currently, the ratio of old people 60 or more years of age to *the left-behind children* is approximately 1:1. Upon returning to his hometown, a *drifter in Beijing*[42] wrote in a blog, "Walking on the road, I saw few people; and of those I saw, it was rare to find one who is young and in his/her prime. In all the villages around, there are basically no men or women under 50 years of age. Those who work the fields were, without exception, old people. While working in the fields, some of the old people have one or two kids on the ridge. After the night falls, the village sinks into a dead silence except for occasional barking of dogs."[43]

As we mentioned earlier, it used to be an ideal of family life in traditional China for old people to have young kids around them, but although this is still true today, it is far from the traditional scene with "four generations under one roof," but one of gloom and sadness. This phenomenon has attracted the attention of the national government, which is trying to pass legislation for building and perfecting a mechanism to provide support to young children

[40] "An Incredibly Desolate Scene Similar to That Resulting from Destruction by War Has Appeared in Some Rural Areas in China," *Tianya Community*, January 2, 2014. http://bbs.tianya.cn/post-free-4053030-1.shtml. Accessed February 6, 2017.

[41] An Qi, "Suggestions on Improving the Living Conditions of the Left Behind Children and the Left Behind Elderly in Rural Areas", October 14, 2011. Website for the Political Consultative Conference of Shanghai Municipality. shszx.eastday.com/.

[42] "Drifter in Beijing," means someone who wants to work in Beijing but, without a steady job, is likely to move often, trying to find housing that is suitable for his/her means, as he/she works on and off at different jobs.

[43] "An Incredibly Desolate Scene Similar to That Resulting from Destruction by War Has Appeared in Some Rural Areas in China," *Tianya Community*, January 2, 2014. http://bbs.tianya.cn/post-free-4053030-1.shtml. Accessed February 6, 2017.

and to old people who were left behind in rural areas when young people went to the city. However, such a mechanism cannot be built in a short time, and we have yet to see any real effect from the government's effort.

The elderly who are in a later stage of their life in old age still retained a lifestyle with an approach to leisure that includes elements of "meticulous cultivation of land" and "finding company in a natural way." The skills they had when young find expression in tending flowers and grass in horticulture. At set times of different seasons of the annual cycle; they worship heaven and earth or the ancestors at family temples, and manage family affairs. In relatively remote areas, this kind of life still continues for many elderly people. If the tradition of "family learning" continues or if the family still holds books of classics, history, philosophy, and literature inherited from the past, the elderly can still live a serene life. Investigation and observation by sociologists show that elderly people much advanced in age tend to have kept to this kind of lifestyle throughout their lives.

These elderly people are accustomed to hard work and a simple life, and have trouble with fashionable and boisterous modern life. This author has had opportunities to visit many elderly men and women in remote areas in southern Anhui, Guangdong, Guangxi, Zhejiang, and Fujian provinces, and was able to see and appreciate the serenity in their leisurely life.

Although it has been quite a few decades since the New Countryside Movement was first started, infrastructure is still very backward in many rural areas, with hardly any recreational facilities for the elderly or for children. In the slack season for farm work, the elderly and children are especially bored and lonely, with TV the only possible channel for some amusement. However, investigators have found that most elderly people have slight interest in TV, for they are not used to the "motionless" way of leisure such as watching TV, and believe one will become lazy and sick that way. The older generation of elderly people usually spends their free time basking in the sun or chatting with neighbors in the courtyard or at the corners of the houses, or they may invite some relatives and neighbors for a few rounds of *mahjong* or *gomoku*. In the summer and the autumn, people's lives seem to be richer and more colorful because there is much to do in the fields.

In traditional China, most villages had their own stages, and migrant troupes came to perform from time to time. That was the time when the villagers were the happiest. This kind of rural life provided fertile soil for Chinese drama to grow. At its height, Chinese drama comprised more than 400 local genres, which nurtured a large number of folk performing artists who brought much fun and vitality to life in rural China. Currently, many local areas are trying to restore this tradition. Up to today, the 24 solar seasons (see Chap. 2) of the agrarian society of traditional China are still very important and very interesting for people in rural areas. They form a rhythm that not only guides people's farm work, but also provides many occasions for festivities for all.

According to the traditional lunar calendar of China, there are 24 solar terms of celestial patterns, which not only serve to indicate seasonal changes and guide the annual cycle of agricultural activities, but also mark days on which people worship various deities and the spirits of ancestors. The most solemn festivals on the lunar calendar are the Spring Festival (Chinese New Year), the Lantern Festival, the Dragon Boat Festival, and the Double Ninth Festival. On these holidays, old people put to work the skills they have inherited from their forebears to create art works such as paper-cuts, New Year paintings, dough figurines, decorated kids' shoes and clothes, embroidery, and so on. These festivals are also occasions for worshipping Mother Nature, for giving thanks to the heavens, for praying to gods for favorable weather for the crops and for bountiful harvests, and for the worship of ancestors to cultivate the relationship among different generations and the continuation of the family line and family traditions.

To take the Spring Festival for an example. During the Spring Festival season, a series of traditional activities, such as worshipping the heavens, worshipping ancestors, ending the previous year and planning for the new year to come, and maintaining the collective consciousness of the lineage groups, are undertaken, all centered on family reunion. The Spring Festival has a history of two millennia in China, and has become a common national symbol, a carnival full of cultural elements, and a spiritual ritual for the Chinese. With the greatly increased mobility of the population today, "Spring Festival transportation" (春運) has become quite a scene in China, with more than three billion people being transported in a period of about 40 days around the Spring Festival, largely from where people work to their hometown for the Spring Festival season, and then back.[44] Although many of the migrant workers bring television sets as gifts to their parents, the latter are not that interested in those, but are more willing to

[44] In the last three decades, the scale of *Spring Festival transportation* has increased from about 0.1 billion to the 3.7 billion in 2015, enough to move the entire population of Africa, Europe, the Americas, and Oceania combined together.

immerse themselves in the traditional way of life—in the festival atmosphere where people from the whole village celebrate and carry out all kinds of exchanges, and in the leisurely and natural way of life embodied in various rituals that have been inherited from the past.

Many contemporary anthropologists, ethnologists, and sociologists are trying to study these activities as important elements of their scholarly research. It is likely only people in their sixties or older still have memories of these activities and the skills needed for them to continue.

Urban Elderly

The elderly in cities have had complex and challenging life experiences, such as the "three years of natural disasters" in early 1960s, and the Cultural Revolution which they all went through. As "educated youths" they had the experience of going to the countryside, where they lived and worked for years, and to the country's border regions to join in agricultural activities as part of the national defense program. They witnessed the reform and opening-up to the outside after Deng Xiaoping came to power, but also went through the hard times when many of them had to retire early and or go unemployed as state-owned enterprises in China went through major reforms, starting in the late 1990s. Most of the urban elderly currently in the early stage of their old age were not able to pursue their studies when they were supposed to be in school, and when they got married the one-child-per-family policy came into effect.

Now that they have begun their life in old age, two thirds of them have pensions of at least 2,000–2,500 yuan a month. They are partially covered by government medical insurance plans and have housing units that were allocated to them in the era of the planned economy. Thus, many of these elderly people actually feel nostalgic about that era, when the government took care of employment, when housing was distributed to employees for free or could be rented at very low cost, when medical care was covered by their work units, and when children went to kindergartens free of charge. They are also nostalgic about the egalitarianism of the Maoist era, when there was little economic inequality among the people, although life was austere.

In the early stage of the reform and opening-up movement, the most entrepreneurial of this generation embraced the opportunities offered by the more liberal government policies and left their jobs in the public sector to start their own businesses or work in the burgeoning private sector. After decades of hard work, they typically have accumulated quite some wealth, each with at least two or three housing units under his/her name and full insurance coverage from commercial insurance companies including life insurance, property insurance, and medical insurance. They make up the main force in the great army of tourists and extravagant shoppers of China. The best thing they did or have wanted to do, though, is to have their children go abroad for a good education, to make up for that of which their generation had been deprived.

In the urbanization process, many older buildings were pulled down to make space for new and taller buildings to be built. Those elderly people who owned apartments in those building typically got very good terms for compensation and became millionaires overnight, able to live handsomely, buying nice cars and jewelry, amusing themselves with curios, and going on trips to other countries as tourists. That is indeed a life full of joy!

Many of the elderly in this generation have blended the traditional and the modern in their thinking. They have the good qualities of the older generation, but are also able to show understanding and appreciation of the choices the younger generation have made in their lives. The better educated among them have shown more independence, with many of them choosing to go to universities for the elderly, especially to take classes in Chinese painting and calligraphy. They are not dependent on support from their children either financially or psychologically. Most of them join group tours to other countries every year, or go abroad on their own to be reunited with their children there. By and large, they live a satisfying life of ease.

The "Chinese Damas [women of middle age and older age] dancing in the streets" also lives a life of ease and satisfaction. Singing and dancing are their favorite leisure activities, and everyday one can see them in various parks. Their presence, indeed, has become a rather common scene in the city life of China. Through singing and dancing, they are able to have social interaction with one another, to give vent to their emotions, to keep up with what is going on in the society, and to have a sense of attainment. They have even staged dancing shows in public squares in Paris, New York, and Moscow. Dressed fashionably and in bright colors, the dancing damas all appear in fine fettle and good health.

Many elderly persons have pets, mainly cats and dogs, who have become important members of their families. They are the best companions to comfort these people in their old age, and also an important part of their recreational life. Of course, some elderly people have been taking care of their grandchildren. According to findings from some interviews, some elderly people believe that helping their children to bring up the latter's children is something they should do as a matter of course, and this practice has been passed down from generation to generation since time immemorial. These elderly people enjoy taking care of their grandchildren and never seem to get tired of doing it. There are others who are not very willing to shoulder that responsibility, but have to share some of the responsibility of their children's families, especially if their grandchildren are only-children.

Some elderly women are in a difficult situation. They did not go to school when they were young; and, because they focused on the family, giving birth to their children and taking care of the whole family, they never held a job, either. Now they live in small and old housing units and are often in bad health, depending on their children for financial support because they have no pensions and low coverage in terms of medical insurance. Those who are in worse situations—the "especially poor" families, families with elderly people with "grave health problems," families who had only one child in compliance to government policy but lost the child, and disabled elderly people are qualified to receive multiple government aids, such as on-the-spot service and medical insurance arranged by the government. The elderly of 65 years of age or older can ride buses for free, can visit parks which normally would charge an entrance fee for free, and can visit museums at half of the normal entrance fees. Those who are 80 or above can get an allowance of 100 yuan a month from the government and those who are 100 or above can get 200 yuan a month. The standards may be different in different cities, but all cities have benefits of this kind for the elderly.

Some of the older elderly have had even richer experiences in their life. Having been through war years, famines, and plagues, they cherish the life today very much. Most of them have retained a lifestyle of hard work and thrift, and are accustomed to treasure all things. They would hate to have leftovers from meals discarded, or old clothes thrown away. In the balcony of an apartment where such an elderly person resides or in the corridor outside it, or even in the corners and nooks of the rooms, there are likely to be many an old bottle and broken jar he or she has collected. They tend to have a large family, with many children and grandchildren, but four generations under the same roof, which was an ideal in traditional China, is now a rarity. For leisure life, this older generation of elderly people like to spend whole afternoons in a park, where they can idly chat on and on with others of their generation.

The elderly of Beijing are particularly interesting in this respect. They often gather in groups to talk about world events, commenting on the pros and cons of a strategic decision made by Obama or Putin, proposing that the wars in Iraq or Syria should end quickly so that their people can live in peace, but also offering sharp criticism on current social problems. To these elderly people, this is a splendid way of life that gives full expression to the human spirit.

Interestingly, most elderly people have strong memories of songs from the former Soviet Union and of songs and drama pieces from the Cultural Revolution period. If one wanders through a park, one is likely to see elderly people reveling in singing those old songs. Some of them never seem to get tired of listening to the eight "model operas" from the Cultural Revolution period. Neither do they just listen to them, but like to sing pieces from those operas. Many elderly people are so familiar with those operas that they can sing very long excerpts from memory.

Other elderly people are fond of traditional drama, especially Beijing opera. When Beijing opera is performed in theatres, about 80% of the audience is likely to be elderly people with grey hair. When the play reaches its climax, the elderly are likely to shout in great excitement like youngsters. Beijing opera is indeed the national drama form of China, in which the nation's cultural spirit finds its expression. In addition to professional performance groups, there are numerous amateur groups organized by fans to perform Beijing opera on all kinds of occasions. In small towns as well as in large cities, there are many groups of Beijing opera fans actively promoting this genre of drama.

Those who have inherited skills for various forms of intangible cultural heritage—art forms such as clay sculpture, colored drawing, kite-making and flying, silk figurines, local drama, miscellaneous folk arts, and connoisseurship—are people aged 60 or above.

Of course, many elderly people are also attracted to TV programs and to *mahjong*. Surveys have shown that the time spent by elderly people in watching TV is usually more than four hours a day, and the favorite programs for them (especially elderly women) are mainly soap operas, which have become a way of life. Elderly people who have watching TV as their main form of recreation have high incidences of high blood pressure, high blood fat, and high blood sugar, stroke, obesity, cancer,and such like, which to a large extent can be attributed to their sitting before the TV sets all day long and the lack of physical exercise and mental activity.

Mahjong has long been popular in China. In the *mahjong* game, four people are engaged for on average 2–3 hours. In most cases, the game is used for gambling. Some people have "put family and work aside" to play the game, which sometimes results in the disintegration of their families.

About seven or eight decades ago, many eminent figures in the cultural circles criticized the addiction of the Chinese to *mahjong* thus, "It results in the wasting of people's time and energy, to the great detriment to our nation." However, this bad habit has continued to this day, which this author thinks is no small matter.

Nevertheless, the life of the urban elderly is still rich and colorful, and everyone can choose his or her own style of leisure life. Traditional activities such as *taiji* boxing, kungfu, and five-animal exercises, which can contribute much to one's peace of mind, are the favorite activities for most elderly people. The traditional approach to leisure and recreation—subduing motion with tranquility—has been continued in this generation.

Conclusion

In traditional China, the standard for material affluence was "two *mu* of land and an ox, together with a wife, some children, and a heatable brick bed to sleep on"; while that for a rich spiritual life was to have "learning and honesty to perpetuate the family." Knowing that "the tailorbird may build her nest deep in the forest, but the nest occupies but one branch; the mole may drink from the Yellow River, but he can take at most a bellyful," who would still want to pursue a life of luxury with so many material fetters? For millennia, the forefathers of the Chinese had maintained a life of self-sufficiency with a balance of material and spiritual life, and had been making many cultural achievements. Today, however, the standard for affluence seems to have gotten lost. When there is a plentitude of material goods, people aspire to material extravagance. This may be what human nature leads us to, but when multitudes of people, driven by a motive for excessive wealth and extravagance, are in hot pursuit of millions and then billions of yuan, the scene becomes one in which "humans are slaves to goods" and "the mind is slave to the body," and in which there is a general feeling of being exhausted and fettered.

Why do people feel exhausted? In order "not to lose at the starting line," little kids have already entered a competition against one another; in order to obtain high scores, students live a monotonous life day and night, hurrying from home to school and back, with their basic need for sleep unsatisfied and their curiosity and interest in play thrown to the wind; in order to survive and have enough money, salary men live an ant-like life, hurrying from their residence to the workplace and becoming narrow-minded, like a "frog at the bottom of a well"; in order to make more money; and out of vanity, the rich are willing to become slaves to their mansions, to their cars, to money, and to their own "face." In order to gain promotion and high status, those in officialdom have to live like lap dogs, forever currying favor with their superiors; in order to gain higher professional titles, academics give up grace and refinement in exchange for grants and money, with their minds crowded with many disorderly thoughts.

And people are fettered with fame, money, and endless desires. Being exhausted and fettered is not limited to a small number of people, but has become the "normal" state for the majority of people.

Now, people in China already have 115 days of weekends and holidays a year, which would give them enough time to nurture their dispositions, to raise themselves to a higher spiritual existence, to cultivate their poetic sense and aesthetic tastes, and to accumulate their cultural capital. However, their neglect of and scorn for leisure, as well as the shallowness of their understanding of it, are perhaps unprecedented.

What does leisure mean in the contemporary world? Government policy has turned it into the "golden weeks" for tourism; society has taken it as the house of pleasure where one can live in luxury and dissipation; common people have taken it to be "TV + cell phone + chatting on the Internet." Although efforts are being made to reverse the tide, the nation has been immersed in such an atmosphere for so long and we still do not have sufficient humanistic ethos, so the true meaning of leisure, or *xiuxian*, is unlikely to be revealed soon.

Xiu (休), in its sense of "leaning against a tree to rest," means the union of humans with nature, and also a leisurely existence in and an intimacy with nature. *Xian* is the metaphor for the delights of life as one wanders "before flowers and in moonshine" and "watching the moon in a leisurely mood." The essence of leisure is that one should "be true to one's own nature and in quietude refrain from impetuosity."

Unfortunately, such spiritual wisdom for life inherited from the ancients has been discarded. Furthermore, the spiritual content and value of leisure has been disrupted and contaminated by consumerism and Mammonism. Fickleness and boisterousness have been the cancer adhering to the fruit of advances in material life in the last three decades, while concepts of "mind" and "quietude" have virtually disappeared. Mammonism and excessive desires, while they seem to have helped to create the prosperity and affluence we see, can also work to empty the Chinese of their soul. The leaders of China really should pay close attention to this phenomenon.

CHAPTER 6

Forces in Conflict

China is now undergoing drastic social transformation, and there are many kinds of conflicts all the time and present everywhere in Chinese society. On the macro level, in the pluralization of Chinese culture, many different kinds of ideas can come into conflict. In particular, with many Western ideas, which belong to a different system and tend toward different directions from traditional Chinese thinking, being imported to China, there are ample opportunities for conflict between ideas from these two systems. That being the case, how to have ideas from these two different cultures interact in a fruitful way against a background of globalization is an important question to be addressed. Again, with respect to the relationship between tradition and modernity, we are faced with the problem of how to have "the traditional" transformed into "the modern" through a continuous process of creativity. How can we ensure adequate continuity as the traditional is transformed into the modern? We are also faced with the problem of how to keep "the material" and "the spiritual" in balance in the face of a powerful commercial society and persistent infiltration of capital into the cultural sphere, so that proper balances can be maintained for human nature and for life.

When we look at contemporary Chinese society, corruption, the huge gap between the rich and the poor, moral decay, pathogenic factors within society, and anomie all pose challenges to the new reforms China is trying to undertake. How can China go beyond the pattern of reforms of the past and

Huidi Ma, Er Liu, *Traditional Chinese Leisure Culture and Economic Development*, DOI 10.1057/978-1-137-59253-8_6

develop institutional arrangements that will effectively stop the rampant corruption? How can the pattern of government functioning be thoroughly transformed so that the power exercised by government officials will be constrained institutionally? How can the hurried and pressurized existence generally felt by people be altered to give them more freedom? How can we help people develop decent and graceful behavior and modes of consumption? Doubtlessly, proper handling of these conflicts and contradictions is likely to help generate new forces to propel the continuous progress of Chinese society.

Chinese Versus Western Learning

First, we should point out that "learning" here refers less to the detailed knowledge of specific things and more to a general way of thinking and viewing the world and the theoretical systems that are historically formed throughout the history of a people. To understand the real history of a country and its people and to be able to see its future, one has to be familiar with their thinkers and the veins of their thought in the history.

There is a famous saying in *The Republic* of Plato: thought is always the ruler of the universe. So, Churchill said he would rather lose India than lose Shakespeare. This shows the importance of theoretical thinking for a nation.

Chinese Learning: Origins and Later Developments

The formation of a nation's theoretical thinking is intimately related to its intellectual heritage from its sages of the past. The theoretical thinking of the Chinese originated with various classics that took shape about three millennia ago, such as the "Six Classics" (六書) of *The Book of Poetry* (詩經), *The Book of Documents* (尚書), *The Book of Rites* (禮記), *The Book of Change* (易經), *The Book of Music* (樂經), and *The Spring and Autumn Annals* (春秋). The contents in these books were preserved from ancient times and, before Confucius compiled them into books, were kept by royal houses and the aristocracy. After their compilation at Confucius' hand, they have been much applauded and greatly valued by the ruling class through the ages, with *The Book of Change* being considered the most fundamental and most important among them.

The Book of Change (or Yi-Jing)

What kind of book is *The Book of Change*? Sima Qian, the great historian of the Western Han Period, said the 64 hexagrams, which are the core of this book, were developed by Ji Chang, or King Wen of Zhou (1152–1056 BC), when he was put under house arrest by King Zhou of Shang. *The Book of Change* we see today is composed of the "Classic of Change" and its "Exegesis." Rich in contents, it has exerted profound influence on the political, economic, and cultural spheres of China for millennia. It is the source for the "hundred schools" of thought that arose later in the Warring States Period, and has also furnished many inspirations for people's daily lives. As a modern scholar puts it, "The philosophical thinking of scholars in traditional China had much of its inspiration from the study of *The Book of Change*, and their ability for philosophical speculation was for the most trained and improved through the analysis of that book and through the scholarly exchange among people with different views."[1]

Laozi, the founder of the Taoist school of thought, infused the essence of *The Book of Change* into his *Daodejing* (The Virtues of the Way, also called *Laozi*), in which he developed a philosophical system centered around dialectical thinking, proposing, "The Dao gives birth to the One, the One to Two (*yin* and *yang*, or the feminine and masculine principles), and the Two to the Three, from which the myriad things are derived," therefore, "humans emulate the Earth, which emulates the Heaven, which emulates the Way, which is its own model."

The Confucian school took the doctrine of the mean as the ultimate moral standard and the highest level of wisdom for dealing with all problems, proposing that one should be impartial in handling all matters, that excess in anything is just as bad as insufficiency. This doctrine, then, is one of the core concept in Confucian ethics.

Buddhism, which originated in India, was transmitted to China at around the same time as the beginning of the Christian era. The Zen Buddhism that evolved in China is a branch of Buddhism with many Chinese characteristics. The famous Zen argument about the movement of wind versus that of a flag seems to concern a problem of physics with regard to the objective world, but was a metaphor with important spiritual

[1] Gao Huaimin, *A History of the Study of the* Book of Change *in pre-Qin Times*, Guangxi Normal University Press, 2007, p. 320.

significance for Zen Buddhism, with emphasis on the power of the understanding of its practitioners.

Yinyang 陰陽 (the masculine and feminine principles) and *Taiji* 太極 (the supreme ultimate) are the key ideas in the "Exegesis" of *The Book of Change*.

Yinyang The ancients of China observed many pairs of natural phenomena that were antagonistic but also connected to each other, such as the sky and the earth, the sun and the moon, day and night, the cold winter and the hot summer, male and female, the upper and the lower positions, and so on. Induction based on observation of these phenomena and their interrelationships gave rise to some important philosophical speculations. The theory of *yinyang* is an attempt in ancient Chinese culture to describe the basic laws behind natural phenomena that are also the forces the propel changes and development of the natural world. *Yinyang* was considered to be the primal motive force for the gestation, development, maturation, degeneration, and fading away of various things. This concept was the core element that laid the foundation for the logical reasoning of the Chinese.

Taiji The concept "*Taiji*" was a category that was used to explain the origin of the world in the philosophy of ancient China, and also a world view and a methodology for the Chinese to understand the objective world. It contains the wisdom that humans should follow the great Way with its perfect virtues, as well as the natural laws, so that they will not be unduly constrained by external things and will eventually reach a spiritual realm of peace and harmony that can comprehend all things of the world. The *Taiji* boxing that has continued to be practiced to this day by many Chinese, for example, embodies the *Taiji* concept in a form of bodily exercise. In doing so, it reflects a kind of life's wisdom of "subduing motion with quietude," "facilitating speed with slow motion," and "overcoming the tough with softness," which helps both to keep one's body strong and to cultivate one's mind.

In its long history of several millennia, the mainstream of Chinese thinking and even the ways of thinking of the Chinese people have been powerfully influenced by this dialectical mode. As the major schools of Chinese thinking, Confucianism, Taoism, and Buddhism have much in common when we get down to their fundamental ideas, although they have developed along different paths and were accorded different degrees of importance by rulers of different periods in history.

Confucianism, Taoism, and Buddhism

Confucianism

In its effort to maintain the "rule of rites" (禮制), its advocacy of "rule through exemplary moral integrity" (德治), its emphasis on "rule of man," and its propositions of "valuing harmony" and the "doctrine of the mean," Confucianism consistently reflects the balance between *yin* and *yang*, the major idea of *The Book of Change*. This school of thought had great influence on traditional China, when it was consecrated as the orthodoxy for a long time. It stresses the individual's responsibility for the society, and is considered a "this-worldly philosophy."

Taoism

With Laozi and Zhuangzi's view of the natural order of things with the Way for its core, this school of thought emphasizes that humans should emulate the Way in their thinking and conduct, "bringing things forth without possessing them, doing things naturally without counting that as one's own deed, and helping things grow without dominating over them" (Laozi). In political philosophy, "governing without making strenuous effort (to change the natural course of things)" is the rule, and "discarding the benevolence and righteousness (as advocated by Confucianism)" was basic to its ethics. After the Han Confucian Dong Zhongshu's proposal of "venerating Confucianism as the sole ideology and exiling all other schools of thought" was adopted by the state, Taoism gradually became a religion for the common people. Considering philosophy to be "otherworldly," it puts its emphasis on what is natural and spontaneous in humans.

Buddhism

After Buddhism was imported to China, its Chinese adherents used terms and ideas from Laozi and Zhuangzi's philosophy to interpret its voluminous sutras, which led to a trend toward convergence between these two schools of thought. The Song scholar Zhu Xi strongly espoused Confucianism as the orthodox thinking perpetuated by a lineage of sages. He condemned Buddhism together with Taoism as heretic, but actually absorbed some ideas from these schools into his own system of Neo-Confucianism. The Buddhists tried to transform the mundane world while adhering to an otherworldly philosophy.

Absorption of Elements of Foreign Cultures

As the mainstream of Chinese culture, Confucianism, Taoism, and Buddhism ran through scholarship, politics, and education throughout history, forming an open system of unique culture, public administration, and political systems. Exchange between Chinese culture and other cultures in the world began two millennia ago.

The "Silk Road" in Traditional China

The earliest cultural exchange between China and the Western world probably began with the "Silk Road" that started during the Western Han Period. The "Silk Road" was a system of trade routes covering many countries of Asia, Europe, and Africa, with multiple routes on the continents and on the seas serving as the main channels of economic, political, and cultural exchanges between the East and the West. Silk products were luxury items requiring exquisite spinning and dyeing techniques and thus became the major items used in trade and cultural exchange when the Chinese government sent diplomatic envoys to countries in Central Asia and beyond. In addition, china, jewelry, and tea were also important trade items demonstrating the rich resources, exquisite craftsmanship, and elegant styles of the Chinese society. Many heads of state and the aristocracy in many countries took the wearing of silk and the using of china from China as expressions of wealth and honor.

The Missionaries

Serious intellectual exchange with between China and other countries began with the introduction of Buddhism to China in the reign of Emperor Ming (65–70 BC) of the Eastern Han Dynasty. This exchange largely came to an end in the Tang Dynasty. Such exchange occurred again in the late Ming Dynasty. The starting point of this period is usually dated to 1583, the year when the Jesuit Matteo Ricci entered Zhaoqing, Guangdong, an event that initiated the dialogue and intellectual exchange between China and the West in the modern era. A large number of missionaries, including Matteo Ricci, Johann Adam Schall von Bell, Giuseppe Castiglione, and Timothy Richard left indelible marks in history for their contributions in the transmission of Western learning to China, bringing new knowledge and new ways of thinking to its intellectual, scholarly, and educational circles on an unprecedented scale.

These missionaries also made great contributions in the transmission of Chinese learning to the Western world. Many of them took large numbers of Chinese books and other documents with them upon their return to Europe and translated those into many European languages. They introduced not only the Confucian classics but also many ideas of contemporary Chinese scholars to Europe, laying a foundation for the rise of Western sinology.[2]

Studying Abroad Funded by the Qing Government

Between 1872 and 1875, the Qing government sent a total of 120 students in four groups to study in the United States. At an average of only 12 years of age, these young students were quick to accept Western education and the American way of life. They not only learned a great deal of new knowledge in natural sciences, but also came in contact with the post-Enlightenment Western culture with its humanities and social sciences. Such changes of these young students in their thinking and their ways of life were deemed intolerable by the Qing government, so the program, which was planned for 15 years, came to an early end in 1881. But a few of the students who participated in this program did later emerge as important figures in modern Chinese history, including the father of telegraphy and modern mining in China, the father of railway in China, the first president of Tsinghua University, and the first premier of the Republic of China.[3]

The Movement to Study Abroad in Late Qing and Early Republican Era

The program of sending young students to study in the USA was part of China's "Self-Strengthening Movement," an effort to "learn the strengths of the foreigners in order to subdue them." The limitations of this movement became apparent with China's defeat in the Sino-Japanese War of 1894–1895. Many Chinese were awakened as if from a dream and those of a more reformist frame of mind started a new movement to study abroad by raising the banner of reform. By a rough count, the number of students who went abroad was 274 in 1901, 1,300 in 1903, and jumped to 8,000 in 1905, the year when the examination system of China, which has lasted for

[2] Yung Wing (Rong Hong), *My Life in China and America*, Translated by Xu Fengshi et al., Beijing: SDX Joint Publishing, 2011, pp. 15–17.

[3] Ibid.

more than a millennium, was abolished, and then took another jump to reach 12,000 in 1906. At that time, the destinations of the students were mostly the USA, Europe, and Japan. In less than two years from 1919 to 1920, 1,600 students reached France on work-study programs. Of the early Communists of China, Zhou Enlai and Deng Xiaoping were among these students, and it is when they were studying abroad that they discovered and accepted Marxism.[4]

The New Culture Movement

The New Culture Movement was started mostly by intellectuals who had had contact with Western education, with Chen Duxiu, Hu Shi, Lu Xun, Qian Xuantong, and Li Dazhao as the representative figures. These intellectuals advocated an intellectual movement to reform Chinese culture, a movement that was "against tradition, against Confucianism, against the old moral order, and against classical Chinese as the written language"; and tried to introduce Western democracy and science to China. This movement went directly against the traditional ethical codes that had ruled China for more than two millennia, trying to enlighten people to democracy and to spread knowledge of modern science in China. It also prepared the intellectual backdrop for the propagation of Marxism in China.

Cultural Enlightenment

However, the radicals in the New Culture Movement tended to become conservative in their later years. They had learned from reality that, although the propagation of Western learning in China was the trend of the day, traditional culture, the rapid diminishing of which they keenly felt, was also indispensable. With that, the effort to combine Western with the Chinese culture and a "creative transformation" of the traditional to the modern became the cause of their old age. "Gu Hongming had devoted himself with great enthusiasm to translating Chinese classics for Western readers, Yan Fu spent most of his time in the study of *Zhuangzi* in his later years, and Zhang Taiyan had backed down from his earlier position of 'scholarship for scholarship's sake' and began to advocate the pragmatic value of scholarship, in the hope that people could learn the methods of the ancients for self-cultivation and for governing the state. A group of scholars solidly

[4] Dick Wilson, *A Biography of Zhou En-lai*, Translated by Feng Changhong. Beijing: International Culture Publishing Company, 2011.

grounded in traditional learning, such as Du Yaquan and Zhang Shizhao, also advocate vehemently the reconciliation between Western and Chinese learning, and between traditional and modern learning."[5]

Feng Guifen, a forerunner of reformist ideas in the Self-Strengthening Movement, proposed, "The Confucian ethics should be the foundation, while the techniques of the powers can be used to increase national power and wealth." Xue Fucheng, another important figure in the Self-Strengthening Movement, proposed, "Now if we take Western techniques for our use, we will be able to guard the Way that has been passed down to us through Yao, Shun, Yu, King Tang, King Wen, King Wu, the Duke of Zhou, and Confucius." All these ideas served as a kind of theory for the Self-Strengthening Movement, and reflect a kind of enlightenment on the part of Chinese intellectuals with regard to Chinese and Western cultures.

Sense of Responsibility for the Country and a Climax of Scholarly Activities

The leaders of the New Culture Movement were all solidly grounded in both Chinese and Western learning, and there are two reasons for the changes in their ideas in their later years. First, with the imperial order having crumbled, the influence of traditional culture had also dwindled, and the cultural heritage of the China, both material and non-material, had lost its appeal to many, and people were faced with task of reselecting their values. With new culture and new ideas ready to surge from the horizon, the time was ripe for leaders of a new cultural movement to emerge who were well-grounded in both Chinese and Western learning. Secondly, the traditional culture of China was deeply rooted in Chinese society. It was a rich and complex entity connected to people's life in numerous ways, and the effort to terminate it in a short time would not only be impossible, but was likely to lead to the breakdown of the whole nation. Thus was born Modern Neo-Confucianism.

The New Culture Movement gave rise to a peak of intellectual innovation in China. "The structure of learning of the scholars of twentieth-century China differs from that of all their predecessors in that their training in Western learning exceeded by far that of the Qing scholars, not to mention the Song and Han scholars.... Living in an open society

[5] Liu Yizheng, "On the errors of recent scholars in their discussion of the pre-Qin philosophical schools," *Journal of Historical and Geographical Studies*, 1921, 1(1).

undergoing tremendous social transformation when many old things were replaced by new things, they not uncommonly went abroad to Europe, the United States, or Japan while still teenagers or in their twenties, and was proficient with one or several foreign languages. The outstanding ones among them often came from families with a strong family tradition with traditional Chinese learning, so they enjoyed exceptional advantages in their education."[6]

It is interesting to note that the highest peaks of intellectual development in Chinese history all appeared at times of great social upheaval and political chaos. This perhaps shows the power brought about by conflicts. At the same time, it also poses the interesting question as to why peaks of intellectual development can be brought about at times of tremendous social upheaval and political disorder.

Tragedies in the History of Chinese Culture

The intellectual achievements of generations of ancient Chinese helped to create the tradition of "a land of courtesy and propriety" and of "venerating teachers and valuing education." But tragedies, even bloody anti-intellectualistic massacres, did happen from time to time. There were, indeed, quite a few such anti-intellectualistic campaigns in Chinese history which are particularly outrageous.

Book-Burning and Scholars Buried Alive (焚書坑儒)

This event was recorded in the *Historical Records* of Sima Qian. Kong Anguo's preface to *The Books of Documents* also states that "When the First Emperor of Qin tried to destroy canons and classics from previous generations, burning books and burying scholars alive in pits, scholars in the whole country tried to escape, going in all directions." In 212 BC, one year after he had begun to commit to fire large numbers of books, the emperor had more than 460 magicians buried alive in pits that had been dug beforehand. This act on the part of the emperor was intended to help maintain political centralization and to dispel political views not in accord with the ideology espoused by the state.

A similar event occurred during the Qing Dynasty and gave rise to the Qianjia school,[7] and has generally been taken to be a product of the

[6] Liu Mengxi, "Modern Scholars of the Faith," Beijing: The Commercial Press, 2015.

[7] This is a school of scholarly research in the Qianlong and Jiaqing reigns of the Qing Dynasty which was focused on philological studies of the ancient texts of China.

Manchu dynasty's effort to suppress the Han Chinese and to control its subjects. The event took place during the Yongzheng and Qianlong reigns. At that time, China was in an era of social stability, but the government adopted a harsh policy against the literati. In the Qianlong reign, there were many literary inquisitions, and the emperor issued several edicts banning and destroying many books. With that, the literati dared no longer to voice their political views or to discuss politics, but rather redirected their energy to the study and compilation of works from the past, which gave rise to an intellectual movement focused on philological studies including minute exegesis of ancient texts, so as to escape from political persecution of the time.

The most recent anti-intellectualistic event of this kind was the campaign to "destroy the 'four olds'" from mid- to late 1960s during the Cultural Revolution. In this campaign, almost all books and documents from the pre-Cultural Revolution times were considered "feudalistic, bourgeois, or revisionist" and committed to the "dustbin of history." "In Beijing alone, the homes of more than 114,000 families were ransacked and searched for any suspicious items, and in the whole country the figure was about 10 million families. No one knows how many books (including old books of great value) and magazines, works of calligraphy and painting, and vessels and accessories of much artistic value disappeared in fire."[8]

In the history of Chinese culture, the greatest tragedies are such campaigns to "burn books" and to kill or persecute scholars, and such tragedies took place in most dynasties. According to Gu Jiegang, a great historian in modern China, "In the three centuries of the Qing Dynasty, numerous documents vanished. Are there other literary inquisitions in history that can be ascertained? The answer is 'Yes!' However, none of them is quite as severe as the one in the early Qing period."[9] Through literary inquisitions, the ruling class could eliminate ideas not in accordance with their own. Thus, autocracy found expression not only in political, but also in cultural spheres, and intellectuals could not escape their fate of being constrained and suppressed under autocratic rule.

[8] Ruan Kaibo, "The greatest catastrophe in the five millennia of China's cultural history—the 'destroying the four olds' movement during the Cultural Revolution," *Tianya Forum*, June 2012.

[9] Gu Jiegang, "A study on the literary inquisitions of the Ming Dynasty," in Zheng Tianting, eds., *Sources for Ming-Qing History*, vol. 1. Tianjin: Tianjin People's Press, 1980, p. 84.

Utterly Useless Are the Scholars?

Starting from the mid-Qing period, the general situation of the literati in the Chinese society can be summarized in two lines from a poem by Huang Jingren[10]:

> Nine out of ten are looked down upon by people –
> Ah, utterly useless are the scholars!

The second line cited above later actually became an axiom about the status of intellectuals and is still in wide circulation today. This axiom seems to be absurd, but in traditional China, "he who obeys the heavens can live, and he who goes again heavens perishes," with the "heavens" basically equivalent to the emperor, the supreme ruler. There were intellectuals who had strong characters, but once they showed disobedience to the emperor, they were likely to get killed without mercy.

In traditional China, there were many intellectuals, basically Confucian literati, who were expected to have a strong character, maintain personal integrity, and be ready to assume responsibility for society. An important part of their social responsibility was to inherit and pass on the Confucian tradition and, when necessary, to develop it creatively. Typically, they began their education early, studying under the direction of family members, or going to private or government schools. After they became officials, they were likely to continue to read books, compose poems, and conduct scholarly studies. The literate "studies when he has leisure from his official duties, and assumes official responsibilities when he can have time away from his studies." From such a way of life was derived the literati's tendency to cultivate and show refinement and good taste, with "valuing the refined and rejecting the vulgar" as a general quality for this class. However, the literati, especially those with a noble character, often had many tribulations in their lives. They may have had lofty ideals of serving the country, but often in vain, because many were never given the opportunity to do so. If they insisted on their moral integrity and offended those in power, they would be demoted or even killed. There were, to be sure, clever opportunists who escaped such fates by currying favor with those in power, but though they were thus able to live on, they had become soulless.

[10] Huang Jingren (1749–1783), a Qing poet, wrote this poem to express his detestation for the world because it did not recognize his talents.

Today there is the view that line "utterly useless are the scholars" has been used to mean "contempt for education, but this is serious misinterpretation." This view has some reason to it, but is also a little forced. It has some reason because it reflects the extent to which education is emphasized in China today; and it is forced because the attitude of most Chinese toward education is too pragmatically bent, too utilitarian, and too lowly—they believe education is useless unless one becomes a high official or makes a great deal of money with his/her education. This is the sad reality. When education is no longer deemed an endeavor worth the most patience and the most careful work on the part of the educator, such as shown in the saying "it takes a decade to grow a tree, but a century to cultivate a noble person," education and reading have already lost their sacredness in people's minds.

In recent years, due to various problems, which can be summarized as the expensiveness of education, the difficulty of finding a job, and the low starting salaries, the view that "education is useless" is again on the rise. On the one hand, the cost for education is very high, and the returns from education is relatively low, which has led to questioning of the utility of education. On the other hand, it takes much time to go through the education process, and those who have gone through the process often have a low capacity for innovation. What they have learned may be useless, while society demands from them something other than what they have learned. In schools, transmission of knowledge has replaced humanistic education, resulting in the typical graduate being unable to establish him/herself in society as a human individual while also being unable to start a good career. That, actually, is the core of the problem. Of course, we should also note the profound effect, which should never be underestimated, that the aforementioned historical tragedies, especially the "destroy the 'four olds'" campaign have had on several generations of people.

Intellectual Mercenaries

Intellectual mercenaries have always existed alongside true intellectuals. These are sycophant literati kept by emperors and lords to sing their praises. They are typically well provided for by their masters, but that has often distorted their souls and diminished their literary talents. They are no more than the mouthpiece of the ruling class and sycophants who try to curry favor from their masters. Such intellectual mercenaries through the dynasties have brought about a rather unwholesome social milieu that works against the development of people with the lofty Confucian ideal of "being the conscience for heaven and earth, being models for the people, carrying on the attenuated intellectual tradition of sages of the past, and laying foundation for a peaceful and well-ordered world that can be perpetuated forever." Such a social milieu also makes much space for irregular practice in the academic world, with scholars becoming fickle and without any coherent and consistent theoretical guide for their scholarly work.

At any rate, the saying "utterly useless are the scholars" contains much prejudice and short-sightedness. In fact, the real intellectuals throughout history have been the backbone of the nation, leaving such famous sayings as "awe-inspiring righteousness," "worry about the world before others realize there are things to worry about, and enjoy life only after all others have an enjoyable life," and "though just a single individual, I must partake in the responsibility for the flourishing or perishing of the world," which have inspired generation after generation of people in their spiritual pursuits and their concern for their dear motherland. No country can be without such an intelligentsia as the backbone of society, for its absence would be disastrous. Does the saying "utterly useless are the scholars" express a dissatisfaction with the lack of a true spirit of intellectuals, a bitterness for the low status of scholars who have to salute the powerful in order to be able to make a living, or just a self-pity of a poor scholar who is yet to win status in society? This is a question that is worth considering for intellectuals.

Of course, the fewer intellectual mercenaries there are, the better it will be for society. Only when the social conditions for intellectual mercenaries no longer exist will there be rich soil for free thinking and an independent spirit.

Western Learning

In the West, a large number of thinkers, scientists, artists, and philosophers were produced in ancient Greece, with the "three Greek wisemen," namely, Socrates, Plato, and Aristotle, being the most outstanding. In literature, art, philosophy, education, ethics, and many other fields, these philosophers made great theoretical contributions that still have a strong influence on the direction of cultural development and spiritual pursuits in the West.

Socrates

Socrates (469–399 BC) is the most important icon in the Western philosophical tradition. He believed that as human beings people were equal and he did not like to have disciples. He never gave students ready answers to questions, but let them reach their own conclusions through their own exploration. This kind of exploration allowed people to maintain their own independence in the process of trying to be united with the Way. His conception of education is for teachers and students to seek truth while trying to tackle difficult questions together, and for each to reach his own independent judgment amidst the painstaking process of thinking when there seems at times to be no way out, in which process they are to discover the logic of things and also the meaning of their existence. To him, education is not for the teacher to instill knowledge into a passive receptacle called "student," but for him to ignite the flame of active thinking in them. "Questions" are midwives who help to bring about the birth of new ideas.

Plato

In his most famous work *The Republic*, Plato (427–347 BC) describes the "perfect" state, or polis, according to his ideal, and poses the questions "what is a citizen?" and "how should the citizen be educated?" For him, the aim of the polis is for all citizens to have the virtues of "justice" and "common good." To attain to that aim, the polis was to establish an educational system with its emphasis on education as a generative process.

Along with this educational system is to be built the best regime, which comprehends the entire way of life and includes the moral and religious practices, customs, mores, and emotions, which make a people what it is. "The polis and the soul are essentially similar. This view is the key metaphor for the entire *The Republic*."[11] But what is the use of a perfect polis? And what end does it serve? The philosopher-king may be a kind of ruler to be yearned and hoped for, but it is also a metaphor to help one understand the education of the soul.

Aristotle

Aristotle (384–322 BC) proposed that the physical and mental development of children goes through different stages. He praises the Athenian education with its focus on the development of physical health and beauty and the harmonious development of the human individual, suggesting that natural endowment, acquired habits, and intellectual development be taken

[11] Steven B. Smith, *Open Yale Courses*, Beijing Joint Publishing Company, March 2015, pp. 57-58.

as the three sources for moral education. He advocates liberal education that facilitates leisure. Later, he proposed that "the good man is also the good citizen," for the virtues for a good man (*agathon*) are also the virtues the polis demands of the individual. He has been considered the father of leisure philosophy with his statement that leisure is the pivot around which all things revolve.

Scholastic Philosophy

This was a kind of speculative philosophy in service of Christian theology. In it, the Christian concept of "original sin" is expressed as "the seven deadly sins" of pride, envy, wrath, sloth, greed, gluttony, and lust, which supplies a set of precepts for self-discipline while laying the theoretical foundations for Christian thinking.

Thomas Aquinas not only succeeded in almost perfectly combining Christian theology with Aristotelian philosophy in his *Summa Theologica*, but, based on Christian doctrines and relevant ideas of Aristotle, proposed that the basic principle for handling economic relationships ought to be equity and justice in distribution and exchange. His thinking has affected the entire cultural history of modern Europe.

The Renaissance

The Renaissance started a new epoch in the modern history of human society. It not only laid foundation for natural science and raised the curtain for the history of modern science and technology, but established "the true, the good, and the beautiful" as the eternal standards for value judgment, and, through numerous works of literature, architecture, sculpture, painting, and poetry, extolled the beauty of nature and the spiritual value of human beings.

In the nineteenth century, historians coined the term "humanism" to summarize the world view of the humanists of the Renaissance. They discovered man and his greatness, affirmed his value and creativity, and proposed that individuals have to be free in order for humanity to gain liberation. As a general movement to give freedom to human beings in their thinking, the Renaissance greatly propelled the development of world culture, providing a lighthouse that gave light to the entirety of Europe and even the whole world.

Mutual Borrowing Between Chinese and Western Learning

Both Chinese and Western learning have helped to foster the world view, the value systems, and the ways of thinking for various nations. Each has its own Way and its own strengths, but both have the same end, though the end is reached through different paths. Chinese learning and Western learning may differ in appearance, but are the same in essence. This essential sameness is what gave rise to the theory of the "axial age" in intellectual history, which proposed that first-rate thinkers, including Shakyamuni the Buddha, Confucius and Laozi of China, and Socrates, Plato, and Aristotle of ancient Greece, appeared in many different cultures in about the same period from the eighth to the fifth century BC. Thus, as an eminent Chinese scholar puts it, "the principles of intellectual activities are the same in the East and the West, and the ultimate Way is no different though there can be southern and northern schools of thought."[12]

In the modernization process of China, great emphasis has always been assigned to the absorption from the West the better parts of its culture and its ideas, its spirit for the rule of law, and its advanced management ideas. Similarly, the West has also tried to introduce Confucian, Taoist, and Buddhist thinking and to study them. The circulation of different translations of Laozi's *Daodejing* is second only to that of the Bible.

Tradition and Modernity

The traditional culture of China does not just consist of the orthodox Confucian Way adhered to by the literati, but is also expressed in family education, family instructions, family-centered learning, and folk beliefs. Chen Yinque, an eminent Chinese scholar, once made the important hypothesis that after the Han Period, the official government school system declined and the center for scholarly pursuits gradually moved from official schools to schools of lineage groups, and thus the lineage group was a very important channel for the continuation of learning and culture in the traditional Chinese society.[13]

[12] Qian Zhongshu, *Essays on Art*. Beijing: Sanlian Bookstore, 2002, preface.

[13] Liu Mengxi, *The Faith of Modern Scholars*. Beijing: Commercial Press, 2015, p. 55.

Folk Beliefs in Traditional Family-Centered Learning

In Chap. 2 of this book, we discussed both the fine sentiments and spiritual pursuits in the life of the literati and Confucian officials of mainstream Chinese culture and the life wisdom of the common folks. In this section, we will focus on folk beliefs and the tradition in family education, so as to gain a glimpse of the role played by the other branch of culture, the folkways, in the cultural traditions of China.

Folk Beliefs

The Gods Are Just Above Our Heads

The saying that "the gods are just above our heads" shows that the ancients imposed a kind of self-discipline on themselves piously and self-consciously. This saying carries three-fold meanings. First, it says the human individual should have reverence for nature and for society, and guard against wanton behavior on his/her part. One cannot assume one can do certain things in complete secrecy and then do whatever one wants. Secondly, one should only do what one can do with a clear conscience. If one harbors any evil thought, one would immediately incur punishment from the gods. When one holds this belief for a long time, one would become accustomed to having strong self-discipline. Thirdly, the "gods" are omnipresent, an idea that puts constraints on one's malicious conduct. Typically, a traditional Chinese family would have in the central hall of its house a small table with an urn on it where one could burn incense to the gods to show one's awe and reverence for them. Such awe and reverence were often written into warning axioms in family instructions for family education. People in the modern world tend to interpret such practices of the ancients from an overly utilitarian point of view, but in fact, the aim of these practices was simply to have self-discipline in both one's mind and in one's outward behavior.

Misfortune May Give Rise to Blessing, but May Also Hide in It

This axiom from Laozi, which contains a simple kind of dialectic thinking among common people, has been used to conceptualize the mutual conversion between blessing and misfortune. The ancients understood that when one's life is full of blessings it may mean some misfortune is coming. Thus, when one has blessings, one ought not to get dizzy about it. But since this dialectic also works the other way: when some disaster falls on one, one ought not to panic, but rather should remain composed and deal with it calmly, in which case one may be able to head off the danger and save the day. The older generation often tells their offspring that, when living a life of great wealth and high status, if the only thing they know is to be happy and merry, that would necessarily incur misfortune. This is a lesson derived from experience, but also a kind of natural law. Therefore, many families teach their children not to be too deliberate in seeking power and wealth, nor to show off the power or wealth they already have.

"The gentleman cultivates himself in quietude and nurtures his moral sense with a life of thrift. Without indifference to fame and wealth his ideal would not be made clear, and without tranquility of mind he would not be able to go far in realizing his ideal." These are words from Zhuge Liang's *Jiezishu* mentioned in Chapter 2. Zhuge left this letter for his son while on his death bed, which shows his noble character and outstanding wisdom. *Jiezishu* has come down to us through many generations and still has profound influence on the Chinese. Many intellectuals and men of letters have noted down "Clarify our ideal with indifference to fame and wealth and work toward the ideal with a tranquility of mind" or "Cultivate ourselves in quietude and nurture our moral sense with a life of thrift" as a motto to be hung in the main hall to encourage and admonish themselves to maintain personal integrity. "Quietude" and "thrift" are the wisdom of our ancestors, and also the necessary conditions for the flourishing of a humanistic culture.

To Suffer Losses Is a Blessing

This is an axiom shared by Confucians, Taoists, and Buddhists alike. The Confucians value righteousness over profit, the Buddhists make light of profit and value righteousness, while the Taoists embrace both. The literal sense of this axiom is that one's losses in making contributions to others and to the common good will be repaid. But the profundity of this axiom rests at a deeper level. Confucius said, "Do not dwell on wealth and power if they have not been obtained in ways that are in accordance with the Way." So the deeper meaning of the axiom has more to do with spiritual cultivation and virtue. It is only human for one to want to gain various advantages in life, but if one does that to the extent of greed, or begins to spend inordinate amounts of time and effort to gain petty advantages, or even be so deeply involved in such undertakings as to lament any small loss, it would not be worth it, for that way one would be losing something very important for the sake of those petty advantages. Therefore, if one can afford to yield three-tenths of a profit to others, one should not try to bargain it down to two-tenths. By thus taking some loss on oneself, one succeeds in cultivating goodwill between the two parties. Is not that something one can feel good about? To suffer some loss is not to be muddle-headed, but shows one's nature as generous and respectful of others.

Modesty Benefits While Pride Hurts

This axiom, which comes from the "Da Yumo" 大禹謨 chapter of *The Book of Documents*, has been used to expound the idea that hubris would lead to damage, while modesty can lead to beneficial results. This axiom has had a powerful influence in China, with modesty becoming one of the virtues most highly valued in the family education of the ancients. Modesty is a virtue important for self-cultivation, and the gentleman is often called "a humble gentleman," referring to the restraint and caution expected of him. Of all the 64 hexagrams in *The Book of Change*, all except one has at least one of its six lines that is inauspicious, and the one exception is the hexagram for "humility." Why is this so? The comments made for this hexagram in the books provide this most exquisite explanation for it: "When the gentleman is in a high position, his humility will add to his appeal; and when he is in a humble station, people would not try to put him down since he is already showing humility, "Xici" in *The Book of Change* (易·系辭). In other words, modesty cannot be conquered.

Success Results from Thriftiness While Extravagance Would Bring Ruin

The following story is told in the "Shiguo" chapter in *Hanfeizi* (韓非子·十過). Once, the Duke of Qin asked You Yu, "Could you enlighten me on the causes for some kings of the past having their states flourish while others had their states go into decline?" You Yu replied, "Indeed I had the good fortune to hear about the causes—normally a king had his state flourish through thrift, and had it go into decline through extravagance." There have even been stories about Yao having to abdicate his imperial throne to Shun, and the latter had to abdicate it to Yu, all because of their extravagancy.

Based on these stories, the Tang poet Li Shangyin wrote in poem:

> From stories of worthy people's deeds with their families and the state
> We see that their success was due to thrift, and failure to extravagance

which provides a warning for later generations. Thrift was considered the source of all virtues. In Chinese history, one can find many a ies of rulers who lived extremely extravagant and luxurious lives and ended up with the perishing of their dynasty and the loss of their own lives.

Time Is Money

The sages considered an inch of time to be more valuable than a piece of jade a foot in size, for time is difficult to get and easy to lose. "Treasure time as much as one does gold" became a motto for the Chinese people. It is often said that time is the fairest thing in the world, for it treats everyone the same way, and is neither so generous as to give one second more to anyone, nor so parsimonious as to withhold one minute from anyone. However, although they all have the same amount of time, some become well learned, while others are not able to accomplish anything.

With Harmony a Family Is Bound to Prosper

The "family" or "household" has many special meanings for the Chinese. Assuming the household and the state are structurally the same, the Confucians believe that if one can put his household in good order after one has properly cultivated oneself, one could use the same techniques to govern a state and pacify the whole world. In traditional China, the public educational system was not very strong, and family learning was therefore rather important. And family learning was pretty comprehensive, covering a very broad range of things from the proper manner for talking and conducting oneself in everyday life, to how to serve the country, with specific instructions and exemplary models for all these areas. The emphasis of family learning is on harmony within the family. Husband and wife are not only to treat each other with courtesy, but also the help each other make progress in their development. Affinity and solidarity are stressed in the family, and, when these principles are applied to the government of the state, can be used to increase the power of the nation as a whole. Harmony is both the starting point and the end for the Chinese in their deliberation on various matters.

"Harmony" is an important category in Chinese philosophy, and it contains much dialectic thinking, as shown in the phrase "[different elements] are in harmony with, but not identical to, one another."

The Gentleman Holds Three Things in Awe

The Analects says, "The gentleman fears three things: the will of heaven, the superior, and the words of sages." This is followed by the statement "The lowly man does not know the will of heaven, and thus does not fear it; he shows no respect for his superiors, and holds the words of sages in contempt."

Of the gentleman's "three fears," the fear of the will of heaven means two things, for "heaven" in Chinese philosophy can mean laws of nature and in folk beliefs can mean the mandate of heaven, the will of heaven, and gods. The "superiors" as the object of the second fear include those in a superior moral stance, the mighty and powerful, the head of one's lineage group, and one's parents. The "words of the sages" include words from sages of the past, from one's ancestors, and from the classics.

The "three fears" are not limited to gentlemen, but are also part of the folk belief system. Those who fear nothing are either lowly men, or those who have psychiatric disorders, or even devils. One who does not know to have respect for others is also one who holds himself in contempt, allowing himself to be ranked with lowly people, mad people, or even devils. The basis for the fears named above is the obedience to nature's laws, to superiors with their superior character, and to the wisdom contained in the words of sages, rather than to wealth, status, power, or to sinful desires.

The Value of Tradition

The power of tradition lies in that "nothing is more visible than the hidden, or more notable than the obscure, and thus the gentleman is very cautious with his conduct while alone" (*The Doctrine of the Mean*). As Lin Yusheng says, this is the "internal transcendence" of the gentleman who "makes his best effort, but knowing the limits of human nature and the will of heaven."[14] Such internal transcendence does not rely on external constraints from institutions with their laws and orders. This may be one of the reasons why historically the Chinese have much neglected the idea of the rule of law.

Many may question the necessity of tradition in modern society. Please note, however, that tradition is a continuous historical process, and what has come down to us must have gone through the test of human nature.

[14] Lin Yusheng, *The Creative Transformation of Chinese Traditions*, 2nd ed. Beijing: SDX Joint Publishing Company, 1992, p. 100.

Guarding the treasures of the nation and passing on the tradition is the most important thing.

Recently, the author has seen an article questioning various folk beliefs, with an attempt to interpret those using the rules of a heavily commercialized society. For example, "the gods are just above our heads" is interpreted as a superstition; "to suffer losses is a blessing" is born of the Ah Q mentality[15]; "the gentleman's three fears" are held to be detrimental to the independence of the individual; and "success results from thrifty while extravagance would bring ruin" is said to be running against the current government policy for a consumption-driven economy. Such readings of tradition out of context and the misinterpretation and warped interpretation of it are the results of the discontinuity that traditional culture has suffered for long periods since the twentieth century, a discontinuity has led to many people being unable to tell true from false tradition, or to distinguish the good from the bad in traditional culture.

How to revive the Chinese culture when many people no longer have any faith and how to ensure sustainable development of the economy is a very important issue faced by the Chinese nation. Regardless of how remote history may seem, how much time has been wasted, and how the society is being transformed, the cultural tradition of a nation is the inner force that sustains its development.

Modern Issues

How to define modernity has been incessantly debated in academic circles. This section is not meant as another contribution to that debate. Instead, using Dr. Sun Yat-sen's Bourgeois National Revolution as the beginning of the modern era in China, the author reflects on and explores some issues since then.

Prelude to the Modern State in China

The Bourgeois National Revolution in the early twentieth century led by Dr. Sun Yat-sen developed the three dimensions of "political participation,

[15] Ah Q is the protagonist in *The True Story of Ah Q*, a novelette by the eminent author Lu Xun in the early 20th century. Ah Q is a peasant with very low status, and meets with all kinds of frustrations in his life, but he always finds a way to deceive himself into believing that those frustrations are actually his victories.

political competition and political control"[16] and served as a prelude to the transition of China from a feudal society into a modern state.

However, the Bourgeois National Revolution did not seem to go well. Where did the future lie in China? Chen Duxiu[17] and Li Dazhao,[18] the earliest founders of the Chinese Communist Party, and returning revolutionists from their overseas studies, introduced the Marxist primer *The Communist Manifesto* to China. It served as a golden key for the Chinese Communist Party to open up and create a New China.

In the beginning of 1920, Li Dazhao and Chen Duxiu agreed that they would stage organizational activities in Beijing and Shanghai separately in order to set up a communist party in China. In March of the same year, Li Dazhao formed the first society for Marxist studies at Peking University. During the late fall and early winter that year, Mao Zedong and He Shuheng secretly established an early communist organization in the city of Changsha, utilizing the key elements of the Society of New Masses as founding members. During the next year, Zhou Enlai[19] and other revolutionaries among overseas Chinese students in Europe formed another early communist organization in Paris, France. The founding of the Chinese Communist Party of China in July 1921 marks the entrance of "the brand new" Chinese experiences and ideas onto the stage of world communist movements.[20]

Mao Zedong and the New China

On October 1, 1949, Mao Zedong declared to the world from the rostrum of Tian'anmen via radio waves: "the founding of the Central People's Government of the People's Republic of China."

Mao Zedong (1893–1976) was the founder of the People's Republic of China. Via his famous theorem that "power comes from the barrel of a gun," he started the new era of people becoming masters of their own destiny and

[16] Kuhn, Philip Alden, 2013. *Origins of the Modern Chinese State*, trans. by Chen Yi. Beijing: SDX Joint Publishing Company.

[17] Chen Duxiu (1879–1942), apostle of the first Intellectual Emancipation Movement in China in the twentieth century; leader of the May 4th Movement; propagator of Marxism; the most important founder of the Chinese Communist Party.

[18] Li Dazhao (1889–1927), well-known Chinese Marxist; outstanding proletarian revolutionist; one of the main founders of the Chinese Communist Party.

[19] Zhou Enlai, the first premier of the People's Republic of China.

[20] "The Chinese Communist Party of China" in Baidu Encyclopedia.

began the difficult and tortuous journey of exploring and realizing socialist democracy. He laid the foundation for the communist party as the governing party and made tremendous efforts toward maintaining the progressive nature and governing status of a Marxist political party.

Mao is also one of the most important historical figures of the modern world. In the 1960s, Maoism became popular in the Western countries and has influenced the thinking on governing of many ruling parties in the world. He has been ranked by the American *Time* magazine as one of the 100 most influential people in the twentieth century for his ideas.

Folklore has it that Mao is "a figure that emerges only once in every three to five hundred years," which expresses the kind of homage that people pay him. In the 1930s, Edgar Snow, an American journalist, felt that Mao exuded a force of destiny when they met for the first time.[21] According to Snow, Mao was an accomplished scholar, well-versed in traditional Chinese studies. He read widely and did serious research on some philosophical and historical issues. His reading was not limited to Marxist philosophers; he also read ancient Greek thinkers, Spinoza, Kant, Goethe, Hegel, and Rousseau.[22] After he came to power, Mao moved his residence to Zhongnanhai compound where he named his private library the "Reading Room of Chrysanthemum Fragrance." It contains over 10,000 titles, totalling about 100,000 volumes. They cover myriad subjects and periods, including Chinese books and translations of foreign books, classics, histories, *belles lettres*, and books on astronomy and geography. Reading was an important part of his life. He once said, "Having accumulated lots of knowledge, one feels like standing on the mountain top and is able to see so many more things in far-away places; a man without knowledge is like moving in a dark culvert by groping around, very hard and difficult indeed."[23]

In the early phase of the new government, Mao said, "What can we make now? We can make desks and chairs, tea cups and tea pots; we can grow grains, grind them to flour, and produce paper; but we cannot manufacture a single car, an airplane, a tank, a tractor."[24] What he had in mind was to

[21] Snow, Edgar, 1937. *Red Star Over China*. London: Victor Gollanca Ltd.

[22] Ibid.

[23] Gong Yuzhi and Shi Zhongquan, *Mao Zedong's Life of Reading*. Beijing: SDX Joint Publishing Company, 2010.

[24] Mao, Zedong, *Selected Works of Mao Zedong*, vol. 5. Beijing: People's Publishing House, 1977.

draw the most beautiful picture on a blank canvas. During the years when he held power, many new and beautiful pictures did emerge; but he also created the cultural tragedies of the "Anti-Rightist Movement" and the "Cultural Revolution."

The Collective Leadership of the Chinese Communist Party

The original *Party Charter* stipulates that the party aims to overthrow the capitalist government, eliminate the private capitalist ownership of the means of production, recognize proletarian dictatorship, and realize communism. The party conference confirms that the party's organizational principle is that of democratic centralism and that the nature of the party is that it is the vanguard of the working class. The Chinese Communist Party's Charter has been enriched and expanded in the course of revolutionary practice. Even though the party has undergone several leadership changes since Mao passed away, the goals of the party have remained the same.

Hua Guofeng

Hua Guofeng, the chairman of the Party's central committee (1976–1981), raised the issue of improving the country's economy through each and every means available. He emphasized on many occasions that revolution means the emancipation of productive forces so that industrial and agricultural production can resume and develop. He said, "We must learn from good foreign experiences, including their science and technology, their administration and management theories and practice, and engage in comprehensive economic cooperation." He urged the party to liberalize the mind further, be more courageous, try out more solutions, and speed up the pace.

Hu Yaobang

Hu Yaobang, the chairman of the party's central committee (1981–1987), presided over and adopted a series of agricultural reform measures and policies that led to rapid economic development in Chinese villages. A good example is his promotion of the rural household contract responsibility system that was fully implemented in Anhui province. He said that the criteria to judge the success or failure of reform measures and policies should be based on whether they help build socialism with Chinese characteristics, whether they are beneficial to making the nation more prosperous, and whether they help make people richer and happier. He is looked upon as the promoter of "liberation of the mind" and "the big debate on the criterion of truth." He added great intellectual vigor and resources to the cause of reform and opening-up.

Zhao Ziyang

Zhao Ziyang, the general secretary of the party's central committee (1987–1989), is known for his lenient and tolerant attitudes toward the students involved in "the June 4 Incident" that took place in Beijing in 1989 during his tenure in the office. As a result, he was removed summarily from his job: "Comrade Zhao Ziyang has committed the error of supporting the riot and splitting the Party at the critical moment of life or death for the Party and the country and played his inescapable role in the formation and development of the riot. The nature of his error and its consequences are extremely serious."[25]

However, this author still remembers that it was Zhao who led the struggle to get out of the leftist tenets and constraints and explored the way to rural reforms with courage. The implementation of the system of fixed output quotas for individual farming households led to greater food production. Finally, the rural population had enough to eat. There was a popular saying at that time, "to feed your people, go and get Ziyang," which just shows what an outstanding achievement he made in agriculture. And his tolerant attitude and care for students will also be forever remembered.

Jiang Zemin

Jiang Zemin, the general secretary of the party's central committee (1989–2002), is the originator of the important ideas of "the three represents": (1) The party should always represent the development needs of China's advanced productivity; (2) it should always represent the onward direction of China's advanced culture; and (3) it should always represent the fundamental interests of the overwhelming majority of the Chinese people.

Hu Jintao

Hu Jintao, the general secretary of the party's central committee (2002–2012), put forward the concept of the scientific outlook on

[25] From the "Report on the Errors Made by Comrade Zhao Ziyang during the Anti-Communist Party and Anti-Socialism Riot" by the 4th Plenary Session of the 13th Central Committee of the CCP, June 23–24, 1989.

development. The basic idea is that all development should be people-oriented, comprehensive, coordinated, and sustainable. The goal is for both social economic development and human development in a harmonious way.

Xi Jinping

Xi Jinping, the general secretary of the party's central committee (2012–now), is the party's present leader. Under his leadership, the Chinese Communist Party is returning back to its source—among the masses, and sharing a common fate with them. It wants to serve the people whole-heartedly.[26]

The Status of the Chinese Communist Party as the Ruling Party

There have been doubts about the legitimacy of the Chinese Communist Party as the ruling party for a long while. The sentiments have deepened over the years because the bureaucratic system and rampant corruption hurt people's feelings. People are unhappy and have become suspicious of the party and its ability to rule. A few years ago, there circulated a popular gag and it went something like this, "It looks like a temple from afar and turns out to be a Party school[27] on a closer look. There are no monks and dogmas inside and only corrupt officials undertaking advanced studies." This satirical comment reflects many negative views that the masses harbour about the party. In fact, many corrupt party elements have indeed gone through training at the party schools, which has raised questions about the usefulness of this sort of training mechanism. Hu Jintao said while in office, "The advanced nature of our Party and our governing party status can never remain stagnant and constant. The advanced nature in the past does not imply the advanced nature in the future; the present modernity does not guarantee everlasting modernity."[28]

On September 9, 2015, during a meeting with foreign representatives, Wang Qishan, secretary of the CCP Central Commission for Discipline

[26] From the article "Xi Jinping's Strategic Thinking on the Party Discipline," *People's Forum*, 2014: 38.

[27] The party school is a communist party institution specializing in training and educating party members and officials. From the central committee to various local governments, there are established party schools.

[28] Hu, Jintao. Speech in Commemoration of the 30th Anniversary of the Third Plenary Session of the 11th Central Committee of the CCP, December 18, 2008.

Inspection, did not avoid the topic of "legitimacy" and said, "The legitimacy of the Chinese Communist Party is rooted in history, has been determined by popular support and chosen by people."[29] Xi Jinping began his term of office with an anti-corruption campaign, for he realizes that while water can float a boat, it can also sink the boat.

"The Two Conferences" (两會)

"The Two Conferences" refer to "The National People's Congress" and "The Chinese People's Political Consultative Conference" and their meetings are very important events in the political life of the Chinese Communist Party. These conferences are held every five years and there is an annual general meeting for each institution. They take place in early March of each fifth year, and last about ten days. The total number of representatives of both institutions is about 6,000. What the representatives do is to convey whatever information and demands they receive from their constituents to the party's central committee. In principle, they are elected by the people, represent people's interests, reflect the people's will, pass on the new policies from the central committee, help formulate and establish new regulations and measures, make policies to address new social problems, and provide solutions to new difficult issues.

Understanding China

Understanding the Party

During the last 95 years, the Chinese Communist Party has had many leaders who together form three generations of core leaderships (officially, Mao Zedong, Deng Xiaoping, and Jiang Zemin are the representatives of these three groups of leadership). As far as the party's general principles, aim, path, and orientation go, they are pretty clear. How is it, then, that things like the "Anti-Rightist Movement," "the Cultural Revolution," and the rampant social corruption and bureaucracy in the last 20 years have occurred one after another. They have caused people to become doubtful about the governing party. What are the problems that have led to these occurrences?

[29] Zhang Feng, 2015 "Dialogs between the CCP and the World." www.rmlt.com.cn. Accessed on September 18, 2015.

Some may say that the problems are a result of the tendency during "the peaceful times" for the Chinese communists to stray from their Marxist and Leninist "tenets." This author believes that several other issues are also worthy of consideration: (1), as the ruling party, the Chinese Communist Party provides its members with the paramount political capital. Many members join the party in order to benefit from this capital, climb up the bureaucratic hierarchy, and gain personal profit; (2), the processes of selection and appointment of party officials at all levels are not open, not transparent, and not democratic, thus causing the whole leadership to be unbalanced and patchy; (3), the way the party system is designed encourages enjoyment of privileges, lack of oversight, and autocratic leadership style, making it vulnerable to corruption and leaving much to be desired in the party's self-improvement efforts; (4), the party leaders at different levels have been isolated from the masses for too long and hence have been divorced from reality. They often govern like tyrannical parents, despots, and feudal magistrates and have deviated from the principle of "serving the people"; and (5), there have been no mechanisms to assure "life-time accountability" and no policy to encourage leaders to take responsibility and resign, thus leaving loopholes for the crooked to evade consequences and proving Dalbert-Acton right that "absolute power corrupts absolutely."[30]

Xi knows the severity of corruption within the party and has laid out the strategy of "the four comprehensives": building a comprehensively prosperous society, implementing comprehensive reforms, running the country according to a comprehensive legal system, and comprehensively disciplining the party with strict rules. He's also proposed that "power should be put back inside the cage of the system." When some people questioned the relationship between the Party and the constitution, Xi said, "the Party leads people in making the constitution and law; the Party leads people in implementing the constitution and law; the Party must function within the constitution and law. The Party should be the real leader in law-making, law enforcement, and law-abiding practice."[31]

[30] Dalberg-Acton, John Emerich Edward (1949), *Essays on Freedom and Power*, Boston: Beacon Press, p. 364.

[31] Xi Jinping's speech on the 30th Anniversary of the Implementation of the Current China Constitution. xinhuanet, 2012:12.4.

However, questions such as "Is the law above the Party, or is the Party above the law?" and "Can the constitution accepts rule of law and guarantee the independence of the judiciary?" still attract lots of attention and cause debates. People are looking forward to Xi's next moves in reforming the political system.

Understanding China

Some people say that Mao Zedong spent 30 years in pulling the country together; Deng Xiaoping spent 30 years in economic development and turning a poor nation into the world's second largest economy. The next 30 years, as a result, should be devoted to social and systems construction. This is crucial to the next phase of China's development.

Obviously, it is very important to balance the relationship between tradition and modernity. Tradition is a gargantuan system, including politics, culture, ethics, morals, and faiths. This author believes that even though carrying on the legacy of the fine cultural tradition needs the will of the state it cannot be done in too ideological a fashion and certainly not in haste. What is needed is setting good examples from the top down in promoting tradition and emphasizing cultivation of temperament, intellect, and virtue. We must also keep reminding ourselves what great damage the Cultural Revolution has done to our tradition and how much it has twisted the national psychology of the people.

It is important to give priority to theory building, especially theories about liberal arts and social sciences. A nation without its contemporary thinkers, theorists, and liberal arts scholars cannot go very far. We need them to comprehensively raise people's standards. After all, no matter how good systems and institutions are, they will be quite hollow without the active participation of the masses. People's high standards come from great education; nurturing students of talent should be our main educational idea. We should train many superior managers and civil servants of the highest calibre for all levels of government instead of bureaucrats found in a feudal society. Education should produce a substantial group of elite liberal arts and social science students who can become the pillars of the nation.

We can draw lessons from foreign experiences and expertise. Building "socialism with Chinese characteristics" does not mean xenophobia. We need not reject all great foreign culture and every idea of how to run a country.

In 1876, Guo Songtao, the first Qing minister to be stationed in a western country, said after witnessing the rise of Great Britain that it is wrong to attribute the Western power and prosperity to their warships and guns only. China cannot make the country prosperous and its military powerful by studying their military science alone. He advocated the value of learning and studying Western democratic politics.[32]

There are people today who argue that China first has to answer whether it wants institutionalized centralization of power or power centralized within individuals. If we want institutionalized centralization of power, it may turn into something permanent in a big country like China. Centralization does not preclude delegation of power and not all the power should be confined within the central committee. Centralization of power is necessary whether in anti-corruption campaigns, top-level design, or eradication of vested interests. Thus, power should be weighted toward institutions, not toward individuals.[33]

History is like a mirror. Learning from history can allow one to foresee the rise and fall of a country's fortune. In the last 100 years or so, in its struggle to become a modern nation, China has travelled some very bumpy roads and paid very heavy prices. During the "Westernization Movement" of the 1860s through the 1890s,[34] including the incident "Scholars' Open Letter to the Emperor"[35] and "the Hundred Days Reform,"[36] numerous

[32] Guo, Songtao, *Memories of the Diplomatic Missions in the West: Collected Works of Guo Songtao*. Liaoning People's Publishing House, 1994.

[33] Ibid.

[34] A westernization movement lasting over 30 years between the 1860s and the 1890s advocated for and introduced Western weaponry, machines of production, and knowledge of science and technology into China. Its goals were to make the country strong and prosperous. The major figures include Zeng Guofan, Li Hongzhang, Zhang Zhidong, and Zuo Zongtang.

[35] In 1895, Kang Youwei, a well-known scholar and political reformer, together with Liang Qichao and thousands of other scholars, submitted a joint letter to the Emperor in protest against signing of the humiliating and sovereignty-forfeiting Treaty of Shimonoseki. Even though the letter was rejected by the government, it had a strong impact and is regarded as the beginning of the mass political movement in China.

[36] It refers to the political reforms carried out by Kang Youwei, Liang Qichao, and other reformists via Emperor Guangxu between June 11 and September 21, 1898. It was fiercely apposed by Empress Dowager Cixi and conservative officials. On September 21, 1898, Empress Dowager issued orders to arrest and execute the six reformist leaders of Tan Sitong, Kang Guangren, Li Xu, Yang Shenxiu, Yang Rui, and Liu Guangdi, signaling the end of the reform movement. However, this is a very important political event and helped push forward the rise of a modern China.

patriots and revolutionary martyrs shed their blood and sacrificed their lives to no avail. China lost great opportunities for modern political reform. We can draw some profound lessons from them and stay vigilant and watchful.

Understanding the Chinese People

Confucianism has remained the mainstream culture in China for over 2,000 years. Confucius laid down the basic codes of ethical behavior and morals that can be summarized as: being benevolent, being righteous, following rules of the rites, being wise, being trustworthy, being temperate, being kind, being courteous, being restrained, and being magnanimous. These have formed the core of Chinese cultural values and traditions and are the basis for different schools of family teachings and good upbringing. Unfortunately, during the last one to two hundred years, the Chinese have strayed further and further away from them.

In 1914, Gu Hongming, a noted cultural eccentric and scholar, published *The Spirit of the Chinese People*[37] in which he has this to say about the Chinese: "now the first thing which will strike you about the Chinese is gentleness. By gentleness I don't mean softness of nature or weak submissiveness. By gentleness I mean absence of hardness, harshness, roughness, or violence. The real Chinaman may be coarse, but there is no grossness in his coarseness. The real Chinaman may be ugly, but there is no hideousness in his ugliness. The real Chinaman may be vulgar, but there is no aggressiveness, no blatancy in his vulgarity. The real Chinaman may be stupid, but there is no absurdity in his stupidity. The real Chinaman may be cunning, but there is no deep malignity in his cunning." This author believes that his understanding of the spirit of the Chinese people is lively and on the whole fits the national characteristics of that time.

Now, more than 100 years later, a well-known contemporary writer Liang Xiaosheng[38] has published the literary works *The Depressed Chinese* and *The Fearful Chinese.*[39] Through them, he discusses all kinds of confusion and bewilderment that have been present in the course of China's

[37] The book was originally published in the English-language newspaper *China Review* in 1914.

[38] Liang Xiaosheng (1949–) as an contemporary writers, has always been regarded as a spokesperson for the common people. The style of creation centers on: the realistic style of the heroic, the realistic style of the civilians, and the realistic style of the allegorical.

[39] Liang Xiaosheng, *The Depressed Chinese* and *The Fearful Chinese*, Guangming Daily Press, 2013.

development. The issues include depression, fear, and lost and bored youths who are life's "onlookers." Though his style is frank and his tone is somber, his words are sharp in analyzing the pressure and anxiety that the Chinese experience in their mental and daily life. His descriptions of social reality and the stratification of Chinese society resonate strongly among his readers. What makes the Chinese depressed? What are they worried about? What are they puzzled by? Has the spirit of the Chinese people changed or not in the span of 100 years? These questions deserve rational analysis and appraisal.

Material and Spiritual

The relationship between the material and the spiritual has always remained a hot topic for debate in academia: from Hegel to Marx, from idealism to materialism, from philosophy to behavioural science, and from consumerism to sustainable development. In 1943, Abraham Maslow proposed his theory of hierarchy of human needs: physiological need, need for safety, needs for love/belonging, esteem, and self-actualization.[40] It is shown as a pyramid of human needs of gradation and coexistence. In reality, the material and the spiritual aspects of life are reflected through people's choice of lifestyles. They are also important dimensions through which to evaluate the superiority and inferiority of a lifestyle.

People's Livelihood and Lifestyles in a Modern Country

People's livelihood and lifestyles are important issues that any modern country has to tackle. How to balance the relationship between the material and the spiritual can be a test of how well a political system and a government works.

Mode of Life in China 1949–1985

Since the founding of the People's Republic of China in 1949 through the early days of 1980, people would automatically add the adjective "bourgeois" whenever the word "lifestyle" was used. Lifestyle meant bourgeois lifestyle. The two words were inseparable. During those times, bourgeoisie and proletarian were opposite classes and the proletarian would never talk

[40] Maslow, A., "A Theory of Human Motivation." *Psychological Review*, 1943, vol. 50, pp. 370–396.

about a lifestyle that they found repulsive. Let me give a concrete example. During those days, women were "half of the sky" and people tried all sorts of means to eliminate anything feminine. When purchasing a bra, female urban residents would pick the smallest possible size in order to press in their breasts and prevent them from growing. Some people even refused sexual intercourse after they got married. Naturally, civilized activities such as dining with friends, learning to embroider, and cultivating good manners were all shunned, because they ran counter to revolutionary zeal.[41] There even circulated such a saying, "We'd rather have socialist weeds than bourgeois seedlings."

Yet, elements of the bourgeois lifestyle still existed and, to some extent, needed to exist. Unfortunately, they became the victim of political and ideological struggles. The class struggle became the "protagonist" in the modes of people's daily lives.

Even when the twenty-first century turned dawned, scholars in the field of leisure studies were still criticized and regarded as "the spokespersons on behalf of the bourgeois lifestyle." In 2006, this author was questioned by a departmental leader as to why "leisure" was translated into "*xiuxian*" and asked to find another substitute word. I refuted his criticism by quoting traditional Chinese documents as evidence. As we can see, the extreme leftist ideological forces are deeply rooted. My little incident also shows that some officials in charge remain very ignorant and know next to nothing about Chinese cultural traditions.

Reforms and Lifestyles

Incorporating style into one's life, being aware of living with grace and harmony, what we may call "lifestyle," has returned to people's lives and also become the subject of academic studies. It began in the early 1980s when Yu Guangyuan, then vice-president of Chinese Academy of Social Sciences, kept calling on social scientists to study issues concerning people's consumption and lifestyles and find ways to make people live better, happier, and healthier lives under the current circumstances, to provide better advice on people's lives but never arbitrarily interfere. "On the one hand, we

[41] Mao says, "Revolution is nothing like dining with your friends, or writing an essay, or painting a picture and doing a piece of embroidery. It can't be done elegantly, without hurry, with good manners, like a gentleman. It is a rebellion, a violent action of one class of people overthrowing another." (Mao Zedong, "A Report after Investigating the Peasant Movement in Hunan Province," in *Selected Works of Mao Zedong*, vol.1, Beijing: People's Press, 1967, p.17.)

should help masses set up correct modes of life, including their aesthetic standards, and let them better arrange their lives; on the other hand, through better balancing production and consumption, we help them make smarter choices on consumption."[42]

As a result, people could find three paragraphs on the issue of "lifestyle" in the report on the 3rd Plenary Session of the 12th CCP Central Committee. (For details, please see the section "The Reform and Opening up of China" of Chap. 3)

During the decade of 1980–1990, research on lifestyle in the Chinese academic circle reached a peak; a large number of valuable research papers were published. However, starting from early 1990s, lifestyle studies gradually faded from research fields. At the administrative levels (including planning, assistance, organization, etc.), lifestyle research was pushed to an obscure corner by heat waves of single-minded economic development that swept across the country.

Consequently, what we have witnessed during almost 30 years of urbanization is the fact that urban planning and design and their guiding principles have deviated further and further away from a city's liveability and humanity. Despite bright and alluring neon lights in commercial and business districts, good taste, sensible design, humanistic atmosphere, and so on are hard to find. And people's lives are filled with haste, noise, confusion, chaos, and general noxiousness. Where is serenity and leisure and enjoyment?

A Brief Look at People's Lifestyle Today

Today, people's modes of life can be described as kaleidoscopic—various, multidimensional, multifaceted, and multimodal. Historically speaking, the changes that we see today are tremendous. However, there are many, many social phenomena that are very worrisome.

Science and Technology Era: "Pie in Sky" and "Traps"

Various achievements of modern science and technology have infiltrated every aspect of our lives: from food, clothing, and housing to recreational

[42] Yu Guangyuan. *Reforms. Management. Life. Construction of Organizations.* Hunan: Hunan People's Publishing House, 1986, p. 350.

activities and life of leisure in general; scientific and technological innovations have impacted them all.

Television has satisfied not only people's entertainment needs but also their needs for learning new knowledge, their demands for instant news. It also provides a new venue to enjoy live performance and even increases their aesthetic standards. Weekly fashion shows in London, Paris, Milan, and New York will see the latest fashions appear in other cosmopolitan centers a week later.

Multifunction mobile phones not only serve as tools of communication, but also meet users' entertainment needs, such as taking photos, chatting online, and sending group messages. In China, everyone seems to have a mobile phone and uses it 24/7.

The spread of cars has changed the way people travel. Now they can go to places that they could not before. Traveling by car is now fashionable. People are no longer content going places within the country; they have gone over the border and can be found all over the world.

Television, mobile phones, cars, and the Internet are some of the most popular innovative products that are closely integrated into people's lives. And they add greatly to the pleasures of a life of leisure. The American writer Jeremy Rifkin says in his book *The End of Work* that science and technology will bring us into a "techno-paradise," a human society of abundance and leisure. Scientific miracles are inexhaustible. It is science, not God, who will be the new Moses to lead God's chosen people into the land of milk and honey.[43]

There is one reality, however, that we cannot ignore: the Internet, mobile phone, social media, the exponential increase of data and information, and television have taken control of people's lives. TV is the "painkiller" for the afflicted, the "companion" for the lonely, and the thief of our free time. Scores of episodes of TV dramas have emptied viewers' brains; mobile phones are as evil as drugs that make users addicted. People start to suffer disorders of anxiety and their mental state from dependency; their ways of thinking and psychological health have been unconsciously but assuredly affected. Cars do not only cause traffic jams; they jam the heart as well. Moreover, their exhaust fumes contribute to city smog and the reduction of natural resources. At the same time, people have willingly given

[43] Rifkin, Jeremy. *The End of Work*. Shanghai: Shanghai Translation Publishing House, 1998.

up their pedestrian rights and are engaging in less and less walking, which has weakened their physical and biological abilities. The Internet seems to link us all together and make us feel that the world is within our grasp, whereas what it really does is to net us all in captivity and put us into a new prison.

It is true that we now possess certain powers that gods did not have, but we are lost in our goals. Where should we go? How do we get there? Why should we take this path? A Chinese saying has it: "Nothing in the world is as dangerous as this."

The triumphs of modern technology have enabled people to revel in continuous partying and have blinded their view of the sorts of problems that Marxism has always been concerned about. As a matter of fact, Marx called on people in his early work to avert the alienation of labor. Later, he said that life is the precondition of all history and developed the idea that the free development of each individual is the condition for the free development of all human beings.

During the rise of the Frankfurt School in the 1930s and 1940s, Herbert Marcuse pointed to the morbid society where the biggest malady is that it turns a person into a one-dimensional man, who's lost his sanity, liberty, virtue, and the habit of living joyously.[44] Eric Fromm shared the same sentiment, believing that because of the one-sided emphasis on physical consumption man has lost contact with himself, with life, and with living. He's also lost his religious faith and various associated humanistic values. He leans on technology and physical values and has lost the ability to experience and feel at a deep level and therefore has lost the feelings of joy and grief that come with those experiences.[45]

We cannot help but wonder how man has become the prisoner of his own creativity: he has triumphed so splendidly over nature and fallen into the most serious danger of destroying himself.

A Case of Women's Lifestyle

Since 1990, The All-China Women's Federation, with The National Bureau of Statistics, has done an investigative survey on "Chinese women's Social Status" every decade as an important project sponsored by the State Social

[44] Marcuse, Herbert 1964. *One Dimensional Man*. London: Routledge & Kegan Paul Ltd.

[45] Fromm, Erich. *The Revolution of Hope: Toward a Humanized Technology*. New York: Harper & Row, 1968.

Sciences Foundation. One of the important indicators in the survey is the issue of lifestyle. This author participated in the 2010 survey and has published a few reports and research papers as a result. Several sets of data and statistics have attracted the author's attention and consideration.

After analyzing the ten-year data between 2000 and 2010, the author discovered that the enjoyment of leisure has not improved during that period. Here is an interesting phenomenon of antinomy: on the one hand, the government has increased the number of statutory holidays; on the other, people feel that they have been trapped into all kinds of time crises: lack of time, pressure of time, decreased value of time, and so on. The statistics show that daily working hours increased whereas the time for leisure kept going down.

People were not very conscious of the value of leisure time and therefore did not have a clear idea as to the daily allocation of their time. Most of people spent their free time watching TV as their main activity. And the statistics show that compared with the previous decade, people during this ten-year period spent 10% more time on watching TV.

There is a difference in the ways urban residents and country people allocate their time. People living in the country spend little time on studying and learning, but still spend a lot of time on household chores. At present, it is a fact that rural areas are still lagging behind cities in development.

Social security plays a significant role in how people allocate their time. According to the data collected, people who have social security and good health have more choices as to how to spend their leisure time and participate in various activities. But statistics also show that these people tend to work longer hours.

Equating leisure with travel and shopping not only resonates in the mainstream, but also portrays many people's patterns of behavior. It has created a booming luxury market, slowed down the downtrend of the world economy, and in the process left behind unflattering images of conspicuous Chinese consumers and wealth-flaunting upstarts. The real concern is that consumption of intangible things such as raising the professionalism of the labor force and developing free and well-rounded persons has not attracted people's attention.

Overall, the concern that emerges from the survey is the following: the general development of women is uneven. In one way or another, most women are still under the influence of the old and traditional ways of thinking such as "produce a child first and live one's life later" and have no thoughts on how to live a leisurely and cultured life. They lack correct understanding of the value of their free time and still identify with popular but restrictive sayings like "To marry well is better than studying well," "Women should take care of home and let men take charge of what is going on outside," and "Why should a beautiful woman worry about intelligence?" These self-degrading sayings of female dependency still enjoy their share of support among women themselves.[46]

Hidden Worries About China's Cultural Capital

The 2,000-year-old Chinese tradition of respecting teachers and extolling education is now being blamed for myriad cultural problems: students reading classics blindly without a critical spirit, universities expanding by lowering standards, exploding numbers of college professors, too many postgraduate degree holders having no job prospects, and so on. Nowadays a university education is treated as nothing more than a stepping stone to a job, just like scholars in the old days writing just for the sake of making a living. Today, the new round of "reading is useless" arguments has hit the masses. In the old days, intellectuals were regarded as the social conscience and backbone of the nation, shouldering the societal responsibilities. They seem to have all but vanished. In their stead, cultural merchants appear on the scene one after another, and dupe the eager but unsuspecting passive receivers. Mass media, pop culture promoters and producers have turned culture's social responsibility into games for snobs and trend followers.

We cannot blame the former British Prime Minister Margaret Thatcher for her curt answer when she was asked to respond to the media question whether she felt threatened by the arrival of the Chinese television sets in Britain. She answered, "Ask me this question when China starts to export their TV programmes to Britain." Hillary Clinton, the former American Secretary of State said something similar while in office: a country that cannot export its values cannot be said to be a strong country.[47]

There is another phenomenon that is equally worrisome. We have turned the three most meaningful holidays (the Chinese Lunar New Year, May 1st

[46] Ma Huidi, "The Lifestyle in Social Transformation, 2 *Academic Journal of Jinyang*, 2013(9).

[47] "Background material for high school students" writing, www.edudo.com/36585. May, 13, 2013.

Labor Day, and October 1st National Day) into "golden weeks." All the media touted in unison: "May 1st Golden Week," "October 1st Golden Week," and "Lunar New Year Golden Week." Before these holidays arrive, people's first response is the desire for travel and shopping. Crowds and money have turned these significant holidays into "golden money holidays." When the holidays are over, the media keep reporting record levels of consumption, reinforcing misguided value judgments and spurring masses further toward the worship of consumerism. As a result, the real significance of the three holidays has been wiped out.

Merchants in the entertainment industry have turned the tradition of leisure culture into the legendary money tree, or gold mine. For profits, they have destroyed homes, towns, the ecological environment, and heritage sites. Instead they have created fake folk customs, built artificial scenic spots, and forged phony historical sites that cater to vulgar tastes. Leisure entails extravagant meals, sensual pleasures, and wanton pursuits at the expense of its implied cultural significance.

There are about 660 cities in China and leading administrators want to turn 300 of them into international metropolises. They want to compete in "heights" (who has higher skyscrapers). No wonder that the American Hollywood star Ben Affleck once exclaimed that one knows what a cosmopolitan city is like only after one has been to Beijing. On the other hand, the Chinese roaming in Beijing feel like they are in Tokyo. And they unashamedly feel flattered by the comparison.

Today, Chinese cities, no matter big or small, look and feel like the same. There are commercial and business districts everywhere, but cultural centers are scarce and rare. Take libraries for example. The total number of libraries is about 3,000 and a large number of them do not make book purchases anymore; they are not open to the public and have few readers. The state of the national readership is a big concern. Most people read fortune-telling tips and prurient gossip columns and hardly ever touch classics and the works of literary masters. In daily life, children's playgrounds, young people's sports fields, and even ordinary rest areas are very hard to come by.

China is now engaged in a state-sponsored culture export project. On the one hand, we are expanding Confucius Institutes overseas. On the other hand, we are buying advertising at prime locations in big foreign cities, sending troupes of artists to perform at foreign theaters, increasing participation in big international bookfairs, and actively engaging in international tourism promotion and sales activities. I am sure that all these are necessary. However, the success of real culture export should rely on winning the recognition and trust of international peers for our ideas, for our scholars, for our new ways of thinking, for the richness and value of our classical heritage, and for our unique angles of social observation. We may close the door and celebrate the success of our projects, but that would be nothing more than self-deception. The increasing status of cultural strength depends on the overall academic accomplishments in sociology, philosophy, arts, and religious studies. Unfortunately, at the international gatherings of important liberal arts scholars and experts, few Chinese figures are seen. This is partly due to limited travel budgets and strict approval mechanisms. However, those lucky few who are able to go often tend to spend conference time on tourism and consequently leave a bad impression among their international peers.

Our understanding of "cultural capital" is still very superficial. We only see tangible "goods" as cultural assets and neglect the existence of cultural capital in the form of national spirit, social systems, and time. This is especially the case in our indifference toward creating a favorable social atmosphere by heeding our ancient wisdom: "intelligence arises from leisure," "observe in tranquility and comprehend with heart," and "inactivity leads to good administration." At present, the whole society is in a state of sound and fury and engaged in consumerism and money worship. Once people sink so low as to become slaves to their money, one can only sigh and ask, "What can be more lonely and pitiable than to find our soul bound and controlled by our physical body?"

Conclusion

Karl Marx is one of the founders of conflict theories. The three conflicts of productivity versus relations of production, superstructure versus the economic base, and interest demands still apply in China, and even worldwide, today. Under certain circumstances, conflicts can act as a warning about problems of social antagonism and animosity. Handled properly, these conflicts can prevent stagnation of social and political systems, promote social fairness, justice, and shrink the gap between different interest groups. Solutions to conflicts must come from concessions and compromises that ruling classes and interest groups should make. On one hand, ruling classes have to improve their policy-making abilities, make the execution of the power mechanism transparent, become more aware of being public servants, and continually engage in system reform. On the other, all members of different interest groups need to stick to rationality and objectivity and fully understand and acknowledge that conflicts are multi-regional, plural, and multifaceted, and can be both uniform and aggregative. Only through such concessions and compromises can conflicts become constructive and beneficial.

Even though they may belong to different categories, sinology and Western studies, tradition and modernity, and the material and the spiritual are mutually dependent and supplementary to each other. In the process of resolving conflicts they may provide a common ground for both sides to come to terms with shared values.

History has proven that any society of outstanding strength (or a power at a certain historical period) is one that learns and borrows from different cultures for its academic ideas and acts as a bridge between tradition and modernity, keeping its national heritage alive while absorbing the newest cultural achievements of all humankind. Such a powerful society can balance the material side of things with the spiritual side and makes sure that people can maintain decent living standards and self-respect while at the same time letting their souls be nourished spiritually. "Academic ideas," "the spirit of tradition and the power of modernity" are the three indispensable pillars of the foundation of national development and are the sources for easing and resolving conflicts.

The lack of coordinated and harmonious development of both the material and spiritual sides of culture remains the main issue in China. This lack reflects the wrong ways of handling the relationship among academic ideas, the spirit of tradition, and the power of modernity. We must admit that today's social conflicts are intense, focused, and complex. To channel them into positive energy requires not only policy-makers to possess wisdom and courage in order to "do better by correcting one's errors and amputate the fatally wounded hand to fight another day," but also it requires all people to cultivate greater spiritual strength.

CHAPTER 7

Conclusion and Further Thinking

China is a country with one of the longest histories in terms of culture, with a rich tradition of leisure, and is widely known as "a land of etiquette and righteousness."

The unity between humans and nature, self-cultivation, and the pursuit of elegance and taste were the foundations of the concept of leisure for the ancient Chinese. The concept of the unity between humans and nature laid the foundations for the Chinese outlook on life and their values; self-cultivation was used to shape the basic principles that the individual identified with in his conduct, and the pursuit for elegance and taste helped to enrich life.

The tradition of leisure culture in China tells us that the wonderful world of leisure has quietly nurtured people's hearts and minds, as well as their moral sense and their moral character, and has silently but also with great strength nurtured and guarded the spiritual home of human beings.

This tradition further tells us that the ancient Chinese understood leisure not simply as a length of free time to be used for recreation, but also a particular state of mind and as an opportunity to nurture one's own character and develop healthy hobbies. It is in this state of mind that people can learn that the coming and going of life is always dependent on spiritual activities beyond the bodily and material realities of life.

The effect leisure has on the human individual cannot be exactly measured, but it is doubtless an important part of human life and of society. Only when sustained by leisure can the dignity of human nature, the

Huidi Ma, Er Liu, *Traditional Chinese Leisure Culture and Economic Development*, DOI 10.1057/978-1-137-59253-8_7

richness and interest of life, and the harmony of society advance to ever higher levels.

For over 2,000 years, those virtues and life wisdoms have nurtured the spiritual world of Chinese people. Unfortunately, since the Opium Wars, those cultural traditions subsequently became distant from the Chinese people, given the fact that China has lived through natural disaster, poverty, war, and corruption over the 100 years, which, as a result, has severely damaged the essence of Chinese cultural traditions, depriving them of the passion for exploring the significance of existence, and the drive for the pursuit of a life of quality.

Since the reform and opening-up over three decades ago, the lives of Chinese people have improved considerably. Leisure as a choice for living and patterns of consumption has been rejuvenated that not only in terms of the comprehensive development, leisure activities, and consumption that drives economic growth, but it is also accelerating the reform of policy-making, public services, social management, and the protection of human rights.

The future of the Chinese economy is facing a dilemma of strategic planning, such as how to transform itself from notions of quantity to quality, from materialistic consumption to improving one's intrinsic character, from hard power to strengthening soft power, from a focus on economic indicators to shifting to humanistic care, from eagerness for quick success to steady growth.

However, it must be admitted that, with the transitional background in modern times, people still hold a very limited knowledge of cultural traditions; they have mainly focused on wealth capital, thus overlooking the cultural capital that the social system, the spirit of humanity and the modern timeframe represents, particularly in neglecting the building of a harmonious and quiet atmosphere. Society has become impetuous and noisy; people excessively worship materialistic goods and consumption, thus making humans the slaves of money.

Nevertheless, the revival of Chinese traditional culture and political democracy is the current objective of China. Although the future looks promising, we must be aware that it is going to be a lengthy and complex journey.

Today, the difficulties faced by China with regard to the sustainability of economic development are also very prominent, such as how to handle the projected unemployment for six million industrial workers as China undertakes to de-stock and de-leverage, and to provide re-employment opportunities for them; how to avoid falling into the "middle income trap" with the accompanying fragility of social institutions; how to keep the livelihood of common people in sight and ensure relatively balanced distribution of wealth as the GDP keeps on growing rapidly, as the nation's wealth grows by leaps and bounds, and as rich people keep on emerging; how to ensure the increase in income for common people which would be annulled by rising price levels; how to encourage financial capital to flow in the direction of the "real economy" and small enterprises; how to have craftsmanship embodied in education, in dedication to work, and in one's disposition and integrity; how to have "entrepreneurial and innovative undertakings by large numbers of people" while avoiding the vulgarization of innovative thinking, and the use by some of innovation for short-term, ulterior purposes; how to increase the willingness of the supply side to provide quality goods and services for customers. In all these areas, China has great challenges at the level of social practice.

In some areas, we still face severe difficulties. For example, society is aging rapidly, with the elderly population projected to increase from 212 million in 2015 to 418 million in 2035. There are more than 60 million children who stay in rural areas while their parent/parents are working in cities as migrant workers and 30 million adults who are bachelors; and one third of the population have health problems in need of treatment. Not one of these problems is likely to be completely and easily solved within the specified period of time.

In the last three decades, China has benefited from the rapid growth of GDP, but the price she has paid is very high—both the natural and the humanistic ecology have greatly deteriorated. Now the Chinese have just realized that people's feeling of "happiness" depends not just on GDP, but has to be supported by many more elements. The "Ranking of Happiness" in the *World Happiness Report 2016* recently published by Sustainable Development Solutions Network (SDSN, a global initiative for the United Nations) and the Earth Institute of Columbia University shows that the sense of happiness is not just used to measure the levels of education, health care, income, and good government, but has to do with the amount of social support, the degree of freedom people have in making life choices, the perceived extent of corruption, and the presence of generosity that helps to reduce inequality. In this list, of the 157 countries surveyed, China ranks the 83rd on the "happiness" scale.[1]

[1] John Helliwell, Richard Layard and Jeffrey Sachs, eds., *World Happiness Report 2016*, vol. 1, New York, Sustainable Development Solutions Network, 2016, p. 21.

This ranking reflects the many problems China has amidst her seemingly splendid economic performance: the rampant corruption despite repeated efforts to eliminate it, the growing inequality between the rich and the poor, the diminishing social justice, the deterioration of natural and human environments, the lack of trust, the existence of many pathogenic factors in the human ecology of society, the dwindling willingness to help others, the low efficiency in government functioning, and the mediocre performance of government agencies in management and in providing services have all negatively affected people's sense of gain from the progress of society.

For many years, there have been widespread inclinations among officials at different levels of government to sponsor vanity projects, to fake figures in favor of themselves, to be formalistic in implementing what higher levels of government demand of them, to aim high and show off grandiosely, to speed up things unrealistically without caring for the actual outcome, to play down tactfully on the policies promulgated by their superiors, and to disperse responsibility so as to avoid penalties for their failures—and these inclinations still exist today. There has also been another form of corruption—the tactic of creating neologisms, new concepts, and new campaigns (propaganda) to cover up the problems and contradictions that exist, while actually changing nothing in an essential way. Such persistent patterns of behavior on the part of government officials, despite the effort of the central government to ban them, have doubtlessly added to the burden of the taxpayer.

And there are other, less visible and perhaps more intractable problems. For example, statistics show that about 85% of private enterprises in China are family owned. In the decade to come, about 75% of these enterprises will face the problem of inheritance.[2] The estrangement and even hatred between the rich and common people stimulated by the showy, extravagant lifestyles of the "rich second generation" is a potential threat to society in the future.

In the area of leisure usage, including the system of vacations, institutional design has not been worked out very well. For many years, the "golden weeks" have resulted in artificially engineered prosperity, but has not brought a level of humanistic care. The government lacks not only the

[2] "Some Rich Two Generations in China Only Eat Kobe Beef and Drink Red Wine of 'Straw, French'," *Reference News*, March 17, 2016.

necessary skills, but also a humane concern for the management of time, and is unable to come up with schemes of staggered hours to lessen traffic flow in rush hours or staggered vacations to avoid transport congestion over the year, or with designs of road systems to eliminate inefficiency. Administrative indolence and barriers hindering effective communication and coordination across different levels of government and across different departments and different regions have led to low efficiency and inaction. On the other hand, most citizens have shown a disdain for the effective use of leisure time, squandering it in playing *mahjong*, in chatting on the Internet or on WeChat, in watching TV, or simply idling it away. The "Statistical Report on the Development of the Internet in China 2016" shows that, as of December 2015, the number of Chinese netizens had reached 688 million, and the amount of time spent on the Internet by the average person had reached 26.2 hours/a week; but this squandering of time, a valuable resource, is no different from slow suicide. The lack of adequate effort on the part of government and schools alike to provide guidance on the rational use of leisure time has not helped with lessening the worship and excessive consumption of material goods or the neglect of spiritual pursuits on the part of people. Devoid of leisureliness, grace, and refinement, contemporary lifestyles have led to hurriedness, boisterousness, and vulgarity, and have thus been weakening the economy and culture of China.

Current lifestyles are generally associated with an imbalance between work and leisure and disorders of both physical and mental constitutions of people. In a nutshell, contemporary Chinese life is one of material abundance coupled with spiritual poverty. Urged on by a mentality of "seeking quick wealth," people are always in a rush, pursuing fame and money in a restless world by all means available to them. Such a mentality has made people short-sighted, with their attention focused only on petty benefits, utterly unable to appreciate any beauty as they go.

In their attitudes toward tradition and modernity, people have forgotten what their ancestors had believed and have shoveled aside their cultural heritage. They have become rootless, floating in the ever-changing world of toady, adhering to hedonism with excessive consumption that seems to give them a sense of their own existence. On the other hand, there has also been much talk about reviving traditional culture in recent years, but when it comes to how to actually effect the revival, people often mistake the forms of certain elements of traditional culture for its essence, failing to engage with tradition seriously and practice what they preach. In education, schools still tend to take a utilitarian approach, trying to achieve quick results without really strengthening the foundations. But a healthy and rational society cannot have economy as the overwhelming concern at the expense of all other realms. Without the flourishing of a humanistic culture, economic prosperity is bound to be short-lived.

Marxism is the theoretical foundation of the Chinese revolution led by the Communist Party of China, and has been with us for a century now. However, the Chinese study of it has been conducted from a very narrow and overly pragmatic perspective, which has yielded only some shallow and fragmented understanding. The essence of Marxism as a systematic view of the world has not been comprehended properly, and, because of that, it is now losing its audience, with many of the younger generation no longer willing to take it seriously; and China has not been able to carry on fruitful dialogue even with Marxist scholars from other countries. On one hand, in-depth exchange with and borrowing from the multicultural humanistic thinking from other countries are missing; on the other, free and independently conducted study carried out by serious Chinese scholars has received little attention. But if no great thinker can emerge in China in our era, it must mean something is seriously wrong with our political and social institutions and the general atmosphere for scholarly research and independent thinking.

In sum, this book traces the sources of the leisure values, philosophy of life, and life wisdom of the Chinese back through China's cultural history. But why have these values gone adrift in modern times? By sifting through extensive historical materials, the author attempts to discover the reasons why those core values have been lost.

In the face of drastic social changes in China today, three questions need to be carefully addressed: (1) what is the best way to integrate tradition and modernity? (2) how can Chinese culture and Western culture join forces and be fused into a stronger culture? (3) does modernization necessarily imply a farewell to traditional cultures? These are issues that need to be considered and solved for the revival of Chinese culture in future.

This is the very reason why China needs to go back to traditional values of benevolence, righteousness, rights, wisdom, and trust, and the traditional virtues of temperateness, kindness, respectfulness, thrift, and magnanimity, which would foster a social milieu where gentlemanly conduct prevails. Whether China can revive these elements of traditional culture will be the greatest challenge and a test the nation has to face in order to achieve sustainable development in the future.

At any rate, while the huge waves arising from a tumultuous river could potentially destroy the river banks we have built, when properly channeled they can also push on and form a most splendid scene of waves following waves to make for continuous and great progress.

INDEX

Note: Page numbers with 'n' denote notes.

Huidi Ma, Er Liu, *Traditional Chinese Leisure Culture and Economic Development*, DOI 10.1057/978-1-137-59253-8

C

Z

CPSIA information can be obtained
at www.ICGtesting.com
Printed in the USA
LVOW05*0123090617
537491LV00033BA/1328/P

9 781137 596604